To Sharon,

Best wishes!

Akiva Tatz

DANGEROUS DISEASE
& DANGEROUS THERAPY

In Jewish Medical Ethics

DANGEROUS DISEASE & DANGEROUS THERAPY

In Jewish Medical Ethics

Principles and Practice

AKIVA TATZ

TARGUM PRESS

First published 2010

Copyright © 2010 by Akiva Tatz

ISBN 978-1-56871-535-3

Published and distributed by:

TARGUM PRESS, INC.
22700 W. Eleven Mile Rd.
Southfield, MI 48034
E-mail: targum@targum.com

Fax: 888-298-9992

www.targum.com

Printed by Chish

Printed in Israel

Cover design: Bracha Erlanger

בס"ד

Dayan Ch. Ehrentreu
Rosh Beth Din

חנוך עהרנטרייא
ראש בית דין

55 SHIREHALL PARK
LONDON NW4 2QN
TEL: +44 (0) 20 8202 2364
FAX: +44 (0) 20 8203 8942
email: dayan@ehrentreu.com

ששת הימים 41
רמת אשכול
ירושלים
טל: +972 (0)2 532 8551
פקס: +972 (0)2 532 8552

Rabbi Akiva Tatz's new book constitutes a valuable and timely addition to literature on Medical Halacha. Precisely because treatments and technologies are changing with such dizzying rapidity in the contemporary world, it is all the more important that we keep our eyes firmly on the fixed points of the compass – eternal Torah values.

In today's post-religious society, the gulf separating the Halachic approach to medicine and the values of our secularised health services seems to be growing ever wider. "Quality of life" seems too often to be more prized than life itself: hence the understanding afforded to those advocating the right to assisted suicide, euthanasia or abortion. In Judaism, however, life itself is the primary value. To give but one example: patient autonomy, one of the key mantras of modern medical ethics, is not necessarily supreme according to Judaism. Indeed Rabbi Tatz notes that in Halacha, therapy can sometimes be imposed against the will of the patient. The body – indeed, life itself – is not man's possession. It is not his to dispose of, nor to mutilate. That is Hashem's prerogative.

Contemporary medical ethics can be as consistent as quicksand. Rabbi Tatz cites the well known case of an elderly Orthodox Jew in Canada whose continuing treatment was deemed by the hospital's hard-pressed and under-resourced clinicians to be "futile". The hospital administrators and doctors determined that ventilation and feeding tubes must be withdrawn, despite the wishes of patient and family. Patient autonomy, it would appear, takes pride of place in shortening life – not its continuation!

Doctors are experts in how to prolong life. But unless they have received a very thorough grounding in religious education, they are not necessarily experts in the meaning or value of life. Rabbi Tatz is well grounded in both disciplines. He can claim first hand experience of many of the Halachic dilemmas of which he writes, as a doctor in both civilian life and in the military. As such, he is as conversant with the latest reports of the Royal College of Physicians as he is with the Radbaz on Rambam. He is a born teacher, simultaneously capable of appealing to Torah scholars and newcomers alike – a point underlined by the large and enthusiastic audiences who gather for his Shiurim at the Jewish Learning Exchange and beyond.

The range of issues addressed in this volume is daunting. When can a physician undertake life-threatening surgery? What level of risk is acceptable? How is such risk calculated? Who is the first in receiving treatment on the battlefield? What are the priorities for physicians after a natural disaster – such as Hurricane Katrina in New Orleans? Interesting as such questions are for laymen, they are absolutely vital for Torah-observant medical practitioners, who may well have to make spur-of-the-moment decisions without recourse to a competent Halachic authority. This work will help them make the right choices. In doing so, Rabbi Tatz brings the spirit of Hakadosh Baruch Hu into our surgeries and operating theatres as never before. I sincerely hope that it will achieve the widest possible readership.

Ehrentreu

Dayan Ch. Ehrentreu

Rosh Beth Din
London Beth Din

בס"ד ירושלים כ"ב כסלו תש"א

ידיד יקיר לי ר' עקיבא הי'

שמחתי מאד לשמוע על הולדת ספוך התם רב המעלות אשליו בדברי תורה והלוע
קבלתיו הדנני רכאה, אך לי אלא לבירך אותך הלב יצך הלמון יהא שען לך ואין
לאודים ובביוך אותכים את הלב והמקבלים האהבה ותן מוצק הלקחותיך, כן תועע להאיר
עוד הגברים של שלם ולוא את אין לחקלא אומר ולוא נועע של אורה דבור נתוך
ותהגולב כך יאיר אור רב אל ציון ונועע עלון אורה לאורו

מאהבה יוהה הכבוד

מאת שלי ירא

Acknowledgments

The assistance of many people has made the publication of this book possible.

I am deeply indebted to Rabbi Moshe Shapira; his teaching has enabled me and many others to see a depth and beauty unique in this generation.

Some of the material presented here derives from the lectures of Rabbi Yitzchak Zilberstein which I have had the privilege of attending for a number of years together with other physicians. I am grateful for his responses to my questions in a number of clinical situations. Where he is quoted as a reference without mention of a particular published work, the information or opinion referenced was received as a personal communication (this is also true of others I have similarly quoted). In many cases his opinion reflects that of his illustrious father-in-law, Rabbi Yosef Shalom Eliashiv (the relevant references indicate where that is the case).

The following people provided essential help and I thank them:

My mother, Mrs. Minde Tatz, for her usual meticulous work on the manuscript.

Michael and Vivien Bonert of Los Angeles, whose generosity has made this book a reality. It has been a pleasure to be associated with them over the years, and it is a privilege to partner with them in this project.

Rabbi Danny Kirsch, Director of the Jewish Learning Exchange of London, a man of remarkable character and vision.

Rabbi Marcel Bordon, whose contribution has made this a far better book. Virtually every aspect has benefited from his suggestions.

Rabbi Aubrey Hersh, whose expert and extensive knowledge has been a valuable resource.

Dr Alastair Santhouse, who has made a number of significant contributions.

I appreciate the assistance of Prof. Avraham-Sofer Abraham, Dr Joseph Adler, Dayan Ivan Binstock, Rabbi Yitzchak Breitowitz, Dr Howard Desatnik, Bracha Erlanger, Rabbi David Frid, Dr Fred Glatter, Rabbi Chanan Gordon, Rabbi Jonathan Rosenblum, Harry Rothenberg Esq., Dr Owen Samuels, Dr Helene Shapero, Dayan Shmuel Simons, Rabbi Yaacov Weiner and Rabbi Nissan Wilson.

I am indebted to the editors of the New England Journal of Medicine for a number of textual quotations.

Thanks are due to the staff of Targum Press; working with them continues to be a pleasure.

More than mere thanks are due to my wife Suzanne. In this book I have labored to present ethics and ideals in principle; she demonstrates those in constant effortless practice.

I would like to mention my father, Dr Koppel Tatz, who inspired and encouraged me in the study and practice of medicine as well as in Jewish learning. Like Dr Bonert's father, he was of a generation of doctors who not only cared for their patients but also cared about them. His relationship with his patients was deeply personal; I remember the distress he experienced when they were not doing as well as he would have liked. The doctor-patient relationship was different then; for various reasons, no doubt, it has changed. This book represents an effort to re-examine the spirit of that relationship in the light of dangerous illness and dangerous therapy in Jewish law; if it merits to revive some of that spirit, it will have been worthwhile.

A.T.
Tevet 5770
January 2010

Contents

Interventions in Pregnancy

Approach to Dangerous and Terminal Illness

PART TWO:
LIFE AND DEATH ISSUES IN JEWISH MEDICAL ETHICS AND THE MODERN WORLD

Appendices

Clinical Cases

Bibliography and Sources

Introduction

This book presents a halachic approach to dangerous illness, dangerous therapy and some related issues. The relevant principles are given in theory, followed by specific clinical applications that demonstrate those principles in action. Discussions of selected issues beyond the halachic and legal dimensions are presented in an attempt to portray the ethos of this area of Torah and to show how it differs from the modern secular one in many ways.

The book is intended to be of direct clinical use; clinical scenarios are presented for the purpose of identifying and analyzing the relevant halachic issues in the context of their usual range of application.

Broader areas of Jewish medical ethics are not dealt with here except where such issues are relevant to questions of risk and danger. Subjects covered in detail in other works are not repeated here; references to those works are provided.

In general, the references given indicate the more comprehensive sources or those that represent the consensus. For those interested in the full array of background detail, the references quoted will lead the reader through the steps that have led to the evolution of the consensus presented here.

Although the aim here is to be clinically relevant, as with all works of this nature the conclusions presented should not be taken as *p'sak,* final rulings to be applied to specific cases – each case needs individual halachic examination by appropriately qualified rabbinic authority, and perhaps nowhere more importantly than in this area of life and death decision making.

Despite that caution, however, the newcomer to Jewish medical ethics should not feel that this material is hardly relevant to him or her. The physician who lacks specific halachic expertise often plays an essential role in arriving at an appropriate clinical ethical decision because the halachic authority called upon to rule in a particular case will need to rely on the clinician for accurate medical information and clinical assessment. It is important, and indeed often critical, for the practising physician to know enough medical halacha to engage in this process – firstly, because it is often the physician who must recognize an ethical question or problem in the first place, and secondly, because when the search for a halachic solution in a particular case is under way, the physician must understand which clinical details are relevant and why.

The book is organized as follows: in Part One general halachic principles are discussed, followed by chapters that consider distinct areas of halacha relevant to dangerous illness and therapy; the sections are followed by clinical case studies that invite application of the principles, together with a detailed analysis of each scenario. The cases presented are real; most are drawn from the personal experience of the author and colleagues.

Part Two presents a number of essays whose aim is to set the principles and issues discussed throughout in the context of a system of values, pointing out where the current secular paradigm is not aligned with Torah values. The Appendices present material relevant to halachic decision-making and background information for some of the areas covered in Part One.

The final section is a collection of the clinical cases described throughout the book, presented without indication of which sections they are drawn from and without their resolutions – this is for the purpose of applied revision for readers who wish to do so. They are also given thus separately and without their "solutions" for the enterprising reader who would like to attempt analysing and resolving them *before* reading the book; many of them are challenging and it is my hope that the reader who struggles with them before studying the material presented in these pages will return to them after doing so with a new-found sense of clarity.

PART ONE

HALACHA – PRINCIPLES AND LAWS

Principles

In forming an authentic approach to Jewish medical ethics in the modern world, a number of basic issues must be borne in mind. The points that follow are relevant to Jewish medical ethics in general and to the halachic principles governing dangerous situations in particular.

Differences between Jewish and Modern Secular Approaches

There are significant differences between the Torah approach to this area and that of the modern secular world; the gap between these positions is particularly wide at present.[1] The principles that underlie this area are very differently defined by these two systems; issues that have primary significance in one may have almost none in the other. This does not simply mean generally divergent worldviews on the theoretical level; there are major practical differences that affect outcomes.

Some of these differences are:

(i) The basic premises of modern medical ethics are very differently defined in Judaism. The pillars of modern medical ethics are generally considered to be the four principles of patient autonomy, non-maleficence, beneficence and justice.[2] Although these are certainly relevant in Judaism, they are all defined and valued radically differently in halacha than in the secular context.[3]

---

[1] See Part II p. 217.

[2] Beauchamp TL, Childress JF, Principles of Biomedical Ethics 5th ed. (Oxford University Press, 2001)

[3] See Life and Death Issues in Jewish Medical Ethics and the Modern World; Part II p. 218.

(ii) "Quality of life": in the world of secular medical ethics, quality of life is often a more primary consideration than life itself. In very many cases in contemporary medicine a life may not be considered worth prolonging when the quality of that life is poor. Judaism, while sensitive to the very real issues of suffering and disability, sees life itself as the primary value. There are certainly specific situations in which the halacha may accord with a secular view in practice; however the basic point to remember is that the default position in Jewish thought is that life itself is a primary value of inestimable worth. To be sure, in halacha not all lives need be prolonged by all means under all circumstances,[4] but the burden of proof must always be borne by the side arguing for quality of life at the cost of life itself.

Age: a specific element within the concept of quality of life is old age. In the secular mode, the quality of life of very elderly patients may be defined as relatively low due the factor of age in itself; advanced age is assumed to detract from the worth of a life. A very old patient with serious illness will be seen differently in the eyes of modern medicine than a younger patient with the same pathology. This is not true in Judaism. Of course, where the patient's age is *clinically relevant* it must be taken into account, and such situations will be demonstrated in the discussions that follow. But to demote a patient's claim to life or therapy based on age as a value in itself has no place in Jewish medical ethics.[5]

(iii) Cost: a major element in modern medical thinking is the cost of treatment (or prevention).[6] A review of modern medical literature shows that cost is almost always a primary concern; the costs of illness to society and the cost-benefit ratio of any given intervention are almost always featured in the literature, often prominently.[7]

---

[4] See Withholding and Withdrawing Therapy, p. 103.

[5] For the possible relevance of age in triage situations, see Triage, p. 182.

[6] See Beauchamp and Childress p. 194 and in particular the analyses on pp. 196 - 199; these are examples of costs involved in saving lives and preventing suffering and the debate surrounding what costs are reasonable or justified here. Note the discussion of "Valuing Lives" on p. 206 and "Quality-Adjusted Life-Years" on p. 209. See also Appendix III: The Dollar Value of Life, p. 313.

[7] The following are examples chosen at random from the recent literature:

"The annual direct and indirect costs for coronary heart disease were $142.5 billion in 2006, and they continue to rise. Determining the respective contributions of prevention and therapy to the declines in mortality from

In some cases, effective screening techniques or interventions are not recommended because they are judged to be too costly relative to the number of lives they are likely to save.[8] This is not the default attitude in halacha. Weighing lives against costs is an odious exercise; life is invaluable in the Jewish worldview.

Cost is certainly relevant in halacha,[9] [10] but the point to remember is that it does not come before the value of life and health in themselves. Major

---

coronary heart disease is therefore becoming increasingly important..." Ford E et al. Explaining the Decrease in U.S. Deaths from Coronary Disease, 1980-2000. N Engl J Med 2007;356:2389.

"The dilemma in managing hemophilia is not whether to use prophylaxis or episodic treatment but how to manage prophylaxis such that the optimal, most cost-effective treatment is provided." And: "...we must await prospective studies that demonstrate the most balanced approach, weighing possible adverse events and cost against benefits." Roosendal G, Lafeber F. Prophylactic Treatment for Prevention of Joint Disease in Hemophilia - Cost versus Benefit. N Engl J Med 2007;357:603-604.

"Prophylactic implantation of an ICD (implantable cardioverter-defibrillator) poses a difficult challenge to health policymakers owing to the high cost of the device and the large patient population in which it may be applied. Even if this approach is used only in patient populations in which it has been shown to be cost-effective, the aggregate expenditure in the United States could easily exceed several billion dollars per year." Sanders G.D, Hlatky M.A, Owens D.K. Cost-Effectiveness of Implantable Cardioverter-Defibrillators. N Engl J Med 2005;353:1471-80.

See also the editorial in that issue: Goldman L. Cost-Effectiveness in a Flat World - Can ICDs Help the United States Get Rhythm? (p. 1513)

Cost features even in otherwise purely clinical discussions: the following exchange appears in the NEJM Case Records, "A Man with Chest Pain Followed by Cardiac Arrest," March 15, 2007; in which a bacterial infection has been diagnosed as the cause of the patient's myocarditis: "Dr H...: 'Dr B..., how expensive was the identification of this organism...?' Dr B...: 'In comparison with the cardiology evaluation, the cost of the microbiology tests was trivial. The PCR amplification and the 16S rDNA studies were performed by research laboratories without cost to this hospital..."

[8] See Appendix III: The Dollar Value of Life, p. 313 for an example of a current approach to quantifying value in this area. See Beauchamp and Childress p. 196.

[9] A family is not obliged to become destitute to provide better treatment for a member when less expensive but fully adequate treatment is available. Families and individuals do not have to incur extremely high costs for a very distant hope

conflicts arise in modern medicine over the factor of cost – many modern medical treatment situations involve major, sometimes huge, costs and these raise real issues for individuals, families, healthcare facilities and society at large. From the halachic perspective however, cost should not be relevant in situations of danger – the default position in halacha is that when life or health are in danger, all costs are reasonable. That position has a number of modifiers (some of these and their practical relevance will be demonstrated in the chapters that follow) but the basic Jewish approach begins with the assumption that cost ought not to limit what should be done for a patient whose life or health are threatened.[11]

---

of cure (and if they choose to do so, this should not be by means of taking loans with no foreseeable means of repayment). (Rabbi Eliashiv).

[10] With respect to society at large, see Gittin 45a and Tosf. there concerning the limits to a community's responsibility to redeem captives at the cost of impoverishing the community.

[11] The modern concern with the costs of healthcare to society may be partially misplaced: by no means all of the costs incurred in a particular prevention or treatment strategy represent resources wasted. Much healthcare spending forms a valid part of the general economy and is no more "wasted" than funds spent in many other areas that are not seen as wasteful; money circulating in the healthcare sector generates employment and maintains valid and intrinsically valuable aspects of the health industry. It is an error to assume that the funds spent on a particular disease management strategy are lost to society *even where those costs could have been saved.* A more relevant measure would be the amount of funds and resources truly wasted, or at the least, funds spent that could have been put to *better* use from a global economic perspective, rather than simply gross costs.

The monetary costs of a particular disease to society are often quoted in the literature with the implied assumption that those costs represent a drain on that society's resources, but in fact much of the cost of keeping a patient with "poor quality of life" alive may be incurred in caregivers' livelihoods and the purchase of goods and services that are worth supporting in their own right and that represent legitimate parts of the general economy. It is far from clear that every dollar spent on such patients could or would have been spent on more necessary ends. To make the argument that money is being wasted in the pursuit of a particular healthcare end, or that the cost of a particular healthcare modality is a burden on society, more evidence is needed than simply a gross accounting of funds spent.

Of course, this consideration applies to costs to society at large. The costs to particular patients or their families is another matter entirely - see note 9 above.

(iv) Judaism posits certain medical ethical principles that are not specifically addressed in the secular world. For example, the Code of Jewish Law [12] states that no physician may treat a patient where there is a more competent physician available – in Jewish law, the patient must receive the best possible treatment. In the secular world, and particularly in the world of academic medicine, relatively junior physicians may treat patients as part of their training. This means that while the junior learns, the patient does not necessarily receive the best treatment available. Now a case may be made for this practice in terms of society's broader needs – junior doctors need to learn, and in the long run training them in this way will benefit patients in the future – but that case would not stand up to Torah scrutiny. In fact, from a Jewish perspective it might be argued that those junior doctors are learning incorrectly: they are learning that the patient does not come first. Of course this approach raises real issues. [13]

Halachic Methodology

Halachic analysis assumes certain methods. [14] A fundamental element to grasp in all halachic investigation and presentation is that halachic principles are derived and demonstrated in hypothetical purity. This

---

[12] Sh. Aruch Y.D. 326 states that the treating physician must be expert, that he may not practice if a more competent physician is available, and that if he is not duly licensed he is liable for damages even if he is expert. ("Duly licensed" means sanctioned by the relevant Bet Din; in modern society this requirement may be satisfied by conventional certification in countries where standards are rigorous – Aruch HaShulchan Y.D. 336.)

Birchei Yosef 336:4 insists that the patient demand the best doctor available; but Tzitz Eliezer 5, Ramat Rachel 22, explains that the Birchei Yosef was dealing with a time and place in which there was no standard certification of doctors and a real danger existed that unqualified personnel would treat patients. In the modern context where controlled standards of supervision and accreditation apply, these may adequately answer the concern of the Birchei Yosef.

Rabbi Eliashiv, based on Sotah 12b (see Maharsha there), makes the point that the "best" doctor or therapy is not always required provided that the quality of care provided meets a certain standard of excellence which is fully adequate.

[13] The exceptions to this rule are: a junior doctor may administer treatment when: (i) all more senior physicians are fully occupied, (ii) a procedure is well within the capability of the junior, or (iii) the junior is under the direct responsibility and guidance of a senior.

[14] See also Appendix I: How a Rabbi Decides an Issue in Medical Halacha.

means that in halachic discussion all relevant variables are assumed to be clear, transparent, stable and guaranteed. Of course, real life is not like that, but one can study a subject objectively only when its elements are fixed – this is nothing other than a well-known aspect of the scientific method: the variables in an experiment are carefully frozen in the artificial environment of the laboratory before the experiment begins. When all is stable and controlled, one variable is carefully shifted in order to study its effect in isolation; when that has been done, that variable may be fixed and another chosen for investigation. This system is highly artificial but it is exactly what is necessary for accurately characterising variables and their effects. In analogous fashion in halacha, when facts and parameters are specified in a halachic discussion they are assumed to be perfect and invariable. Doubts and unknowns are not to be added to the mix – all is assumed to be exactly as specified for the purpose of clear analysis. Once the outcome is achieved and the principle at hand clarified, the real-world factors of doubt and unknown elements can be introduced; in fact, there is an organized halachic approach to the subject of doubt itself. But the principle remains: even when an extremely artificial situation must be constructed or assumed, that will be done in the laboratory of halacha in order to conduct a meaningful experiment.

Of course, that is how medicine is taught too: clinical principles are presented in glorious clarity; anatomy and physiology are taught in pure tones of black and white. But when the physician approaches a real patient in a real clinical setting all the variables may be swimming in shades of grey. In fact, that is exactly the test of clinical expertise; when things are clear, experience and expertise are far less relevant. In halacha, senior judgment is needed for exactly that purpose: a primary reason for seeking senior halachic opinion and guidance is to gain clarity in those situations that are complicated and confusing, where the operative variables are vague and conflicting and mature judgment is necessary.

In medicine, consultant expertise is an extremely valuable commodity; there is no substitute for the depth of wisdom in clinical judgment that comes with years of thoughtful experience. In halacha, in a more profound sense, there is no substitute for the depth of opinion of senior Torah authority; in fact, in an essential way, that opinion *is* halacha. In halacha the opinion of a duly qualified *posek* (halachic decisor) is not only an assessment of the facts, it is deeply definitive – the halachic reality is deeply sensitive to the specific ruling itself.[15]

In real-world halachic application it often happens that the relevant principles are clear, but how they are to be applied is not. Not infrequently a case falls on the borderline between halachic territories because the *medical* situation is subject to doubt so that it is unclear which halachic principle to apply. This is of course a problem not unique to halacha: within medicine itself there is very often uncertainty concerning diagnosis or therapy when a case falls in the "grey zone" between clear-cut medical categories. And again, this is precisely where mature judgment is necessary. In fact, a primary reason for consulting Torah sages should be exactly for the purpose of seeking their judgment when these difficult decisions must be made.

---

[15] Unlike in medicine where the expert assesses the reality, in Torah the authority who decides *adds* an aspect to the reality of the situation. A fuller explanation of this facet of halacha is beyond the scope of this work; but see Chapter 1 of this author's *Worldmask* (Targum Press). Here, one brief illustrative example will be given. In Torah, what is dominant: a majority of competent opinion or a minority of superior opinion? The general resolution in the Talmud favors the majority (even where the minority opinion can apparently adduce objective demonstrations of its validity – Bava Metzia 59b). What is the Torah approach to the analogous situation in medicine? If two senior consultants were to recommend a particular course of action and a single, more senior, consultant recommends differently, how should this conflict be resolved? This author had occasion to seek Rabbi Eliashiv's ruling on such a conflict: two consultant cardiologists recommended the use of a plastic prosthetic valve for aortic valve replacement in a particular case while one more senior authority recommended a porcine valve. Rabbi Eliashiv ruled that the decision should rest with the patient. In deciding a Torah matter of this kind, the majority is definitive; in medicine, that is not necessarily the case.

(It is important to realize that in this case Rabbi Eliashiv was asked to decide between options neither of which was presented as objectively superior in terms of survival; the question was which combination of risks and benefits would be preferable where both are acceptable medically – on the one hand the risks of anticoagulation in the case of a plastic valve which would probably last for the patient's lifetime, and on the other, the risk of possible later re-operation in the case of a porcine valve which may not remain functional permanently but which requires no anticoagulation. Since both options are medically legitimate, it is entirely appropriate that the patient makes the choice.)

It is a general feature of the real world that clearly defined categories meet at an interface that may be blurred. Categories may be indistinguishable where they meet and overlap. This is well known to all practising physicians – at some point cellular anaplasia becomes frank carcinoma, but exactly where that point is may be impossible to define. At some point a blood test becomes abnormal, but exactly where that point is may be difficult to say – the normal values given by any laboratory do not distinguish *exactly* between normal and abnormal except by convention; in the close vicinity of the published norm clinical relevance is always a matter of judgment. Similarly, halachic categories may be sharply defined, but exactly where the application of one ends and the next begins in the blurred and often messy material world may appear impossible to identify, and it is here that senior halachic opinion is necessary.[16]

Dispute and Opinion

Many issues in medical halacha are subject to dispute or sensitive to particular expert opinion. Within the world of legitimate halachic opinion more than one position may be encountered. In some cases discussed in this book a definitive approach is given; occasionally one is not. Where a clear consensus is not indicated, the individual physician must seek personal guidance in arriving at a definitive approach by consulting competent halachic authority. The purpose of including issues that are not resolved in the discussions here is to educate the student of Jewish medical ethics about what constitutes a valid question in this area of halacha and what are the facts and details relevant to the question so that the student can become *learned in the questions* – at the least this will enable asking questions correctly. This, too, is part of the necessary wisdom in this field.

Risk

Many medical situations involve risk, and virtually all therapies have inherent risk.[17] It is difficult to think of a medical or surgical intervention that is entirely risk free – whether it is the administration of a common

---

[16] See for example Approach to Risk in Halacha, p.45. The level of risk that can be justified for a particular benefit is very often a matter for Torah judgment; in the wide "grey zone" of this field senior Torah stature is often called upon to render decisions.

[17] See Approach to Risk in Halacha, p. 45.

medication, the injection of a local anesthetic or even the simple setting of a fracture, all have risk.[18]

One of the meanings of the injunction of "*v'rapo y'rape* – and you shall heal"[19] is to allow human involvement in seeking and providing healing. Perhaps the best-known interpretation of these words is to allow man to act in healing when God has caused illness – lest one think that there may be a prohibition here, the Torah sanctions human involvement in healing.[20] But another meaning is to permit healing activity although such activity inevitably confers risk; the Torah sanctions and obliges[21] attempts to heal despite the fact that virtually all healing modalities have inherent risk. One who reasons that it would be better not to engage in the practice of medicine for fear of causing unavoidable harm is reasoning incorrectly: the Torah specifically allows the practice of medicine despite that risk.[22]

Another facet of this mandate is to allow the specific medical interventions of each generation: although we note that the Torah allows healing, how do we know that a *particular* therapy is allowed? After all, the briefest examination of the history of medicine shows that virtually all therapies adopted as standard in one era are superseded in a later one. In fact, very many standard therapies are later shown to be at best ineffective and at worst harmful. How can we administer any current therapy while acutely aware that in a few short years that form of therapy is likely to be shown to be inappropriate or harmful? Many modern interventions become widespread only to be shown to have serious side-effects, not infrequently within the space of a few years or less. Here the Torah says "*v'rapo y'rape* – and you shall heal...;" that is, you are to

---

[18] Ramban, T. Ha'Adam: "With regard to cures there is nothing but danger; what heals one kills another." See Ran, Sanhedrin 84b with regard to medical error.

[19] Exodus 21:19.

[20] B. Kama 85a; Rashi, Tosf. and Rashba there.

[21] There is debate over whether this verse gives dispensation or posits an obligation. The Ramban (T. HaAdam) states: *"hai reshus, reshus d'mitzva hi...–* this permission (or authority) is a mitzva." The Ramban acknowledges that there is an obligation here but shows that less intervention may be appropriate for those whose spiritual level is adequately developed (see Ramban on Leviticus 26:11). See Rambam, commentary on the Mishna, Pesachim 4:9.

[22] Ramban, T. HaAdam (2:43); Sh. Aruch Y.D. 336:1. See Shach there (sub. para. 1) who explains the Sh. Aruch thus.

engage in the practice of medicine using the best investigations and therapies currently known despite the awareness that in a subsequent period those maneuvers are likely to be discarded as useless or worse.

The philosophy underlying this process (and it forms an essential element in understanding the Torah approach to all human endeavor) is this: it is not the particular therapy that heals in the first place, it is God who does. The small white tablet that the patient swallows is not the ultimate cause of the cure; it is God's intervention that is effective. Yet man must act; there is an obligation of human effort. So a schizoid approach is required: the physician's attitude must be: "I am not the healer here; God is. Whatever happens to my patient is in His hands, not mine. *And yet I will treat the patient as if his every breath depends on me....*" The standard of care must be the best that modern medicine has to offer; the fact that the details of that standard will change is irrelevant. The physician must provide the best of current investigations and therapies; if healing results it will come from the only real Source of healing. Current therapies are simply the means for Divine intervention to manifest, and those means are not specifically indicated in themselves in an absolute way. Next year's drugs will be the correct ones to prescribe next year, when today's drugs will be obsolete and indeed wrong to use. The physician's obligation is to use the best means currently available in applying *v'rapo y'rape;* that injunction mandates the attempt to heal and allows those means to be used as the medium for that effort despite the knowledge that they are very likely to change.

The Primary Value of Life

In the hierarchy of Torah values the saving of life is a priority. It supersedes virtually all other obligations and mandates virtually unlimited effort.[23] With very few specific exceptions (murder, sexual

---

[23] In the prioritizing of lifesaving, the following limitations should be noted:

(1) These extreme measures apply only where a dangerous entity is present or may be expected to supervene – see further discussion in this chapter.

(2) A specific identifiable individual must be at risk – there is either a patient "in front of us" (*lefaneinu*) or a real and present danger that threatens (see Clinical Case 21, p. 191).

(3) Even in high risk situations there is a limit to obligation set by the standard of care – see Standard of Care, p. 39.

immorality and idolatry) one is generally obliged to transgress all else in the attempt to save life and there are virtually no limits to the effort required by halacha in such attempts (exceptions and limitations are clarified in the chapters that follow). These extreme principles apply:

(i) *even where the risk to life is small or unclear* – virtually any risk to life mandates extreme effort to avert that risk;

(ii) *even where there is no guarantee that the life at risk will be saved* – even a small chance of success mandates extreme effort to save that life;

and even when (i) and (ii) co-exist; that is, where the risk to life is small or indefinite *and* where success is unlikely in the event that the risk turns out to be real;

(iii) *even where the life to be saved is of "low quality";*

(iv) *even where the life to be saved is expected to be of short duration;*

and even when (iii) and (iv) co-exist; that is where a life of very poor quality can be extended only for a very short period.[24]

The laws governing the saving of life are operative even before an acute threat to life is present: an insulin-dependent diabetic who is due to receive a dose of insulin and has none available is regarded as if in danger immediately – the Sabbath may be desecrated to procure that dose right now; one does not wait until clinical signs manifest and coma is imminent. Since it is clear that a danger to life will develop later if no treatment is given now, that danger is regarded as present.[25]

The priority of saving life in halacha has unique features: for example, although the rule of following a majority has extremely broad application

---

(4) Where the effort to save life involves risk to the physician or others – see Risk to Caregivers, p. 55.

(5) Where therapy may or indeed should be withheld according to halacha, for example in certain situations of terminal illness – see Approach to Dangerous and Terminal Illness, p. 101.

[24] Yoma 85b – this Talmudic discussion indicates that where a life needs to be saved, even if that life is of extremely low quality and subject to extremely short prolongation at most, neither factor negates the obligation to desecrate the Sabbath in the attempt.

[25] Inevitable future danger is regarded as if present: see Minchat Avraham 42, Achiezer 3:72; cf. Seridei Esh 3, p. 320.

in halacha, it is generally irrelevant in lifesaving.[26] In situations of danger to life even a small minority has significance. A danger to life in a particular medical situation must not be ignored on the grounds that most such situations turn out to be non-lethal; even a small minority of lethal outcomes makes it obligatory to treat *each* case of that sort as if it is likely to be lethally dangerous. One may desecrate the Sabbath for *any* patient with pneumonia although most patients with pneumonia recover – since a minority of patients with pneumonia succumb to the disease every case is regarded as a possible danger to life in halacha. Generally, one should prioritise lifesaving efforts regardless of whether there is a statistical majority in favor of survival or not.

Note however, that this applies where a situation of danger or possible danger *already exists*. Where the danger is not yet present, for example, where a question arises concerning undertaking a course of action *that may bring about* a dangerous situation but where no danger presently exists, majorities may in fact be relevant.[27] A journey may be undertaken even where it is known that the traveller may possibly encounter danger (and even where the statistical risk of encountering such danger is significant). Binyan Tzion[28] discusses the question of a woman who wished to become pregnant against medical advice; he allowed her to do so despite the possible danger to her life that a pregnancy might cause. In the course of his analysis Binyan Tzion points out that although one may not rely on a majority in a case of danger that is already present, one may undertake sea and desert voyages where danger may develop during the voyage because in those cases the danger is a future possibility and not a present threat.[29] Likewise, entering a pregnancy that may prove dangerous could be acceptable under certain conditions.[30]

The Talmud clearly states the principle that majorities are not determinative with regard to danger to life: "We do not follow the

---

[26] Yoma 83a and 84b; Ketubot 15b; Shevet HaLevi 1:40.

[27] This is not to be confused with the case of the diabetic patient mentioned above – in that situation although clinical signs are not yet manifest, a pathological process that endangers life is already in progress.

[28] Binyan Tzion 137.

[29] See Approach to Risk in Halacha, p. 45 for other considerations.

[30] See Interventions in Pregnancy, p. 89.

majority in lifesaving."[31] The reason for this is:[32] "And he shall live by them"[33] – and not die by them; meaning that we must not allow *any* possibility of death.[34]

Is there a limit to this principle – is there a minority so small that it can be considered null? Divrei Malkiel[35] demonstrates that there must be some limit, and debates what that limit must be. A vanishingly small chance of danger (one in many thousands) may usually be discounted – such distant risks do not ordinarily constitute *pikuach nefesh* (concern for danger to life).[36]

A useful principle here is that even the smallest likelihood of danger must be taken seriously *where the cause of danger exists;*[37] however, some situations that may become dangerous need not be regarded as presently dangerous where the cause of danger is not present. For example: not every upper respiratory tract infection should be regarded as a potential danger to life on the grounds that some of these infections will proceed to

---

[31] Yoma 84b; Ketubot 15b.

[32] Tosf., Yoma 85a.

[33] Leviticus 18.

[34] Other sources can be adduced for a majority probability of safety not being enough to allow danger to life: in a ruling (B. Din *piskei dinim* 8:216 under R. Zevulun Graz) concerning forcing a divorce where a husband was exhibiting dangerous behavior, the suggestion is made that a minority cannot be ignored in situations of danger to life based on Avk. Rochel 213 who quotes a responsum of the Radbaz stating that a *s'fek s'feka* ("doubt within a doubt") remains significant (although ordinarily such a doubt is discounted) because the Ramban (Chullin) states that doubtful status (concerning impurity) in a public domain is forbidden in certain cases where the Torah states that "guarding" is required, even though such doubt in the public domain is usually permitted. It appears from here that in cases where "guarding" is required there must be certainty; a majority assumption is not enough. Now the obligation to avoid danger to life is expressed in the Torah as "Guard your souls well..."; since the term "guard" is used, this possibly indicates that certainty and not majority is required.

[35] Divrei Malkiel 5:35.

[36] Ch. Sofer YD 338; see also Ch. Sofer YD 245.

[37] Aruch HaShulchan (O.C. 316:22) states that although many layers of doubt do not extinguish the obligation to take danger to life seriously, there may be some limits where a source of possible danger is not evident. See Nishm. Avraham (Vol. 1, p. 191) for detailed discussion and references.

pneumonia. That is usually too distant a concern. However, if pneumonia is already present, no matter how apparently mild and uncomplicated, it should be regarded as a potential danger to life. The distinction is this: in the case of an upper respiratory tract infection, the dangerous entity (pneumonia) is not present (although there is a small chance that it will develop). In the case of pneumonia however, *the element of danger is already present;* the chance that it will become a threat to life may be small, but that is irrelevant – pneumonia can certainly be dangerous and that is enough.

Of course, where a non-dangerous entity *commonly* leads to a dangerous one, then even where the specific danger is not yet present the patient must be regarded as in danger – an immunocompromised patient with a simple upper respiratory tract infection should certainly be treated as in danger. In such a case the danger is present. Similarly, the diabetic patient who has no insulin (mentioned previously) is regarded as presently in danger even though it may be many hours before signs manifest – one must not wait until overt signs of pathology develop before desecrating the Sabbath, for example, to obtain insulin.

There are also special halachic dispensations designed to facilitate lifesaving and obviate any potential hesitancy on the part of lifesaving personnel:

(i) A midwife may accept a fee for Sabbath work.[38]

(ii) Those who must travel to attend to a case of danger on the Sabbath may return on the Sabbath.[39]

(iii) Someone who pursues a dangerous aggressor is exempt from any damages caused in the attempt to prevent disaster.[40]

(iv) Physicians are exempt from liability for unintentional harm arising during treatment of patients.[41]

---

[38] Mishna Berura 306:24.

[39] Eruvin 44.

[40] Sanhedrin 74.

[41] Tosefta Gittin 3:13; Sh. Aruch, Y. D. 336.

Statistics

Halacha does not relate to statistical values and probabilities in the same way that secular thinking does. Statistical tools are basic to modern medicine in research, diagnostic and prognostic assessments and virtually every facet of medicine. As will become clear in the sections that follow, there are numerous applications in halacha of rules governing majorities and minorities of various types, and it is true that probabilities often feature prominently in questions put to halachic decisors, but the application of a statistical probability derived from large samples to a specific case is not done in quite the way that medicine does.[42]

Unknown Benefit, Unknown Harm

There is a halachic principle that resolves the dilemma of certain dangerous situations where the possible benefit or harm of a particular intervention is not known: in situations where an intervention may save a life if successful but endanger or terminate that life if not, the halacha forbids action.[43] To state this principle in general: if it is not known whether an intervention will help or harm, where all else is equal it is better to have harm result through non-action than to cause (equivalent) harm through well-intentioned but mistaken action. For example, if a patient has been injured and it is not clear whether a particular injury has been sustained that makes a certain manipulation lifesaving if that injury is present, or life-threatening if it is not, it is better to accept the risk of harm through non-intervention than to assume the risk of causing harm by inappropriate action.

---

[42] Exploration of the reasons for the halacha's circumspection and even occasional skepticism regarding modern medicine's pervasive application of statistics to individual cases is beyond the scope of this work. For limitations to the validity of statistics in prognostication in the general literature, see Ware, JH. Statistics and Medicine: the Limitations of Risk Factors as Prognostic Tools. N Engl J Med 2006;355:2615.

[43] Achiezer, Part 2, Y.D. 16:6, based on Avoda Zara 27b and Sh. Aruch Y.D. 155:1. Achiezer states that where it is not known whether a patient will live or die (untreated) and an operation can be performed that will result in permanent cure if successful but may result in immediate death, the operation is forbidden. (However *where it is clear that the patient will die without it* he allows such a procedure - see Risky Treatment in *chayei sha'a* Situations, p. 118.)

A theoretical clinical example may help to clarify this: if a patient has sustained a neck injury and it is unclear whether a spinal fracture is present that threatens to disrupt the cervical spinal cord and cause death, and the clinical dilemma at the scene of injury is whether to gently align the patient's neck to relieve cord pressure before immobilization and thereby avert imminent death, or to immobilize the neck without an attempt at alignment to avoid causing a cord injury which is not yet present, all else being equal it is better to accept the risks of non-manipulation than to take the risk of causing catastrophic injury actively. Put more starkly: if neither of the two options (action or non-action) has a greater chance of saving life, it is preferable that the patient dies because the attendant fails to act than that the patient dies because the attendant kills him.

It is essential to understand that this applies *only where all else is equal:* in our scenario we are assuming that the best possible medical assessment cannot determine whether the patient is surviving because no manipulation is being undertaken and in fact any such manipulation would be lethal, or the patient is dying and the manipulation would be lifesaving. In other words, the best possible assessment suggests that the patient has a 50% chance of survival no matter what is done: there is an equal likelihood that he will survive because we do not act as that he will survive because we do. It should be clear that we are not affecting his chances of survival by our choice at all – in either case he has a 50% chance of survival; on the side of survival the only difference is whether we save him by our action when he would otherwise have died, or whether he survives because we do not act when he would have died had we acted. In these circumstances, since we are unable to increase the patient's chances of survival either way, intervention is prohibited.

A medical (as opposed to surgical) example might be that of a patient with a condition that may remit spontaneously or progress to death, with a 50% probability of either. If we could offer the patient a therapy that would be curative in the event that the disease progresses but lethal in the case that remission is imminent, all else being equal it would be better to withhold the therapy. Again, the reasoning is that we are unable to affect the overall chance of survival; all we can do is choose to allow a passive danger if we are wrong on the one hand or to be the active agents of danger if we are wrong on the other. In either case there is a 50% chance of death: either due to disease progression that we failed to avert with therapy or due to the lethal effect of our therapy when we failed to wait for the spontaneous remission that would have occurred. Here again we should opt not to be the active cause of the negative outcome. And again, this is only where all else is equal – if we could sway the probabilities even slightly a very different halachic handling may be mandated (such scenarios will be presented in the chapters that follow).[44]

Standard of Care

Widely accepted norms have halachic significance.[45] Where a certain standard of care is widely practised it becomes the minimum standard that is halachically acceptable – doing more is praiseworthy but not obliged; doing less is negligent. This applies even in critical situations: an ICU (intensive care unit) must be run at a level of excellence that forms the professional standard demanded in the best institutions. Anything less would be regarded as inadequate professionally and would therefore be unacceptable halachically. An ICU team that works to an even higher standard is extremely meritorious in halachic terms, but such outstanding practice cannot be demanded.

In working through diagnostic algorithms the same consideration applies: certain protocols are accepted in building a differential diagnosis, such as excluding more common conditions before less common ones, or using simple and inexpensive diagnostic tests before more complex and expensive ones. These patterns are acceptable halachically not because they are the best possible but because they define normal practice. It should be noted that this approach means that serious and urgent diagnoses will not always be made in timely fashion: the occasional rare but serious diagnosis will be missed until too late where a higher index of suspicion that would have led to more extreme diagnostic efforts may have been successful; nevertheless the doctor who works to the normal

---

[44] Perhaps the secular medical correlate of this halachic principle is the notion of *primum non nocere* - "First, do no harm." This often-quoted maxim is usually assumed to be Hippocratic; in fact it does not appear in the corpus of Hippocratic writings, although a related idea does: "I will use treatment to help the sick... but I will never use it to injure or wrong them." (The principle is vague and unqualified; modern ethicists therefore question its applicability.) See Non-maleficence, p. 224.

[45] See for example the definition of minimal risk, p. 45.

professional standard will not be considered halachically negligent in those rare cases.[46] [47]

In all areas of medical practice, the halachic standard of care must be the very best currently available; more is optional and greatly to be admired, less is negligent and culpable.

Clinical Logic

The notion of a generally accepted standard can be extended to the principles of clinical decision-making. Diagnostic and treatment decisions based on a broadly recognised set of rules[48] that are practical and based on sound empirical evidence are unremarkable halachically, unlike decisions that are inherently value-laden.

Be Prepared

It should go without saying that the physician must be prepared – in the field of dangerous illness clinical changes can occur rapidly and the clinician may not have time for the luxury of lengthy consultation with

---

[46] It might seem that all efforts, no matter how extreme, should be required: perhaps every diagnostic workup should include an immediate and exhaustive search for every conceivable diagnosis (at least all those that are critical and treatable) giving no more weight to common diagnostic possibilities than rare ones and abandoning the usual step-wise process of excluding diagnostic possibilities in logical sequence. Such extreme attempts to ensure that no urgent and treatable condition is ever missed may be praiseworthy, but they are not required – that is not the approach taken by the best clinicians in the best of academic medical settings, and it is therefore not halachically obligatory (Rabbi Chaim Greineman).

[47] This "standard of care" criterion is not valid, however, where halacha specifically mandates a higher level: where a standard of care is based on statistical majorities, for example, and the halacha specifically excludes relying on majorities in situations of danger to life, the common standard is halachically void.

[48] Such as those expressed by these well-known aphorisms:
- Exclude common conditions before uncommon ones.
- Exclude urgent uncommon conditions before less urgent common ones.
- Rare presentations of common conditions are more likely than common presentations of rare conditions.
- If a test result is surprising, repeat the test.
- If a test will not affect management of the patient, do not perform the test.

halachic authority. A life-threatening emergency may leave no time for protracted dispassionate analysis and the opportunity to ask detailed halachic questions. In such circumstances there is no substitute for being prepared; there is no excuse for not studying this material in advance. Just as every physician must know how to handle any clinical emergency that is likely to arise in his field of practice without recourse to texts, second opinions or senior help in circumstances that preclude such assistance, so too every physician who will have to apply the halachos of acute life and death situations must be prepared in advance. The minimum preparation required is that which will enable the physician to respond in all clinical situations in accordance with halacha at least until the medical situation has stabilized enough to permit consultation with senior opinion. The basic principles of *pikuach nefesh* (lifesaving) and their common clinical applications must be second nature to the practising physician no less than the ability to react to sudden cardiovascular collapse or impending tracheal obstruction.

Clinical Cases – Principles

Clinical Case 1: Benefit or Harm?

A 35 year old man's isolated lymph node swelling was diagnosed as an indolent lymphoma. One expert advised chemotherapy, another advised watchful waiting with no therapy. Their respective reasons were: immediate chemotherapy may avert or delay the change to an aggressive form of the disease; on the other hand chemotherapy is unlikely to eradicate the disease entirely, and if aggressive transformation takes place it may be less responsive to therapy because tolerance is likely to have developed due to the earlier therapy, so it would be better to hold chemotherapy in reserve for use when it is most likely to be effective.

In addition to these considerations, the patient had recently married and was concerned about the damage chemotherapy would almost certainly cause to his fertility. He sought halachic guidance and was advised to obtain a third expert medical opinion. The third consultant agreed with the strategy of withholding chemotherapy, and the patient was halachically advised to follow the majority medical view.

It is now five years later. The disease is stable, although one superficial lymph node may have enlarged slightly; the bone marrow is clear. The same three experts all maintain their original recommendations. The patient now has children, but is still desirous of maintaining fertility. He again seeks halachic guidance.

How should he be advised?

Analysis:

The proposed chemotherapy may help or harm; which outcome is more likely is a matter of opinion. The halachic principle governing situations where it is not known whether an intervention will cause benefit or harm is to avoid causing damage actively – it is preferable that harm occurs due to lack of intervention than due to actively causing it.

In addition to the question of chemotherapy and disease arrest or progression, there is also the question of fertility impairment that must be taken into account. A certain amount of risk would be acceptable halachically to avoid this complication.

Where medical opinion is split, seeking a third opinion is often recommended halachically. In this case that has been done; there is a clear and consistent majority view, and it is halachically appropriate to favor this majority.

Therefore in this case, after five years of stable disease, and in view of the preponderance of expert opinion and the patient's desire not to compromise his fertility, the correct decision is to omit chemotherapy for the present.

Approach to Risk in Halacha

Correct application of much of the material in the chapters that follow depends on an accurate understanding of the halachic approach to risk. This section considers risk in general, indicating the medical relevance of its various elements.

Risk can be stratified into three broad categories from a halachic perspective.[1]

Minimal Risk

Activities included in this category are those commonly undertaken in society at large without consideration of risk – *dash bo rabim,* or those areas that "the many tread." The operative halachic principle here is that "God protects the simple" (or innocent) who do what is normal and broadly accepted in their time and place.[2]

It is noteworthy that the risk constituting this category is not measured statistically,[3] but rather by common practice. This measure is unfamiliar to modern medicine; in present-day medical practice risk is categorized by actuarial statistic. For example, in modern genetic counselling a risk of congenital abnormality of less than 5% is conventionally regarded as low and above 10% as substantial. In medicine (and many other fields), risk-benefit ratios are considered in statistical terms. The halachic standard for

---

[1] See Doubtful Danger, p. 59 for the approach to situations in which a clear risk level cannot be assigned.

[2] Shabbat 129b; Yevamot 12b; Ketubot 39a; Nidda 31a. See Darchei Teshuva Y.D 155:1:2.

[3] See p. 37 and note 42 there.

low risk, while certainly requiring a low absolute risk, is defined more by common practice than by statistical value.

An example of activities that fall into this risk category would be use of a motor vehicle in normal circumstances. Travelling in a motor vehicle has definite risks which can be quantified by statistical analysis; however, such travel is halachically permitted because this is a risk that society at large has accepted. One need not assess the risk-benefit relation of an ordinary motor vehicle journey before undertaking it; it is permitted regardless of that risk. Scheduled airline travel would be another example; modern society at large accepts the small risk associated with air travel and that is enough to permit it halachically.[4]

Medically related examples might be the ingestion of food additives or other products whose safety may never have been conclusively demonstrated. If those products are routinely used in general society such use would be halachically sanctioned. Of course, if real evidence appears suggesting harm, that evidence would have to be evaluated before continued use of such products could be allowed; if the evidence proves valid, the practice may become halachically unacceptable. A standard based on widespread practice makes an activity permissible only when that activity is broadly known to be safe; where harm is known to occur in the majority of instances, as in the case of smoking, the practice becomes forbidden, even when that harm will not manifest immediately.[5]

Another common example is childhood immunization.[6] The following case is illustrative of how normative practice forms the standard of care in Jewish law, and brings out the broad applicability of the accepted norm.[7]

---

[4] See Appendix V: Transport Modes – Risks. When planning a journey one is not obliged to compare the relative safety of flying and driving – since both are very widely used both are allowed with no further reservation.

[5] See R. JD Bleich. Smoking. Tradition Vol. 16:4, 1977, pp. 121-123.

[6] See also Prevention and Screening, p. 207.

[7] For discussion of the concept of defining danger by popular perception and behavior, and with specific reference to childhood immunization, see Minch. Shlomo 2; 29:4. It is possible that Minch. Shlomo would agree that even where people regard a particular activity as risky enough to refrain from in general, where people would engage in that activity *where they have a good reason*, that activity becomes permitted by the same criterion of *dash bo rabim* (that is, the majority undertake it freely) discussed above – one would be allowed to

Parents of a particular family in this author's practice objected to the administration of pertussis (whooping cough) immunization to their children on the grounds that the pertussis vaccine was thought to confer a risk of neurological complications in a small but definite percentage of children immunized.[8] Conventionally, pertussis vaccine is given despite this possible harm because the risk of a young child's contracting pertussis and suffering severe complications is greater than the risk of the vaccine.[9] However, in discussion with the parents a challenging observation was made: the risk of the disease and its complications is greater than the risk of the vaccine *only in unimmunized populations* – but when most children have been immunized the risk to the remaining few is greater *from the vaccine than from the disease* because there will be no outbreak of disease in such a population.

This raises an obvious ethical question: is it proper to impose immunization on an unwilling minority when the population they are part of is already immune to the degree that no epidemic is likely occur? On the one hand, why impose such an action? The minority is not endangering the majority which is already immune. But on the other hand, is it moral for such a minority to "ride" on the immunity of the majority which has been achieved at risk to each of the individuals comprising that majority? And of course there is always the danger that the minority will grow to a critical proportion such that an outbreak of disease becomes possible.

---

undertake such activities *where good reason exists* but not otherwise (R.Y Zilberstein; R. JD Bleich). This would be an alternative approach to allowing entering situations of some danger to that suggested in Moderate Risk below. See there for discussion of what might constitute "good reason" for permitting some danger. See also p. 51 and note 23 there.

(For a discussion of immunization in general, see Tif. Yisrael Mishna Yoma 8:7 Boaz 3 who allows smallpox vaccination with a mortality of 1 in 1,000 where the mortality of the disease is higher than this.)

[8] Figures available at the time suggested a risk of serious harm attributable to pertussis immunization of approximately 1 in 10,000 to 1 in 20,000 cases.

[9] Children younger than 18 months, and particularly those under 12 months, who contract pertussis are at higher risk of life-threatening complications. See Halperin, SA et al. Epidemiological features of pertussis in hospitalized patients in Canada, 1991-1997. Clin Infect Dis 1999;28:1238; and Pertussis, United States, 2001-2003. MMWR Morb Mortal Wkly Rep 2005;54:1283.

The question was put to Rabbi Eliashiv, who ruled that the parents should accede to immunization despite their concerns. When asked if the reason behind his ruling was the issue of fairness and the obligation to share responsibility, Rabbi Eliashiv indicated that it was not; his reason was that *since immunization of children is normal practice* throughout the world, one should follow that normative course. In fact, Rabbi Eliashiv went so far as to assert that failure to immunize would amount to negligence.[10]

In the modern health context this normative principle would mandate abstaining from those activities and practices that are established to be damaging, for example smoking, and conversely to engage in those that are thought to be salutary by a consensus of experts and broadly accepted by the population at large. If particular trends in diet, for example, based on good evidence, become broadly accepted in a particular era then those recommendations should be taken seriously. Conversely, one is not required to be concerned with fringe movements recommending various health modalities as long as those modalities are not broadly established as valid.[11]

Moderate Risk

This category comprises activities that, although having a relatively low absolute risk, are not commonly undertaken by a majority of society without special reason. The general halachic attitude here is that such

---

[10] A philosophical question arises here: what would be the correct analysis of a situation in which normal practice were followed and harm in fact ensued? That issue is beyond the scope of this work (but see this author's "Risks in Medicine and Surgery" in the Glatter Series "Medical Halacha" audio recordings for an approach to that question).

[11] Refusing childhood immunizations on the basis of unsubstantiated fears of vaccine side-effects is irresponsible and out of order halachically. The danger of precipitating epidemics of measles, poliomyelitis and other diseases with potentially devastating complications is far more real than the dangers attributed to vaccines on the basis of anecdotal claims. Until objective evidence to the contrary accrues, the halachically correct approach is to do what is normal. In addition, a legitimate government's legislation concerning standards of medical conduct adds weight to their halachic acceptability (R. SZ Auerbach).

activities may be undertaken only for sufficiently compelling reason. The classic example of such compelling reason is earning a living – the Talmud states that one may pick fruit from high tree branches where there may be a danger of falling, if one is doing so professionally.[12] [13]

An example from the classical halachic literature is provided by a responsum of the Nodah b'Yehuda.[14] He was asked by a professional game hunter whether the risks of his profession render such activity prohibited. The Nodah b'Yehuda answers[15] that the risk would preclude such activity were it to be undertaken outside of a professional context, but that if one earns his living from it, the risk is acceptable.

Rabbi Moshe Feinstein allows participation in professional sport despite the risk of incurring injury (and the risk of injuring others) of "one in some thousands;" since the activity is undertaken in the pursuit of a livelihood it is acceptable.[16]

Although the case of sufficiently compelling reason discussed in the Talmud is that of earning a living, halachic authorities understand this broadly: other genuine needs would similarly constitute good reason. The need to marry, for example, certainly constitutes a valid reason to undertake certain risks in the search for a suitable partner.

In the context of medicine, therefore, a patient may undertake moderate risk for a good reason. Major cosmetic surgery for a frivolous indication would not constitute a good reason; however, relatively major cosmetic surgery for the purpose of enabling a patient to obtain employment, to find a suitable marriage partner or other significant purpose would.[17] Other examples of valid reasons for the assumption of significant risk are given in the chapters that follow. Undertaking such risk for no good

---

[12] Bava Metzia 112a; Shulchan Aruch Y.D. 116:5.

[13] See Appendix IV: Risks Associated with Some Current Dangerous Occupations for relative risks of selected modern occupations.

[14] Nodah B'Yehuda, Mahadura Tinyana Y. D. 10.

[15] He also admonishes the questioner by pointing out that hunting is not an appropriate profession for a Jew.

[16] Igr. Moshe Ch. M. 1:104. See below, p. 161 and note 26 there.

[17] Or to relieve the suffering of restricted social interaction due to disfigurement; see Shabbos 50b (Tosf.) on emotional suffering. See Cosmetic Surgery, p. 197.

reason would constitute a transgression of the injunction to "Guard your souls well," but for good reason such risks are acceptable.

The cases discussed in the classical halachic literature deal with ocean voyages (or other activities) that carried risk in the relevant historical periods; such voyages involved significant risks. The responsa that permitted those activities set halachic precedents – the limit of acceptable risk undertaken for good reason would be whatever risk was involved in ocean voyages, for example, during the era of the relevant responsa. It therefore becomes important to know how risky those activities were.

Exactly how dangerous they were is difficult to quantify, and it may be hard to know where to draw the line as a general rule. The Imrei Esh[18] sets a limit at 1 in 6, but this is higher than many other authorities would allow (and in fact does not accord with the majority view). In the ruling of Rabbi Moshe Feinstein quoted above concerning professional sport, Rabbi Feinstein rules that such activity is acceptable where the danger of serious (life-threatening) injury is one in some thousands, based on B.M. 112, and mentioning the Nodah B'Yehuda. Rabbi Feinstein points out that the risk of causing injury to others must also be considered (where others enter the relevant situation knowingly) and that such risk would be permitted at the same low level of probability as that which justifies exposing oneself to risk. Rabbi Feinstein would allow a danger of 1 in 1,000; he mentions "one in a few thousand" only because that was the figure presented to him in the specific question.[19]

This figure of 1 in 1,000 is corroborated by R. Akiva Eiger[20] and Magen Avraham.[21] (Sefer Chassidim expresses concern about dangers that are 1 in 1,000; however Shem Aryeh[22] explains that the Sefer Chassidim is setting a limit beyond what is strictly required.)

A general medical application of this category of moderate risk would be general anesthesia (although there are authorities who feel that modern

---

[18] Imrei Esh Y.D. 52. See note 31 below.

[19] As understood by Rabbi Y. Zilberstein.

[20] R. Akiva Eiger resp. 60.

[21] Magen Avraham O.C. 316:23.

[22] Shem Aryeh 27.

anesthesia under ideal elective conditions is safe enough to be classed in the minimal risk category).[23] [24]

In more general terms, to apply a therapy that is generally considered safe but has a small known risk, the relevant principles are:[25]

(i) The therapy must be known to be safe *in the relevant clinical situation* and not by theoretical extrapolation from dissimilar situations such as from experience with patients who are younger, healthier or at different stages of the relevant disease condition;

(ii) The therapy must be known to be beneficial in a majority of cases – over 50%;

(iii) The patient must consent to the treatment.[26]

What is the upper bound of this risk category – what statistical risk separates moderate from high risk? Here again, it is important to note that the boundary is not set at a clear-cut statistical value. Firstly, as noted above, the halacha does not relate to statistical values in the way that secular thinking does.[27] Secondly, there is a relatively wide range of opinion on this matter among halachic authorities. Generally, this is an area that must be approached on a case-by-case basis; halachic judgment must be brought to bear on each specific case. Nuances of a case can make a significant difference; there is no absolute mechanical rule here. Nevertheless, a general approach to quantifying the levels of moderate and high risk and separating them into distinct halachic categories is given in the following section.

---

[23] R. JD Bleich. These authorities hold that even moderate risk can be undertaken on the basis of *dash bo rabim* (activities that are so broadly accepted that they are permitted as discussed in Low Risk above) because where such risks are broadly taken *in particular circumstances* (that is, where sufficiently good reason exists to justify that risk in popular practice) they are regarded as normal (but of course only when they are taken *in those circumstances*). The distinction is largely academic because both approaches would allow moderate risk in appropriate circumstances. See pp. 46-47 for a fuller discussion.

[24] See below, p. 81 note 2.

[25] R. M Feinstein in Hershler RM ed., Halacha and Medicine Vol.4 (Regensburg, Jerusalem, 1985).

[26] See Coercion and Consent, p. 155.

[27] See above, Principles p. 37 and note 42 there.

High Risk

This category comprises activities that carry a high absolute risk. Ordinarily, placing oneself in such situations is forbidden, even for such purposes as earning a living. Whether one is permitted, or indeed obliged, to expose oneself to such risk to save life is the subject of a disagreement between the Jerusalem Talmud and the Babylonian Talmud; the opinion of the Jerusalem Talmud is that one is obliged to assume high risk to save a life, the opinion of the Babylonian Talmud is that one may not.[28] The definitive opinion to be followed here is that of the Babylonian Talmud; hence one may not gravely endanger one's life in an attempt to save another, and even where it seems certain that that other life will be lost.

(Some authorities understand that even the Jerusalem Talmud obliges a risky lifesaving attempt only where the victim would certainly die otherwise and where it is certain that the attempt will succeed;[29] some understand that this obligation extends only to risk that is below 50%.[30])

What degree of danger defines high risk? One authority[31] suggests that 1 in 6 (16% – 17%) is the threshold for a definition of high risk for matters

---

[28] See Aruch HaShulchan Ch. M. 4 who mentions this implicit dispute and the definitive ruling of the Babylonian Talmud and points out that the matter always needs careful weighing – one should not desist too readily from attempting to save life on the grounds of danger. See Tzitz Eliezer 9:45 who gives the specific references in the Jerusalem and Babylonian Talmuds and discusses them in detail. Although later sources and the halachic codifiers (B. Yosef Ch. M. 426 in name of Hag. Maimon.) mention the opinion of the Jerusalem Talmud, they (including Rif, Rambam, Rosh and Tur) do not include it in their codes. This omission makes it clear that the opinion of the Babylonian Talmud is definitive. The Radbaz 3:627 (brought also in P. Teshuva Ch. M. 426 and Y.D. 157) states explicitly that it is forbidden to enter certain danger to life in the attempt to save life. (But cf. Chav. Yair 146 and Teshuvot Nishmat Chayim, Derushim, p. 11a.)

[29] See R. JD Bleich, Contemporary Halachic Problems Vol. IV (Ktav, 1995) pp. 275-279 and note 8 there for discussion and references.

[30] See Shevet Halevi 5:119 who allows a risk of up to 50% in practice.

[31] Imrei Esh Y.D. 52 refers to Shevuos 35b where a proportion of 1 in 6 is mentioned with respect to military losses in a war undertaken by a king; Imrei Esh is discussing the permissibility of Jews finding employment in a (non-Jewish) national army and concludes that such employment is in order, implying that even where there is a risk as high as 1 in 6 of dying in a military campaign undertaken by such an army, that risk is acceptable.

such as earning a living; activities involving risks above that level would be forbidden in the course of seeking a livelihood; up to that level would be acceptable. Rabbi Eliashiv holds that this figure is far too high.[32] For such purposes, in his opinion, the upper range of permitted risk would be approximately 1 in 20 (5%).[33] However, a risk of 1 in 6 may be appropriate in the attempt to save life.[34]

A rough rule has been suggested: if one would undertake a particular risk *to save all one's possessions*, one should undertake that same risk in the attempt to save a life. If, however, one would forego all one's possessions in the face of a particular risk, one may desist from entering that same level of risk to save a life.[35] One should not be overly cautious in the attempt to save life when making this calculation.[36]

Rabbi S. Wosner[37] considers a higher level of risk acceptable in the attempt to save life: he states that there are three categories of doubtful danger – a majority risk of harm, equal risk, and a minority risk. Now ordinarily the rule of majority does not apply to lifesaving;[38] however that is where only one danger is relevant, for example, the danger to a patient

---

[32] R. Y. Zilberstein. Rabbi Eliashiv rejects the derivation of the Imrei Esh, pointing out that Shevuos 35b is dealing with governments and armies in non-Jewish countries.

[33] Rabbi Y. Zilberstein. This is based on Mishk. Yaakov Y.D. 17 (p. 206), who refers to Bava Basra 93 regarding minority probabilities: in certain situations a proportion of more than 10% is regarded as significant, whereas one of less than this is not. It is evident that an event with a probability of more than 10% must be reckoned with; one with a probability of less than 5% may be disregarded. (Based on this and other factors, Rabbi Zilberstein permitted an Israeli bomb disposal expert to function; the danger quoted in that instance was less than 1%.)

[34] This level of risk may also be acceptable in the attempt to save a limb – see Danger to a Limb, p. 73, and to relieve severe pain – see Pain Relief, p. 71.

[35] Shevet MiYehuda (1:9, p.23) suggests that the rescuer should consider whether he would undertake the equivalent risk to save a prized possession; if so, he should undertake that risk in the attempt to save a life – the life to be saved should be no less cherished.

[36] Mishna Berura O. Ch. 329:8; P. Teshuva Ch. M. 426. See also Aruch Ha-Shulchan Ch. M. 4.

[37] Shevet HaLevi 5:119; also in R. M. Hershler, Halacha and Medicine Vol. 4, p.139.

[38] See Principles pp. 33-34 and note 26 there.

in usual circumstances – there we are concerned with safety and seek to protect the patient from any risk, even very distant and unlikely risk. One must go to extremes to avert risk to life, ignoring the relative safety conferred by majorities. But here we are dealing with a risk to the life of the rescuer or physician too; and in this situation the consideration of majority and minority risks comes back into play. So here we must ask: what is the risk to the rescuer? If it is equal or higher (50% or greater), the rescue attempt is forbidden. However if it is less than equal, that is, where there is a majority chance of the rescuer's surviving while saving another from certain death, the rescue is permitted.

Other authorities, while agreeing that that there is no obligation to endanger one's life in the attempt to save another, allow it as discretionary.[39] Some limit this permissibility to situations in which the rescuer will be exposed to less than a 50% risk.[40] Others require that the rescuer be exposed to less risk than the victim.[41] Some stipulate that a rescuer may enter danger only where it is certain that the victim will be saved.[42] One may not enter a situation of certain death to save another. [43]

These considerations apply to doctors and others incurring risk in the course of lifesaving activities[44] as well as to potential organ donors.[45]

Although a rescuer may choose to enter danger in order to save life, he may not significantly endanger others in the attempt. Thus if a rescuer wishes to undertake a risk of danger that is close to 50%, for example, he may not do so if others will be endangered to the same degree; in fact he has no right to cause even far less danger to others than this.[46]

---

[39] Minch. Yitzchak 6:103.

[40] R. S. Wosner; see pp. 53-54 above and note 37 there.

[41] R. M. Hershler, Halacha and Medicine Vol. 2, p. 123.

[42] Minch. Yitzchak 6:103.

[43] See Igr. Moshe Y.D. 2:174 for discussion. However, to save a group or community this would be allowed.

[44] For the question of risk incurred in treating patients in general, see Risk to Caregivers below.

[45] See Organ Donation with Danger to Life, p. 81.

[46] R. Y. Zilberstein. An ambulance or rapid-response vehicle driver may drive at speeds that endanger himself, but not when this will expose bystanders to any significant risk.

Risk to Caregivers

How much risk to his own life and health is a doctor permitted, or indeed obliged, to accept in the course of treating patients? The practice of clinical medicine poses certain risks: those posed by infection[47] (AIDS, hepatitis, tuberculosis) contracted through contact with patients' blood and other body fluids[48] and possible violent behavior of patients.[49] There

---

[47] "119 cases of tuberculosis were identified in healthcare workers, including 61 nurses and 42 doctors. The crude notification rate in healthcare workers was 11.8 per 100,000 per year (95% confidence interval 9.8 to 14.1) compared with 3.3 per 100,000 per year (2.9 to 3.6) in other professional and associate professional occupations... The relative risk...was 2.4 (...2.0 to 3.0) This study shows that rates of notified tuberculosis in healthcare workers in England and Wales were two to three times those in other socio-economically comparable occupational groups." Meredith S, Watson J, et al. Are healthcare workers in England and Wales at increased risk of tuberculosis? BMJ 1996;313:522-525.

This study considered all UK healthcare workers; among those specifically exposed to tuberculosis the relative risk is likely to be far higher – see next ref:

"Of an average 267 employed HCWs (healthcare workers), pulmonary TB occurred in nine (six nurses and three laboratory technicians). Cumulative incidence for HCWs was 3,451/100,000, compared to 454/100,000 in the general population, for an incidence rate ratio of 7.6. The risk of TB among HCWs employed at the Institute for Pulmonary Diseases of Serbia in Belgrade is 7.6 times higher than that observed in the general population." S⌣kodric V, Savic B et al. Occupational risk of tuberculosis among health care workers at the Institute for Pulmonary Diseases of Serbia. The International Journal of Tuberculosis and Lung Disease 2000;9:827-831.

[48] Needlestick injuries and HIV: "Of 699 respondents, 582 (83%) had had a needlestick injury during training; the mean number of needlestick injuries during residency increased according to the postgraduate year (PGY): PGY-1, 1.5 injuries; PGY-2, 3.7; PGY-3, 4.1; PGY-4, 5.3; and PGY-5, 7.7. By their final year of training, 99% of residents had had a needlestick injury; for 53%, the injury had involved a high-risk patient." Makary MA, Al-Attar A et al. Needle-stick Injuries among Surgeons in Training. N Engl J Med 2007;356:2693-9.

The per-exposure risk of transmission of HIV is about 0.3% – see next citation.

"Health care workers are at risk for at least 25 different occupationally acquired infections... The per-exposure risks of transmission of HIV (0.3%), hepatitis B (2-35%, depending on e-antigen status) and hepatitis C (3%) have been well-characterized." Sepkowitz KA, Infectious Risks to Health Care Workers. Intersci Conf Antimicrob Agents Chemother 2000;40:544. Mem. Sloan-Kettering Cancer Ctr, New York.

may be a risk of injury when attending to the injured in motor vehicle accidents or other dangerous circumstances, in the course of dangerous rescues requiring on-scene medical assistance, and others. The considerations discussed above apply to the practice of medicine no less than to another profession – moderate risk is certainly acceptable in the pursuit of medicine as a profession. In addition, it could be argued that the physician has a professional duty to expose himself to some risk in caring for patients, and moreover, the practice of medicine involves mitzva activity (healing is a mitzva obligation).[50]

How do these factors summate? A doctor may be exposed to risk in two broad categories: (a) in lifesaving activities, and (b) in the course of treating patients who are not dangerously ill.

(a) For parameters governing the incurring of personal risk in the attempt to save life, see the discussion of high risk (above).

(b) Whether a doctor may (or should) assume personal risk in the course of treating patients in general is discussed at length by Tzitz Eliezer[51] and others.[52] Tzitz Eliezer concludes that a doctor has a duty to enter danger in the course of treating patients; this is allowed in the pursuit of a livelihood[53] and mandated by a number of factors including the

---

[49] "All nurses will be affected by violence and aggression at some stage in their career. One in three nurses will be attacked and their colleagues may well have witnessed these incidents and have had to come to their aid. This week, figures revealed there were 20,000 attacks on healthcare workers in Scotland last year and an average of 400 staff are the victims of violence and aggression every week." Royal College of Nursing report, 28 September 2007.

[50] See note 54 below.

[51] Tzitz Eliezer 9:17 part 5. This particular responsum addresses the context of treating dangerously ill patients, but much of the discussion would appear to apply to treating patients who are not in immediate danger too.

[52] See R. AS Avraham, Nishmat Avraham (ArtScroll, 2000) Vol.1, pp. 216-217.

[53] Tzitz Eliezer makes the point that this is true even when the doctor is involved in the care of patients where no payment is being made; since there is a general professional obligation to treat patients and factors such as professional accreditation depend on the discharge of these duties, effectively all of the doctor's work is classed as the pursuit of a livelihood with respect to the permissibility of entering danger.

commandment to heal.[54] He quotes sources that discuss the duty to attend to patients during epidemics of infectious disease; and while there may be discussion of whether a particular congregation has the right to require the doctor who is exposed to such infection to absent himself from their immediate vicinity for fear that he may be a source of active infection and therefore constitute a danger to them, it is clear that it is permitted for him to attend to the ill in such epidemics and that all the relevant commandments apply.[55] [56]

Another perspective on the question of risk that should be incurred in the course of treating patients may be derived from the principle of "Whatever is worth returning of yours, return to others" found in the laws of returning lost objects.[57] It should be remembered that one of the sources for the obligation to heal is found in the commandment to return a lost object;[58] in that obligation a criterion that defines which objects must be returned is this: any object that one considers valuable enough to cause one to desire that it be returned to oneself must likewise be returned to its owner when found. This reciprocal value can perhaps be applied to the question of healing in situations of danger: if one would enter a certain level of danger for one's own need (a general need; not necessarily lifesaving), one should be prepared to enter that same level of danger for another's equivalent need. If a doctor (or people in general) would undertake a certain level of danger for a purpose that is not necessarily lifesaving such as protecting one's property or earning income, or more specifically to attend to the medical needs of a family member (again, needs that are not necessarily lifesaving) then the doctor

---

[54] Kovetz Shiurim (Pesachim 8:32) and Atzei Arazim (E. HaEzer 17:122) address the issue of exposure to danger in the fulfilment of mitzvos (commandments) in general. The Nesivos (Ta'alumos Chochma on Kohelet) deals with the philosophical question of harm occurring where, according to the principles of Kovetz Shiurim and Atzei Arazim, there should be protection. See note 10 above, and see this author's "Risks in Medicine and Surgery" in the Glatter Series "Medical Halacha" audio recordings for a related discussion.

[55] R. C. Pelaggi, Nishmat Kol Chai.

[56] R. Chaim Soloveichik required doctors to attend to patients during a cholera epidemic despite the risk of infection.

[57] See Rambam Hilch. Gezeila v'Aveida 11:13.

[58] Sanhedrin 73; "lost" health too, must be "returned."

is obliged to undertake that level of danger to treat his patients (even to provide treatment that is likewise not lifesaving).[59][60]

Yet another approach to providing routine treatment to patients in the face of appreciable danger has been suggested.[61] Perhaps the concept of *dash bo rabim* can be broadened somewhat: the usual understanding of this concept is that activities that are accepted by society at large are halachically permissible, that is, activities that people do with no regard to their risk are considered as if the relevant risk is negligible. But perhaps things that people do freely *in situations of appreciable risk* should also be considered to be in the category of *dash bo rabim;* that is, included in this category should be activities that people do not ordinarily undertake because of risk but that they do undertake when a good reason exists (where, in the popular mind, the reason justifies the risk). If, for example, the journey to a particular place is known to be somewhat dangerous[62] to the extent that people do not undertake that journey if they can easily avoid it, we would consider taking that journey too risky to categorize as *dash bo rabim;* after all, "the many" are not "treading that path," and hence it would ordinarily be forbidden. But what if "the many" do tread there *for good reason*? If people regularly undertake that journey for special family gatherings or to attend to ill relatives or for other special needs (even though they do not travel there due to the risk when they do not have such special cause), perhaps those circumstances render that journey *dash bo rabim* – commonly undertaken – *in those circumstances* although it would not be considered so in their absence.[63]

---

[59] R. Y. Zilberstein; see Clinical Case 2, p.60.

[60] It is incorrect to conclude that there is no obligation to prevent suicide because there is no obligation to return a lost object to an owner who does not want it – see below, Lifesaving Interventions, p. 61 note 5.

[61] Shevet HaLevi 5:119; also in R. M. Hershler, Halacha and Medicine Vol.4, p.139.

[62] See Clinical Case 2, p. 60.

[63] Following this approach, one would not need the dispensation granted by the commandment of returning a lost object of the kind that would cause one to enter appreciable danger for one's own similar object (see above) in order to undertake such activities; as long as these are commonly done when the need is perceived as adequately compelling, one would be allowed to do them (but only, of course, in such circumstances).

Doubtful Danger

What is the halacha when it is not known whether there is any danger at all? Where there is a clear diagnosis, risk can often be assigned, but where the diagnosis is unknown (where it may prove to be a dangerous condition or a non-dangerous one) it is not clear what quantitative risk can be assigned. The general approach here is that such situations are regarded as dangerous until proved otherwise.[64]

Risk in Military Situations

Risk and danger in military situations are handled differently than in civilian situations.[65] Although one's own life takes precedence over saving another in civilian life, in military situations one is obliged to endanger oneself to save a comrade.[66] This obligation includes soldiers and military physicians.

---

[64] See Shulchan Aruch O. C. 328:5, Rema and Magen Avraham there and Machz. Hashekel.

[65] See Military Triage, p. 183.

[66] Tzitz Eliezer 12:57.

Clinical Cases – Risk

Clinical Case 2: Risk to Caregivers

A civilian doctor is called to attend to a patient where the only access to the patient is by driving along a road that is exposed to occasional shooting from hostile villages. Is the doctor obliged to comply?

Analysis: [67]

If the risk is small, where perhaps one in a thousand may be injured, the doctor is obliged. Even if the general population avoids using that road unnecessarily, if they use it in circumstances of need such as to obtain medical treatment or to provide medical or other assistance to friends and relatives (that is, for needs other than emergency or lifesaving in nature) he would be obliged. Just as one must return a lost object of sufficient value to cause him to desire his own object of like value to be returned, so one must expose oneself to a danger that one would undertake for one's own needs in the course of providing treatment to others. [68]

In the fulfilment of a mitzva, in this case that of healing, it is entirely appropriate to undertake danger as long as the danger does not amount to *sh'chichi heseika*, a high risk, or clear and present danger. [69] Here, a risk of less than 5% should not preclude the attempt to reach the patient. [70]

These considerations apply to general medical treatment. If however the patient in question may be dangerously ill, incurring a higher level of risk to the treating doctor would be appropriate. [71]

This discussion refers to the duties of a civilian doctor. Military situations mandate acceptance of far higher risk than civilian situations. [72]

---

[67] R.Y. Zilberstein, quoting R. Eliashiv.

[68] See above, p. 57.

[69] See note 54 above.

[70] See above, p.53 and note 33 there.

[71] See High Risk, p.52.

[72] See Risk in Military Situations, p. 59 and Military Triage, p. 183.

Danger to Life and Lifesaving Interventions

There is a Torah obligation to save and preserve life;[1] this obligation takes precedence over most others.[2]

Lifesaving Interventions with Low Risk

Where a lifesaving intervention is not itself risky (that is, where the intervention does not risk shortening life) one may not reject it. In principle, such intervention may be forced on a patient;[3] the secular principle of autonomy is not relevant in halacha where that autonomy is expressed as the choice to die when a painless and safe lifesaving option is available.[4]

Examples would be an attempted suicide that can be averted simply,[5] or a potentially lethal medical or surgical problem that can be treated

---

[1] Rambam H. Rotzeach 1:14; Sh. Aruch Ch. M. 426:1. For analysis of the details and extent of this obligation, including the obligation to incur costs in its fulfilment, see Margal. Hayam on Sanhedrin 73a and Lev Aryeh 1:42.

[2] See above, The Primary Value of Life, p. 32.

[3] See Coercion and Consent, p. 155.

[4] See Autonomy, p. 219.

[5] Tzitz Eliezer 9:45:8 states that the obligation to save life includes the prevention of a suicide. One may erroneously assume that there is no such obligation since a basic source for the obligation to heal is found in the injunction to return a lost object to its owner (and this certainly includes "lost" health; see Sanhedrin 73) – one may assume that since there is no obligation to return an object to an owner who clearly does not want it, there is no obligation to save an individual who clearly wishes to commit suicide. Tzitz Eliezer demonstrates why this conclusion is incorrect.

painlessly with no additional risk, such as major hemorrhage that can simply and easily be controlled. Receiving a blood transfusion, despite the small risk involved, is obligatory when clearly lifesaving.

Lifesaving Interventions with Low Risk where the Intervention is Painful or Mutilating

Where the intervention is painful or mutilating, forcing the patient to undergo such intervention may not always be halachically sanctioned.[6] [7] A patient who refuses lifesaving therapy due to fear of pain, discomfort, disability or mutilation is acting improperly in the eyes of the Torah and should be counselled to accept the therapy or procedure despite the pain. The patient should be assured that the saving of life overrides his other considerations; if the patient's continued refusal is unreasonable, the therapy should be administered despite the patient's refusal unless this will cause distress to a degree that itself may be dangerous.

Margal. Hayam Sanhedrin 73a takes issue with Minch. Chinuch 237 and concurs with Ein Eliyahu on B.M. 28b and Teshuv. Maharam Bar Baruch 39 that saving a suicide is obligatory.

Radbaz on Rambam, Sanhedrin 18:6 indicates that there is certainly an obligation to prevent a suicide: any exemption from returning a lost object to its owner is irrelevant since one's life and body are not owned in the first place – these are not within a person's domain to discard.

(Although one's life and body are not owned to the degree that they may be discarded or harmed at will, they are in one's jurisdiction for a number of purposes, including the authority to make certain life and death decisions – for examples, see Approach to Dangerous and Terminal Illness, p. 101. The fact that life and health must be "returned" in parallel with the obligation to return lost objects demonstrates at least that the individual is their "keeper.")

[6] See Coercion and Consent p. 155.

[7] Rabbi Eliashiv was consulted about an elderly man who refused ventilation due to fear of the pain and discomfort involved; Rabbi Eliashiv stated that the patient was clearly acting improperly in the eyes of halacha but despite this he should not be ventilated against his will, and although he would be seriously derelict in his responsibility to care for his own life, he is not considered to be committing suicide. (Rabbi Y. Zilberstein.) It is likely that other authorities would advise ventilating this patient against his will; refusal here, while perhaps not tantamount to suicide, may be seen as unreasonable. See note 11 below.

Lifesaving Interventions that Add Immediate Risk

Where the intervention adds risk, with or without inflicting pain or mutilation, the patient should undergo the procedure where the added risk is small. Where the risk is significant, the patient cannot be forced.[8]

An example would be a patient whose gangrenous limb threatens life and who refuses amputation[9] – if amputation will add new and immediate significant risk in addition to pain and mutilation, the patient cannot be coerced to undergo that procedure although the amputation would be sanctioned and indeed obliged by halacha[10] in the absence of any alternative lifesaving option. If however the amputation is judged to carry little risk, it should be done against the patient's wishes; in the eyes of halacha it is not reasonable to choose certain death rather than many years of life without a particular limb.[11]

A patient may not be forced to accept therapy that is of doubtful or unestablished efficacy or subject to expert disagreement.

Danger to Life in Halacha: Specific Causes

What exactly constitutes danger to life? In addition to the dangers that are recognized by modern medicine, halacha recognizes a number of others. The Talmud and later sources categorize a number of specific conditions, signs, lesions and injuries as dangerous to life. These include:[12]

---

[8] See Approach to Dangerous and Terminal Illness, p. 101.

[9] A case at Hadassah Hospital some years ago occasioned vehement public debate on this subject: an elderly woman with gangrene of a leg refused amputation, saying she wished to die intact ("I lived with this leg and I am going to die with it"). The more religious factions in Israeli society felt that the patient should be pressed to undergo surgery; the more secular elements (and the law) sided with her right to refuse. Amputation was not performed; she died shortly thereafter.

[10] See commentaries on Sh. Aruch Ch. M. 420:31.

[11] Discussing the case of a 20 year old patient who refused amputation of a leg, thereby choosing death over living with a prosthesis, the Magen Avraham (O.C. 328:6), quoting the Radbaz, states that the amputation should be performed despite the patient's refusal. See Mor U'Ketzia 328.

[12] Meiri Av. Zara 27a - 28b discusses a number of the items listed here as well as some other pathological signs and symptoms. See Nishm. Avraham Vol. I pp. 182-231 for detailed discussion.

1. Danger to an eye.[13]

2. Blindness.[14]

3. A fractured long bone.[15]

4. Lesions of the back of the hand[16] and foot.[17] Even where modern medicine does not see a threat to life in any particular case involving one of these, one should be more cautious and ready to treat these as potentially dangerous due to this Talmudic concern.

5. Serious mental illness.[18]

6. Internal injuries or lesions: from the lingual aspect of the teeth inwards is considered "internal."[19] This category does not require a gross anatomical injury or lesion; physiological derangements are included.[20]

7. Fever with rigors and certain other types of fever.[21]

---

[13] Av. Zara 28b, citing a connection between the eye and the heart. It is not clear whether this refers to the common vagal innervation of eye and heart (pressure on the eye slows the heart rate). Alternatively, the eye's proximity to the central nervous system makes this concern understandable due to the possibility of serious orbital infections leading to central nervous system involvement or cavernous sinus thrombosis. Sh. Aruch O.C. 328:9 and M. Berura 22 there.

[14] See Shevet MiYehuda (1:1:21) who states that blindness constitutes danger to life but remains in doubt on the question of loss of sight in one eye.

[15] This danger is in fact well recognized medically: blood loss and fat embolism are among the potentially serious complications of long bone fractures.

[16] Sh. Aruch O.C. 328:6. See Case Records of the Massachusetts General Hospital: A Man with Pain and Swelling of the Right Hand and Hypotension, N Engl J Med 2009;360:281; in which minor trauma to the back of the hand leading to infection rapidly developed into a life-threatening emergency. It is noteworthy that in this case the infection spread rapidly to the whole forearm but spared the palm; it has been theorized that the direction of lymphatic drainage of the hand from ventral to dorsal aspects may be the cause of this pattern of spread and that this may be at least part of the clinical basis for the Talmud's circumspection about these infections.

[17] Sh. Aruch O.C. 328:6.

[18] Igr. Moshe E.H. 1:65; Minch. Yitzchak 1:115; Tzitz Eliezer 9:51:3.

[19] Sh. Aruch O.C. 328:3.

[20] Zer Zahav, Issur v'Heter 59:9.

[21] See Meiri Av. Zara 27a – 28b.

8. Certain specific types of wound.[22]

9. Danger to a limb: although some authorities hold that danger to a limb in itself allows (and obliges) the same dispensations as danger to life, [23] this is not the normative opinion.[24] However, that is only where the danger to the limb is clearly not endangering life; in most cases danger to a limb may in fact constitute a real danger to life.[25]

10. A woman in labor or after delivery (including miscarriage).[26] Acute danger persists for the first three full days after the birth and to a slightly lesser degree from then until seven days after birth (from then until thirty days some minor danger continues).

11. A newborn infant.[27]

12. Infants, young children and the elderly are considered to be more fragile in situations of medical danger. Patients in these categories should be regarded as dangerously ill more readily than others (this is common clinical experience quite apart from being halachically mandated).

13. Fear or anguish may be life-threatening in certain situations.[28]

14. Any condition declared by a doctor or duly qualified expert to be dangerous; whether internal or external including dermatological.

15. Doubtful danger is treated as real until proved otherwise.

Obligation to Incur Cost to Save Life

One is obliged to incur cost to save life.[29] One is obliged to spend all one's wealth, if necessary, to save one's own life;[30] where a person

---

[22] Meiri above ref.

[23] Meiri above ref.

[24] Igr. Moshe YD 2:174.

[25] R. P. Scheinberg in R. M. Herschler Vol. 4, p. 125.

[26] Sh. Aruch O.C. 330. See Nishm. Avraham Vol. I pp. 221-226 for details.

[27] Nishm. Avraham Vol. I p. 211.

[28] A terrified child is considered in danger – the Sabbath may be desecrated to free a young child who is locked in a room (Mishna Berura 328:13). Fear, anguish and despair are also additive lethal factors in any dangerous illness.

[29] Sanhedrin 73a and Margal. Hayam there. The negative commandment of "Do not stand idly by the blood of your brother" adds the obligation to incur cost to the positive command that mandates lifesaving. The general rule is that to avoid transgression of a negative commandment one is required to expend all one's

chooses to die rather than spend his funds to save his own life, others[31] are obliged to intercede against his wishes and appropriate his funds for that purpose.

When faced with a specific obligation to save a particular life, one is obliged to spend all one's wealth if necessary, according to many authorities.[32] The person saved must then compensate the one who spent the funds on his behalf.[33] Some authorities however do not require the expenditure of one's entire fortune to save another,[34] except in the case of a husband's obligation to save his wife, where all agree that one is ordinarily required to do so (a husband is generally required to pay for all his wife's medical needs),[35] and one's own children.[36] However, up to one fifth of one's wealth is certainly obligatory.

---

wealth if necessary. See Lev Aryeh 1:42 for detailed derivation. Cf. however below and note 34.

[30] Even to save one's life in the short term (to prolong *chayei sha'a*) – this obligation can be derived as follows: one is obliged to spend all one's wealth to avoid desecrating the Sabbath; however, the Sabbath must be desecrated to save even the briefest short-term life. Thus if saving life takes precedence over the Sabbath, it must certainly take precedence over expenditure of funds, and even all one's funds even for *chayei sha'a* (Rabbi Zilberstein).

[31] For example, a wife where a husband refuses to spend his own money preferring to die and leave his funds for her and his children to inherit. The wife should authorize the necessary expenses; saving the patient's life takes precedence over his wishes regarding his possessions.

[32] Rama Y.D. 157:1 and Shach there (para. 3); Igr. Moshe Y.D. 2:174 (4); Lev Aryeh 1:42; Ahavat Chesed 20:2. But cf. other opinions listed in Nishm. Avraham Vol. I pp. 217-218.

[33] Rosh on Sanhedrin 73a. See Nishm. Avraham Vol. III pp. 309-311 for details.

[34] Maharsham (5:52), based on Raavad (in Ran on Rif, Succa 83 and in B.Y. O.Ch. 656). Rabbi Eliashiv does not require a family to become destitute in order to provide extremely expensive treatment for a family member (even when the treatment may be lifesaving).

[35] Ketubot 52b.

[36] Minch. Yitzchak (6:150) discusses a father's obligation to pay for the care and medical expenses of a severely handicapped child; he shows that Ran and Rosh disagree about the derivation of a father's financial obligation to his young children: according to Ran this obligation derives from the father's obligation to his wife (if he does not support his children, his wife will feed them from her

Incurring Costs or Damages to Others to Save Life

In general, one may not steal or incur costs (that will not be repaid) to unwilling third parties even in the course of saving life; for example, a doctor may not order a very expensive, non-standard intervention against hospital rules (Rabbi Eliashiv ruled that a doctor would be out of order if he ordered helicopter evacuation of a civilian patient at hospital expense where standard road ambulance transport was available and hospital payers had disallowed the much more expensive air evacuation option, even where that would be clearly more effective in an emergency situation).[37]

Similarly, public funds may not be used where duly appointed authorities disallow such use (although it is entirely proper to press for liberal authorisation of lifesaving expenses).[38]

One may, however, incur costs to a third party where that third party would also be obliged to save the life presently in danger.[39] One is obliged to save life at the expense of a third party when necessary where one intends to repay the costs.[40]

---

own portion and go hungry); according to Rosh he has a primary duty directly to his children. One practical difference is that according to Ran the father's duty to his children would end in the case of divorce; according to Rosh it would not. Another is that according to Ran this obligation is more extreme; it would extend to all one's wealth as does the obligation to a wife. Minch. Yitzchak demonstrates that in fact both Rosh and Ran may agree on this particular point.

[37] See B. Kama 60b. Rashi and Tosf. HaRosh disagree on whether the question there relates to the permissibility of saving oneself at the expense of others (and the conclusion is that one may not), or whether it is clear that one may and the question is only whether one must later pay for the loss or damages (and the conclusion is that one must). Sh. Aruch Ch. Mishpat 359:4 rules that one may appropriate another's property in the course of saving one's own life (or another's life, as explained by Pilpula Charifta B. Kama 6:12:8) only with the intention to pay but not otherwise. (See Yerushalmi Shabbat 14:4, Korban HaEda and Maharsham 5:44 for the rationale behind these rulings).

[38] Rabbi Y. Zilberstein.

[39] See Clinical Case 3, p. 69.

[40] See note 37 above.

Obligation to Incur Discomfort or Minor Illness to Save Life

There is an obligation to donate blood where a specific patient needs that blood, even where the donor will suffer weakness and discomfort.[41] In addition, there may be an obligation to incur minor illness in the effort to save life.[42] One is also obliged to experience embarrassment or indignity if necessary in order to save life.[43]

Endangering Others in the Course of Saving Life

What are the limits to lifesaving activity where bystanders may be endangered? At what risk to others may one attempt to save one's own life? Generally, where the risk to others is small, the activity may be undertaken.[44] [45]

---

[41] R. S. Wosner in R. M. Hershler, Halacha and Medicine Vol. 4, p. 139 (but cf. R. E. Waldenberg in the same volume with regard to a very frail donor; p. 143).

[42] For a wide-ranging discussion of the possible obligation to incur illness (but not danger to life or limb) in the fulfilment of commandments in general, see R. P. Scheinberg in R. M. Hershler, Halacha and Medicine Vol. 4, pp. 125-138.

[43] Lev Aryeh 1:42.

[44] R. Y. Zilberstein was asked whether an individual living in a city that is experiencing an outbreak of H1N1 influenza ("swine flu") may flee to another city that has no known cases in order to escape infection. Although he is presently well, he may be unknowingly incubating the disease and consequently begin an epidemic in the second city, endangering many. On the other hand, if he is not yet infected he will be saving himself from personal exposure to danger. Rabbi Zilberstein's opinion was that the individual may flee in view of the many levels of doubt that intervene between his action and any danger that may materialize to people in the destination city.

[45] Thus, as noted above (p. 54 note 46) an ambulance or rapid-response vehicle driver may choose to endanger himself in the course of attempting to rescue a patient but may certainly not expose members of the public to any significant danger while doing so.

Clinical Cases – Lifesaving Interventions

Clinical Case 3: Incurring Cost to a Third Party to Save Life

An employee is a "Hatzola" (community paramedical organization) volunteer. Responding to emergency calls during working hours means interrupting his work whenever he is called. His employer objects and wishes to dismiss him, claiming that he is not required to suffer the loss to his business caused by the employee's frequent absences. In addition to the question of dismissal itself, a likely consequence is that the volunteer may choose to give up his lifesaving work to avoid losing his income.

Is the employer correct?

Analysis:

In general, lifesaving activity should be facilitated; numerous measures were enacted by the Sages to ensure this.[46] In this case, Rabbi Eliashiv ruled that the employee cannot be dismissed because the employer too, has an obligation to save life in this situation – he cannot dismiss his employee for doing what he himself is obliged to do. He must stop work to save a life when called on, and he must likewise allow his employee to do so.

However, he is not obliged to renew the employee's contract when it ends. At that time he will be free to employ another worker who is not a volunteer instead. The measures instituted by the Sages to ensure lifesaving work apply to situations where there is a specific obligation to save life; but there is no obligation to put oneself into a situation that will involve lifesaving in the first place. For example, there is no obligation on any particular individual to study medicine in order to be able to save lives.[47] The employer must allow his worker to save life while he is employed; but engaging him as an employee in the first place is entirely at his discretion; he is not obliged to employ a worker who saves lives.

---

[46] See Principles, p. 36 for some of these.

[47] See Taz Y.D. 339:3 in the course of presenting a rationale for allowing physicians to accept fees.

Pain Relief and Functional Improvement

Where the indication for treatment is alleviation of pain or functional improvement, the default position in halacha is that therapies involving moderate risk may be permitted, but not those with high risk. However, the border between moderate and high risk is not sharp; each case must be decided individually after weighing the degree of pain or functional limitation against the risk.

Pain Relief

In addition to the attempt to cure, palliation and the alleviation of pain are parts of the healer's responsibility in Judaism.[1]

Pain relief and palliation in life threatening conditions

This is discussed in Approach to Dangerous and Terminal Illness.[2]

Pain relief and palliation in non-life threatening conditions

In non-life threatening circumstances such interventions are permitted if their risk is not more than moderate and the pain indicating the intervention is significant. As discussed in the section on risk, moderate levels of risk are acceptable where a good reason for undertaking such risk exists; the alleviation of significant pain is certainly a good reason.

---

[1] See Palliation of Pain in R. JD Bleich, Bioethical Dilemmas Vol. II p. 163 for extensive discussion of the derivation of this obligation.

[2] See Analgesia in Dangerously or Terminally Ill Patients, p. 112.

However, interventions that carry high risk would not be halachically acceptable where the indication is pain or dysfunction with no threat to life.

Where severe pain can be relieved only at the cost of risk to life, this may be allowed; there is debate about the level of risk that may be permitted.[3]

Functional Improvement

The general principle to be applied here is that life may not be placed at high risk for functional improvement (where the functional impairment does not itself pose a threat to life). In this area, the default position is to prohibit significant risk for benefits other than lifesaving; this default may be shifted in individual cases where the risk-benefit ratio is low enough in the eyes of mature halachic judgment.

An illustrative example from the responsa literature:[4] Rabbi Moshe Feinstein was asked about a major surgical intervention for a patient who was permanently bedridden but not in danger.[5] The surgery, if successful, would have allowed the patient normal mobility, but at the cost of serious ongoing risk to his life. Rabbi Feinstein ruled that the surgery should not be performed. In these circumstances long term life with significant limitation is superior to the possibility of improvement in function that may be gained at the risk of death where that risk is high and ongoing.

---

[3] It is well known that Rabbi SZ Auerbach underwent a head operation for pain. The Rema (Y.D. 241:13) permits amputation of a limb to eliminate pain; it is not clear how risky such a procedure that was in his day, but it seems the risk would have been significant. See Mor u'Kezia 328, who states that high risk to relieve severe pain (such as that due to kidney stones) is "close to forbidden" but does not categorically forbid it. See Tzitz Eliezer 4:12; She'arim M'tzuyanim B'Halacha 190. See "Risk-taking for Pain Palliation" in R. JD Bleich, Bioethical Dilemmas Vol. II p. 182 and p. 253 for discussion of risk levels and further references.

[4] Igr. Moshe Y.D. 2:36.

[5] Although the medical facts as presented in this particular question are certainly arguable, the principle enunciated in the responsum is clear: it is generally not permitted to seriously risk life itself for an improvement in the quality of life. Put differently, a relatively poor quality of life is preferable to a high risk of losing life entirely.

Danger to a Limb, Organ or Faculty

Cases of threat to an organ or limb can be divided into two categories: where the threat to the limb also constitutes a danger to life, and where the threat is limited to the limb or organ alone.[1]

Threats in the first category are handled no differently in principle than threats to life in general.[2][3]

A threat to a limb that poses no danger to life would permit interventions of moderate risk, as discussed in the section on risk.[4] In principle, interventions that impose a high risk to life are not permitted to avert danger to a part, as discussed there; interventions involving high risk to life are acceptable only where the indication for that intervention is itself a danger to life.

---

[1] Note that in general, risk to a limb may entail risk to life in the eyes of halacha; see R. P. Scheinberg in R. M. Hershler, Halacha and Medicine Vol. 4, p. 135. See also Nishm. Avraham Vol. I, p. 204. Concerning this and the question of whether danger to a limb is considered inherently a danger to life in halacha, see Shach on Sh. Aruch Y.D. 157:3; Meiri Av. Zara 27a – 28b; Seridei Eish 2:34 (p.420). See also above p. 65 and p. 73.

[2] See p. 61.

[3] See also pp. 64-65 for specific limb lesions and injuries that halacha regards as dangers to life.

[4] A lethal risk of 16%-17% may be acceptable to save a limb, according to R. Y. Zilberstein based on Imrei Esh Y.D. 52. See p. 50, note 18 and p. 52, note 31 in Approach to Risk in Halacha.

Examples of conditions in this category would be a nerve entrapment or injury threatening to result in paralysis of a limb; or a spinal or cauda equina lesion threatening lower limb paresis or paralysis without any direct threat to life. Where a procedure required to remove these threats does not present a high risk to life, it is certainly permitted.

Where vascular compromise of a limb threatens viability of the limb in the short term but may result in gangrene of the limb and certainly constitute a danger to life later, that is to be considered in the general category of danger to life; therefore a procedure designed to reverse totally occluded arterial supply to a leg would justify far more risk than a procedure that aims to save only a limb.

Where a condition threatens the sight of an eye, if there is no threat to life moderate risk is allowed in preventing its progression. However, in general, danger to an eye is considered danger to life in halacha.[5] Certainly where the condition may lead to a more general danger such as in the case of intraocular infection, higher risk would be allowed. Where the sight of both eyes is becoming compromised, this may be categorized as a danger to life (blindness is considered a potential danger to life; according to some opinions this includes even unilateral blindness).[6]

Incurring Cost to Save a Limb

In general, one is obliged to spend up to a fifth of one's wealth to save another's limb, organ, faculty or health. For a possible obligation to spend more than this for one's spouse or child, or to save life, see Obligation to Incur Cost to Save Life.[7]

---

[5] See p. 64 and note 13 there.

[6] See p. 64 and note 14 there.

[7] Page 65.

Risking or Sacrificing an Organ or Limb

Endangering or Sacrificing a Limb to Save Life

A relatively common scenario that presents this issue is the need to amputate a gangrenous limb to save life. In obstetrics, uncontrollable postpartum hemorrhage may occasionally necessitate an emergency hysterectomy.

Amputation of a gangrenous limb to save life is an obligation.[1] Even the amputation of a healthy limb, where necessary to save life, would similarly be obligatory.[2] The Radbaz allows the sacrifice of a limb even to save *another* person's life;[3] he mandates it to save one's own life. It seems clear that this is an obligation.[4] Should such a procedure be carried out on a patient who cannot choose – for example a child or an unconscious patient? Where a choice is necessary, Rabbi Feinstein states that parents can make such choices on behalf of their children.

---

[1] Sh. Aruch Ch. M. 420:31; Magen Avraham O.C. 328:6, quoting the Radbaz, states that the amputation should be performed despite the patient's refusal. See Mor U'Ktzia 328; Maharam MiRotenberg 39.

[2] For example in the face of advancing fire or other lethal danger where the only possibility of extrication involves amputating a limb. The obligation would extend to the victim himself, if he were capable of the procedure, as in the following reports:

"Rock climber cuts off own arm to save himself. A rock climber... cut off his own arm to free himself after he became trapped under a fallen boulder... [where he was] pinned for five days." ABC News; 3 May, 2003.

"Farmer saves himself by cutting off arm. An American farmer whose hand became stuck in a corn harvester was forced to cut off his own arm to save himself after the machine burst into flames." Telegraph; 27 Nov. 2007.

[3] Radbaz 3:627.

[4] May such an amputation be coerced? See note 1 above and Coercion and Consent, p. 155.

Endangering a Limb to Save Function of that Limb

May a limb (or residual function of a limb) be endangered in the attempt to preserve or improve function of that limb? This type of situation arises where an operation on a limb can be performed that will preserve function if successful, but is likely to cause more severe damage if it fails. A surgical example would be a complex operation on the palmar aspect of the hand to save function of the hand, where there is a real danger of tendon sheath adhesions developing as complications of surgery that may leave the hand with significantly worse function than existed pre-operatively.[5] Should one risk certain but limited function in the attempt to cure? Subject to medical and halachic judgment, there is no specific objection to this type of procedure in principle.

Sacrificing a Limb or Organ to Save Another Limb or Organ

A clinical example would be the question of enucleating a diseased eye in an attempt to prevent the development of sympathetic ophthalmia in the other eye.[6] Where sight has been lost in the injured eye the issue is largely cosmetic; where sight is retained or expected to improve, the decision is more difficult – if the injured eye is allowed to remain, sight in both eyes may be lost. Is it proper to sacrifice the remaining partial sight in the injured eye to preserve full function of the other eye? Here, the halacha will be sensitive to the degree of probability; since this complication is rare, the correct approach may be conservative (and particularly since options for delayed treatment exist). However, where the risks are higher, a more aggressive approach would be appropriate.

---

[5] "Injuries of the hand involving zone II [the so-called "no-man's land"] are burdened by a significant number of treatment failures... around 10% of tenolysis and tendon repair interventions fail due to breakage or lockage of the tendon due to the development of adherences in surrounding tissue." M. Riccio et al. Definitive Results of the SICM multicenter study on tendon adhesions in zone II of the hand. Riv Chir Mano Vol. 43 (3) 2006.

[6] Sympathetic ophthalmia (SO) is an inflammatory condition that affects both eyes after a penetrating injury to one eye. (It is thought to occur as a result of autoimmune damage resulting from exposure of ocular antigens to the immune system as a result of the injury.) It is rare, affecting 0.2% to 0.5% of non-surgical eye wounds, and less than 0.1% of surgical penetrating eye wounds. Prevention requires enucleation or evisceration of the injured eye soon after the injury (although a modern alternative is to treat SO with immunosuppressives when it occurs rather than remove the injured eye).

Saving Life – Risking and Donating Organs or Limbs

Risking an Organ or Limb to Save Another's Life

Serious risk to a part should generally be approached in similar fashion to donation of a part; see below.

Donating or Sacrificing an Organ or Limb to Save Another's Life

Is there an obligation to donate a limb or organ in order to save another's life? Probably the commonest instance of this question is that of organ donation by live donors.

There are two categories here: donation of an organ or limb with no (or minimal) danger to the life of the donor, and donation that involves a danger to life (the latter is discussed in the next section).[1]

Organ donation with no (or minimal) danger to life

1. Regenerating organ

Where the part in question regenerates and there is no danger to the life of the donor, such as in the case of blood donation, there is an obligation to donate when a recipient is present who needs that donation.[2]

---

[1] See p. 81.

[2] R. Wosner, Part 5. R. Wosner adds that this obligation extends to procedures such as platelet donation despite the associated discomfort. Rabbi Waldenberg however, holds that blood donation is not an absolute obligation (in R. M. Hershler, Halacha and Medicine Vol. 4, p. 143). With regard to donating blood to a blood bank for possible future use, see Igr. Moshe Ch. M. 1:103.

Bone marrow donation: there is no absolute obligation to donate bone marrow, particularly where a general anesthetic is required, but one who does is certainly performing a highly meritorious act.

2. Non-regenerating organ

Loss of the organ or limb: considered in isolation, what is the halacha regarding the donation of a part to save a life? In other words, if a limb could be given to save a life with minimal danger to the donor's life, would such a donor be allowed, or indeed obliged, to donate the organ?

Here, two types of situation are possible: one, where the organ or limb is given to the recipient (as in transplant surgery), and second, where the organ or limb must be sacrificed but not necessarily in the course of a transplantation procedure. An example of the second category would be where an individual is threatened with the choice of losing a limb or having another individual killed instead. There is at least one such question recorded in the responsa literature, and although this type of setting is criminal rather than medical, it is instructive to consider.

The Radbaz[3] received a question along these lines: what would be the halacha in a case where a dictator ordered amputation of a limb (say a hand) of an individual, with the condition that the victim's failure to

---

[3] Radbaz, Responsa 3:627. But see Rekanti (Piskei Rekanti 470). Yad Avraham YD 157:1 (printed in Vilna Sh. Aruch) quotes Be'er Hetev who states that one must allow his limb to be amputated to save another's life; Yad Avraham disagrees. The normative position as accepted by many subsequent authorities is that of the Radbaz; see for example P. Teshuva who cites the Radbaz in YD 157:15. See Igr. Moshe Y.D. 2:174 (4) for analysis.

Hagahot Mordechai (Sanhedrin, 718) states that one may amputate another's limb to save his own life. This is not the normative position.

In the case of multiple pregnancy where an intra-uterine operation will save one fetus but damage others, Rabbi Y. Zilberstein forbids the procedure, pointing out that even according to the opinion of the Rekanti it would be forbidden: it is the obligation of the individual himself to give his limb (he is bound by the prohibition of "Do not stand idly by..." according to the Rekanti) but a third party has no such obligation in these circumstances. Bystanders (medical personnel and the mother) cannot do this harm; it is only those fetuses who would have an obligation; we cannot impose it on them. But see p.93 concerning fetal reduction.

comply would lead to the execution of another individual? Would the first person be obliged to lose his limb in order to save his fellow?

The Radbaz rules that the individual is not obliged to sacrifice his hand, but would be performing an act of outstanding righteousness if he did. In other words, according to the Radbaz the halacha allows such an act of sacrifice but does not mandate it. This of course means that the individual in such a situation would be faced with an agonizing choice; but that choice would be his. Even where the risk to life is minimal and the donation is permitted, there is no absolute obligation to lose a limb or undergo mutilation in the attempt to save another's life.[4]

---

[4] See Ohr Somayach H. Rotzeach 7:8 and Igr. Moshe Y.D. 2:174 (4).

Saving Life – Risking Life for Others

The general principles governing this area are given in Approach to Risk in Halacha.[1] Here, the application of those principles to organ and tissue donation is considered, as well as some further aspects of risking life to save or benefit others.

Organ Donation with Danger to Life

1. Regenerating organ

Where the part regenerates but the donation carries a danger to the donor's life, the degree of danger is the deciding factor. Where the danger is small but significant such danger is acceptable and the donation is permissible and indeed constitutes a meritorious act.[2] Where the danger is great, the donation would not be halachically sanctioned.

---

[1] See High Risk, p. 52.

[2] Bone marrow donation that necessitates a general anesthetic carries a small risk. Modern studies give a risk of death due to elective general anesthesia of between 1 in 20,000 to 1 in 40,000. Such donation is certainly allowed and highly meritorious but not absolutely obliged. Harvesting of stem cells from peripheral blood (which requires no anesthesia but does require stimulatory drug

2. Non-regenerating organ

Where a threat to life accompanies the sacrifice of the limb or organ, what is the halacha? In the course of his analysis, the Radbaz[3] states that the amputation of a limb could certainly constitute a danger to life; in fact he reports personally witnessing a fatality that resulted from blood loss as the consequence of relatively minor superficial injury. He goes on to state that if danger to life exists, the procedure would be forbidden, and he classifies one who seriously risks his life in the attempt to save another as a *chassid shoteh*, a "righteous fool." The Radbaz concludes that in this situation, one's own "doubtful" life should come before another's certain death (*s'feika didei adif mi'vadai d'chavrei*).[4] [5]

However, where the risk is small enough it may be undertaken. In organ donation the degree of risk is critically relevant; the halachic ruling for the potential organ donor is highly sensitive to the degree of risk that would be incurred. Where the donation carries a small but significant risk to life, the donor may undertake that risk in the course of the attempt to save a life; where the risk is high, the donation would be prohibited (as discussed in more detail in the section on risk).[6]

Perhaps the most common example of the former in the modern medical context is the donation of a kidney. Here, the risks to the donor are small but real.[7] The general ruling followed today[8] [9] is that these risks are small

---

therapy) is thought to carry very low risk; if experience confirms that the risk is indeed minimal, this form of donation is very much to be encouraged.

[3] Radbaz, Responsa 3:627 and 3:1,052.

[4] Some authorities hold that there is an obligation to enter danger to save life; however, the position of the Radbaz has been widely accepted as definitive. See above p. 52 and note 28 there.

[5] Igr. Moshe Y.D. 2:174 rules that one may undertake risk to save life although one is not obliged to do so and gives the rationale for this permission.

[6] High Risk, p. 52.

[7] Cecka J.M. Kidney Transplantation from Living Unrelated Donors. Annual Review of Medicine 2000;51:393: "Risks to the donor are low (<0.005% mortality and <0.3% serious complications) but not absent."

Donnelly P. K, Clayton D. G, Simpson A. R. Transplants from living donors in the United Kingdom and Ireland: a centre survey. BMJ 1989;298(6672):490: "...one in 1600 donors die after nephrectomy... Postoperative morbidity has been

enough to make donation permissible, but significant enough to mean that such donation is not obligatory.

(This means that the potential donor must choose to donate; here the problem of potentially coerced choice is encountered – a common problem is how to give the potential donor the opportunity to choose without coercive psychological pressure from the recipient or others, usually family members. The procedure that is commonly followed is to refrain from disclosing which family members match the recipient

---

estimated to be 1-2%, the main problems being deep venous thrombosis, pulmonary embolism, and wound infection."

Ross L.F. et al. Ethics of a Paired-Kidney-Exchange Program. N Engl J Med 1997;336:1752: "Recent surveys show a perioperative mortality rate of 3 deaths per 10,000 donors. Other major complications (such as pulmonary embolus) occur in less than 2 percent of cases."

Ibrahim H.N. et al. Long-Term Consequences of Kidney Donation. N Engl J Med 2009;360:459. This study showed no excess morbidity or mortality in long-term follow-up of more than 3,600 kidney donors, and no long-term compromise in renal function; in fact, the health of these donors for the parameters measured was better than that of the general population. However, the reason for this is that individuals accepted as donors are healthier than the general population due to careful screening. A control group of people who have not donated a kidney but have similar health status to donors would be required to measure the relevant risk. This study followed only long-term survivors; it reveals nothing about short-term mortality and complications.

[8] Tzitz Eliezer 9:45, quoting the Radbaz and others, says that one should not give a kidney where the donation constitutes a real danger to the donor's life, but where the consensus of expert medical opinion is that such donations are safe, it is permitted but not obligatory. This is particularly true in organ donation since not all organ transplants are successful – the risk to the donor is being undertaken with no guarantee that it will save the recipient.

Tzitz Eliezer points out that where a donor is forbidden to donate, the doctor who performs such a procedure is also guilty of a serious transgression.

Tzitz Eliezer 10:25 is an update on 9:45 which reaches substantively similar conclusions. He writes that when medical science reaches a point where the clear expectation is that both donor and recipient will survive, such donations are permitted. This responsum was written some time ago; it is possible that Tzitz Eliezer would regard current results as having reached that point.

[9] Many modern authorities explicitly allow kidney donation. For a list of some of these, see R. JD Bleich, Contemporary Halachic Problems Vol. IV, p. 281.

antigenically; disclosure is made only to the potential donor. This means that the donor can make a choice with the knowledge that if he refuses, no-one will know that he was eligible in the first place.) [10]

Liver donation: the risks of partial liver donation are higher; in 2002 the estimated risk of death associated with donation was 1 in 300, with approximately 20% having a measurable complication. These figures are approximate; and they may be expected to improve with time. [11]

---

[10] A related question is whether the party applying psychological pressure that results in reluctant donation transgresses the prohibition of "Do not covet." (This transgression can take the form of pressing someone to part with something so that he agrees, but unwillingly. No theft has been committed because acquiescence was forthcoming; but coveting has been committed by the one who extracted the gift through duress.) Rabbi Zilberstein was asked by parents whether they would be permitted to urge their eighteen year old daughter to donate a kidney to her younger brother – their concern was not to transgress this prohibition by applying such pressure. Rabbi Zilberstein replied that they would not be guilty of this infraction; urging a lifesaving donation does not take the form of avaricious pressure to extract for personal gain.

[11] Surman O.S, The Ethics of Partial-Liver Donation. N Engl J Med 2002; 346:1038: "...risk entailed by the donation of the right hepatic lobe for transplantation is not adequately documented. At present, there have been seven reported deaths among donors in the United States who have participated in all types of partial-liver donation. The incidence of death among right-lobe donors is probably 1 percent or more — far higher than that for kidney donation, which has a mortality rate of 0.03 percent and a very low rate of serious complications. In two known cases, donors of a right hepatic lobe had to undergo liver transplantation themselves because they were left with insufficient liver volume. The most recent donor to die in relation to partial-liver transplantation was a 57-year-old man who donated a lobe to his brother, a New York physician... About 100 liver transplantations from living adult donors had been performed at the hospital, making it one of the highest-volume centers in the country. This tragic case places in stark relief the potential risk of partial-liver donation, even at a very experienced hospital."

Trotter J.F. et al. Adult-to-Adult Transplantation of the Right Hepatic Lobe from a Living Donor. N Engl J Med 2002;346:1074. "...The most common complication is a bile leak from the cut surface of the liver, which occurs in approximately 5 percent of donors. Between 9 percent and 19 percent of donors have other complications related to major abdominal surgery, including wound infection, small-bowel obstruction, and incisional hernia... Among the reported cases of living-donor liver transplantation, 2 of 706 donors died (0.28 percent).

Lung lobe donation: living lobar lung transplantation places two donors at risk for each recipient (each donor gives a lung lobe). Lung transplantation is newer than kidney transplantation; risks can be expected to change as experience grows.[12]

In summary, where risk is low, saving life is an obligation. Where a non-regenerating limb or organ can be given to save a life and the danger inherent in the donation is small but real, the donor is free to agree to the procedure but is not obliged to do so. Where the danger to the donor is high, donation would not be halachically approved.

Non-sentient and Minor[13] Donors

Many of the situations encountered in this area involve donor decisions. What is the halacha where the potential donor cannot choose? What is the proper course of action where a potential donor is a child, mentally incompetent or unconscious and therefore unable to choose?

In general, where a potential donor cannot choose, where the organ is non-regenerating or where the donation involves danger, such donation may not be accepted from a donor who lacks legal capacity or the conscious ability to choose.

However, the exact risk of death among donors has not been established... the actual mortality rates may be higher than the reported rates."

[12] Bowdish, ME et al. A Decade of Living Lobar Lung Transplantation: Perioperative Complications after 253 Donor Lobectomies. Am J Transplantation 2004;4:1283: "...253 donor lobectomies [have been] performed at our institution during our first decade of living lobar lung transplantation. There have been no perioperative or long-term deaths. 80.2% of donors (n = 203) had no perioperative complications, while fifty (19.8%) had one or more complications. The incidence of intraoperative complications was 3.6%. Complications requiring reoperation occurred in 3.2% of donors. 15.0% of donors had other perioperative complications; the most serious were two donors who developed pulmonary artery thrombosis, while the most common was the need for an additional thoracostomy tube or a thoracostomy tube for ≥14 days for persistent air leaks and/or drainage."

[13] For Jews, the age of legal competence (bar mitzva) is thirteen years for males and twelve for females. The halachic age of legal competence for non-Jews is not fixed at a particular statutory age; in each case a judgment of maturity is necessary.

However, exceptional circumstances may raise the question of acceptability of an incompetent individual as a donor: where an incompetent person can donate an organ to a recipient in such a way that the *donor* benefits, such donation may be worthy of halachic consideration. For example, where a child could save the life of a sibling by donation of a kidney, and preservation of that sibling's life would clearly be in the best interest of the donor child, an argument could be made permitting the donation. Similarly, where a mentally incompetent person is dependent on another individual who develops the need for a donated kidney and the incompetent person's kidney is a good antigenic match, an argument can be made that giving away a kidney in this case will materially benefit the donor: preserving the life and health of the incompetent donor's benefactor is very much in his own interest.

There is another approach to potentially permitting an incompetent individual to donate: if it can be determined that the incompetent person *would have been willing* to donate if he had been competent, such "substituted judgment" may have halachic merit. An even broader standard for "substituted judgment" may be appropriate: where *most people would be willing* to donate, accepting a donation from an incompetent donor may be in order.[14]

A further question, related to that of substituted judgment, arises here too: may parents agree to a child's donating marrow or an organ where the donation is expected to be lifesaving? Exactly how far does halacha countenance parents' responsibility for their children: does parents' authority extend to decisions that will impose an injury on their child that is not in the immediate best interest of that child?[15 16]

---

[14] R. M. Meiselman in R. M. Hershler, Halacha and Medicine Vol. 3, p.121.

[15] These questions are addressed in an extended discussion in R. JD Bleich, May Tissue Donations be Compelled? Contemporary Halachic Problems Vol. IV, pp. 273-315.

[16] R. Y. Zilberstein (in R. M. Hershler, Halacha and Medicine Vol 4, p.156) rules that a child's kidney may not be taken for the purpose of transplantation even where both the child and the parents agree to the donation: firstly, the child has no halachic capacity to make the donation (or any gift, for that matter); secondly, the child is not obliged in the fulfilment of commandments; and thirdly, the parents' consent is irrelevant – they have no capacity to sanction an injurious action that is not for the benefit of the child on whom that injury is imposed. In contrast, however, parents can consent to the performance of investigations on a

At present the halachic consensus is that a kidney may not be taken from a minor. In the case of a regenerating tissue with no danger to life, however, such as in the case of blood donation by a minor, there is no reason obstructing such donation. It may also be acceptable for a child to donate bone marrow, subject to certain conditions.[17] [18]

Risking Life for Another's Benefit (not to save life)

How much risk may be undertaken to benefit another where the benefit does not amount to the saving of life? One version of this question is that of medical personnel accepting personal risk to treat patients whose lives are not in danger.[19]

Donating tissue for non-lifesaving purposes would raise this question. Transplantation of part of an ovary from a fertile woman to her infertile identical twin to enable the twin to conceive has been performed;[20] while such procedures raise serious halachic concerns (mainly due to the question of establishing maternal identity), as far as the question of risk is concerned it would appear that no prohibition exists as long as the procedure is clearly safe.

---

child against the child's will, even where discomfort may be involved, where the investigations are being done for the benefit of that child (p.157).

[17] See R. SZ Auerbach quoted in Nishm. Avraham, Ch. Mishpat 243:1.

[18] The ethics of conceiving a child expressly for the purpose of tissue donation to an ill sibling is often debated – is it ethical for parents to bring a child into the world only because an existing child needs that tissue? In Judaism this is a non-issue: bringing a child into the world fulfils a commandment; it is meritorious in itself even where no sibling needs a tissue donation. Bringing children into the world does not need ethical rationalization in Judaism; it is good in itself. Put differently: in secular values, justification is necessary to conceive and bear a child; in Judaism justification is necessary to desist from that activity.

[19] See Risk to Caregivers, p. 55.

[20] Silber SJ, Gosden RG. Ovarian Transplantation in a Series of Monozygotic Twins Discordant for Ovarian Failure. N Engl J Med 2007;356:1382-4. This report describes a series of 6 twin-to-twin ovarian tissue transplants. In each case a slice of ovary containing ova was transplanted from a fertile woman to her identical twin who was unable to conceive due to premature menopause; in each of these cases the recipient subsequently conceived and delivered a live child. A later report (Silber SJ, Grudzinskas G, Gosden RG. Successful Pregnancy after Microsurgical Transplantation of an Intact Ovary. N Engl J Med 2008;359:2617-2618) describes the successful transplantation of an entire ovary.

Interventions in Pregnancy

The subject of terminating a pregnancy to avert danger to the mother is presented in detail in other works.[1] This section focuses on the subject of allowing or causing risk to the mother for the sake of preserving a pregnancy and some related issues.

What degree of risk or harm to the mother is acceptable in the attempt to enter or preserve a pregnancy?

Undertaking Risk to Become Pregnant

A woman may expose herself to risk in order to become pregnant where the risk is moderate.[2] Binyan Zion states that where the relevant danger lies in the future, such danger may be hazarded. (He similarly allows a traveller to undertake a journey where danger may arise in the course of

---

[1] See Abortion in Halachic Literature in R. JD Bleich, Contemporary Halachic Problems Vol. I, p. 325 for an extensive review; see also Nishm. Avraham and A. Steinberg, Encyclopedia of Jewish Medical Ethics (Feldheim, 2003).

[2] Binyan Zion 137 assesses the risk to the woman in the case presented to him as less than 50% (although the case was said to involve higher risk; he gives reason for doubting that assessment). Because the danger is not immediate (see above p. 34) Binyan Zion holds that majorities are relevant despite the fact that majorities are usually not relevant in situations of danger to life.

the journey because any danger that may materialize is both unlikely and not imminent.) A woman may therefore embark on a pregnancy that is more dangerous than usual within these limits – the danger is both far from inevitable and will be encountered, if at all, as a future consequence of entering the pregnancy.

Various authorities permit entering such a pregnancy based on other considerations.[3]

Allowing high risk is more problematic; this is generally prohibited. However, in certain exceptional cases relatively high risk may be acceptable: Rabbi Eliashiv was consulted about a 37 year old diabetic woman who wished to become pregnant. She had diabetic complications including near-total blindness, severe impairment of kidney function and hypertension which were well-controlled but expected to become unstable during a pregnancy as she would have to stop her current anti-hypertensive medication due to the possibility of fetal complications or abnormalities. She was extremely keen to have a child and was likely to become severely depressed if she were prohibited from the attempt. Rabbi Eliashiv ruled that it would be permissible for her to enter a pregnancy if the risk to her life was thought to be less than 50%.[4]

Prevention of Pregnancy to Avoid Risk

The subjects of contraception and sterilization (both male and female) have been extensively reviewed elsewhere.[5]

---

[3] See Bleich R JD, Bioethical Dilemmas Vol. II, pp. 242-246 for discussion.

[4] (Rabbi Zilberstein). Rabbi Eliashiv's reasoning was that although this woman's medical condition would ordinarily require her to desist from attempting a pregnancy (and her husband would be required to ensure adequate contraception), since there is (1) a real risk of severe depression if she is not allowed to proceed, and (2) since she will not be the direct and active cause of danger to herself – that is, the pregnancy will generate a situation in which danger may supervene because she will stop certain medications in order to ensure fetal well-being (the pregnancy itself would not destabilize her condition if she remained on her regular medications) – in such a set of circumstances she may be allowed to proceed.

[5] See A. Steinberg, Encyclopedia of Jewish Medical Ethics; Nishm. Avraham.

Screening and Diagnostic Investigations in Pregnancy

1. Invasive testing

Amniocentesis[6] and chorionic villus sampling[7] (CVS) performed for the purpose of detecting fetal abnormalities should not be done where the information gained will not affect management of the pregnancy – if a fetal abnormality is suspected that would not justify abortion it is inappropriate to subject mother and fetus to an invasive procedure for its detection. There is no point in any investigation whose result will not be used; an invasive investigation whose result will not be used is certainly contraindicated. Invasive investigations may be justified only where there is no non-invasive alternative and where the investigation is necessary in the diagnosis of a condition that may permit abortion or significantly affect management of the pregnancy.

2. Non-invasive testing

In addition to other routine antenatal tests, ultrasound scanning has become routine in prenatal care and has no known risks. Scanning yields significant clinical information that may be decisive in the management of pregnancy and delivery, including assessment of fetal size and gestational age, placental localization, fetal presentation, fetal movements, liquor volume, diagnosis of multiple pregnancy and diagnosis of uterine and pelvic abnormalities. Such non-invasive screening should be performed and indeed may be halachically obligatory.[8]

---

[6] The risk of fetal loss due to amniocentesis is approximately 0.5% - 1% (recent studies indicate that the risk may be lower; CVS probably has a higher risk than amniocentesis). Besides miscarriage, complications include infection, amniotic fluid leakage with oligohydramnios (which may result in fetal hypoplastic lungs), infection, fetal trauma and alloimmunisation (leading to Rh disease).

[7] The risk of fetal loss due to CVS is approximately 0.5% - 1%. CVS may also lead to infection or amniotic fluid leakage with oligohydramnios. There is also a risk of digit-reduction defects in the fetus if performed before 11 weeks (0.07%-0.10%).

[8] Accepted "best-standards" care is generally halachically obligatory; see p. 39.

Obligation to save a Fetus and Appropriate Interventions

In general, danger to a fetus is treated as danger to life even when the mother's life is not at risk; thus Sabbath and other laws are set aside to save a fetus.[9]

Cesarian section against mother's wishes

May one intervene to save a fetus against the mother's wishes – for example, may a cesarian section (which imposes some danger on the mother)[10] be performed to save the child where the mother refuses?

Ordinarily, a mother is obliged to undergo a cesarian section if necessary to save her child – although she is not obliged to marry in the first place, once she is married she is halachically required to submit to the normal risks of pregnancy and delivery.[11] Cesarian section is a very common procedure in the modern context and although it carries a higher risk than normal delivery, it is within the limits of what is considered usual and ordinary; therefore a married woman cannot refuse it by claiming that it presents an unusual or extreme danger.[12]

However, a mother is not considered a *rodef* (pursuer) on her fetus such that she can be subjected to an operation against her wishes (due to the operative risk) and certainly not for a fetus that has life-threatening abnormalities.[13]

---

[9] BeHaG in Rosh, Yoma 85:13; Biur Halacha 330 states that Ritva rules like BeHaG in Nidda 44.

[10] The maternal mortality rate for normal birth is under 1 in 10,000; for cesarian section it is probably 3 to 4 times higher.

[11] A woman does not have a right to be negligent with regard to her pregnancy – quite apart from the question of the rights of the fetus, Judaism recognizes a right of the father here too.

[12] R. Y. Zilberstein quoting R. Eliashiv. But cf. R. SZ Auerbach quoted in Shm. Shabbat K'Hilch. 36 note 4.

[13] R. Eliashiv: she is not obliged to endanger herself for a fetus that is unlikely to survive. The Maharit (99) states that a woman is not obliged to suffer an unusually difficult and painful pregnancy; and although there is dispute over this Maharit (many authorities disagree with it and R. M. Feinstein is of the opinion that it is not authentic; however R. Eliashiv points out that it is quoted by the Kness. HaGedola) it is likely that all would agree with this position where the

If the doctor did in fact operate against her wishes and delivered a healthy child, she has no claim of damages (for pain and the surgical scar) against the doctor (and the doctor can claim a fee). If the operation was performed against her wishes and a handicapped child was delivered, it is not clear whether she has a valid claim for damages (and it is also not clear whether the doctor can claim a fee). If the doctor is obliged to pay damages, he can claim the cost of the damages from the child later (and also his fee).[14]

If the mother is unconscious, the cesarian section may be performed where it can be assumed that the mother would have consented; tacit consent can normally be assumed.[15]

In the case of an abnormal fetus, the mother should agree to a cesarian section despite its small risk where that will give the fetus a better chance – there is an obligation to save such a fetus; but she cannot be forced to do so. Once the child is born, however, the parents have no right to deny it due care; any correctly indicated care both to prolong its life and improve its health must be given. If the parents refuse, suitable proxies should be appointed.[16]

Fetal Reduction

Where high-order multiple pregnancy presents a danger to all the fetuses (where none will survive without intervention) it is permitted to cull one or more to save the others.[17] As few fetuses as possible must be removed; those most accessible or whose removal poses the least threat to the others should be chosen to minimize danger to those remaining. If a

---

fetus is unlikely to survive. A woman is not obliged to submit to an operation (no more preferable an option than a difficult and painful pregnancy) against her wishes to improve the survival chances of such a fetus.

[14] Rabbi Y. Zilberstein, quoting Mechilta, Mishpatim 8:7.

[15] R. Y. Zilberstein; who states that the doctor should consult with colleagues before proceeding.

[16] R. Y. Zilberstein. See pp. 111-112 for withholding painful treatment from a newborn and note 41 there for limits to parents' proxy role.

[17] Nishm. Avraham Vol. III, p.16 and p. 295; A. Steinberg, Encyclopedia of Jewish Medical Ethics Vol. 1, p.12; see R. JD Bleich, Bioethical Dilemmas Vol. I, pp. 269-281 for a review.

choice must be made between fetuses where all else is equal, there is no specific prohibition in selecting a male or female fetus for removal according to the parents' preference (gender is generally not a factor in triage decisions).[18]

Operating on a Fetus in Utero

Where an intrauterine fetal operation is necessary (where maternal risk is acceptably low) in a situation of multiple pregnancy, the procedure may not be undertaken if the other fetuses will be damaged.[19]

---

[18] See Triage, pp. 181-182.

[19] R. Y. Zilberstein. Even according to those authorities who hold that one must undertake risk or damage to help another, that obligation devolves only on the one who must undertake that risk; no outside party may impose it. If there were an obligation here it would be that of the other fetuses; no other party may impose risk or damage on them (see p. 78, note 3).

This prohibition is not to be confused with fetal reduction (see above) which is permitted in a situation where all the fetuses will die if no action is taken.

Clinical Cases – Interventions in Pregnancy

Clinical Case 4: Obstetrical Risk

A woman presents in her eighth week of pregnancy with an intra-uterine contraceptive device (IUCD) seen in situ on ultrasound examination. The question of extraction of the device is raised, and the following risks are ascribed:

Risk of aborting the pregnancy during extraction of the device: 25%

Risk of spontaneous termination of the pregnancy due to the device if retained in utero: 35%

An obstetric consultant recommends extraction of the IUCD (after careful localization by ultrasound) on the grounds that the overall risk to the fetus would thereby be minimized (25% vs 35%).

A second expert states that the cumulative risk of abortion and premature birth due to retention of the IUCD would be approximately double the risk of accidentally terminating the pregnancy during extraction, and that in addition the following approximate quantitative factors should be considered:

Risk of amnionitis due to retained device: 10 - 15%

Risk of future fertility problems as consequence of infection: 5%

Risk of prematurity: 10%

The woman seeks halachic guidance.

How should she be advised?

Analysis:[20]

Considering the risks to the fetus in isolation: on the one hand, it is preferable to avoid being the active cause of harm – it is better that harm should occur because of failure to act than causing equivalent harm actively.[21] However, the fetus' chances of survival would be improved if

---

[20] Rabbi Y. Zilberstein.

[21] See Principles, p. 37-39.

interference were attempted – the harm here is not equivalent. On this basis, perhaps the interference is obligatory.[22]

To this it may be objected that the risk of interfering actively here is destruction of the fetus: in the event that removal of the IUCD destroys the pregnancy this will constitute an act of killing the fetus – perhaps that puts this intervention beyond the reach of the usual permission granted to the physician to act (even in the attempt to save life one is not always allowed to act – for example, it is forbidden to sacrifice one person in order to save many,[23] despite the apparent logical challenge that it would seem preferable to have one die rather than many, and particularly when that one will die anyway with the rest if he is not sacrificed). Perhaps when the unintended harm will be an act of killing, this may not be allowed in these circumstances. On this basis it would be better to accept that since the majority probability is that the pregnancy will survive if nothing is done (65%) and there is a chance of killing the fetus actively (25%) if intervention is attempted, it is better to remain passive.

The risk to the child as a result of premature delivery due to the retained device is probably not enough to change this conclusion. Where no other factors are relevant, this would be the proper approach.

(It is important to note that if the chances of the pregnancy aborting spontaneously due to the retained IUCD were over 50%, its removal would clearly be indicated halachically. Here the interference would be considered lifesaving since failure to act condemns the fetus to a majority chance of death.)

Thus far with regard to the fetus.

With respect to the mother:

If the device constitutes a real danger to the mother, its removal would be indicated despite the danger to the fetus,[24] and here in fact we have a risk to the mother – the risk to her life and health due to possible ascending infection causing amnionitis, and the risk of future fertility problems due to such infection.

---

[22] Despite the risk of actively causing harm – the doctor who fears acting in general lest he cause unavoidable harm is out of order since the Torah mandates therapy despite the inherent risks. See Principles, pp. 30-31 and note 22 there.

[23] Maimonides, Laws of the Foundations of Torah 5:5.

[24] Where the mother wishes to accept risk to preserve a pregnancy, see p. 98.

Overall, the risks can be tabulated as follows (values approximate):[25]

	Retained IUCD	Removal of IUCD	Suggested weighting
Abortion	40%	25%	5
Amnionitis	10 - 15%	0	10
Fertility problems	5%	0	3
Complications of prematurity	10%	0	3

It can be seen that the cumulative risks under "Retained IUCD" are significantly greater than those under "Removal of IUCD":

Retention: 40 + 12.5 + 5 + 10 = 67.5

Removal: 25 + 0 + 0 + 0 = 25

This gives a ratio of 2.7:1. If the suggested weighting factors (more or less arbitrarily chosen, to indicate that the pro-rata risks to the mother should be accorded more weight than those to the fetus) are applied, this ratio becomes larger (close to 3:1):

Retention: 200 + 125 + 15 + 30 = 370

Removal: 125 + 0 + 0 + 0 = 125

On this basis the obstetrician recommended attempting removal of the IUCD provided that three-dimensional scanning indicated a low risk of perforating the amniotic sac.

In the opinion of Rabbi Zilberstein, in view of the cumulative risks to mother and child, and particularly due to the 10 - 15% risk to the mother due to infection, the proper approach here would be to attempt removal as suggested.

---

[25] The risk of abortion is given here as 40%; together with the 10% risk of prematurity this gives 50% – reflecting the expert opinion given above that these risks together amount to double the risk to the fetus of accidentally terminating the pregnancy during removal of the IUCD (25%).

Clinical Case 5: Delaying Chemotherapy to Preserve Pregnancy

A 42 year old woman who has one child from a previous marriage has recently remarried. She is 12 weeks pregnant when a breast carcinoma is discovered; she undergoes immediate mastectomy while pregnant. She is advised to terminate the pregnancy and begin chemotherapy; however she wishes to continue with the pregnancy and delay chemotherapy until after delivery. Is her choice halachically acceptable?

Analysis:

This was a particularly precious pregnancy for this 42 year old woman with newly diagnosed malignant breast disease; she strongly desired to carry it to term even if delaying chemotherapy increased her risk of recurrent disease.

The first stage in approaching this problem is to define the respective levels of risk for her various options. In this particular case, after comprehensive disease staging, the probability of untreated tumor-free survival for five years was estimated to be approximately 80%. More accurately, that is the estimated survival in non-pregnant women at the equivalent stage of disease; survival figures in pregnancy are difficult to assess because malignant breast disease in pregnancy is relatively rare. Some studies indicate slower rates of disease progression in pregnancy, indicating that the hormonal profile of pregnancy may have beneficial effects in slowing tumor growth. Other studies however indicate the opposite, namely accelerated tumor growth in pregnancy. There are currently no clear means of determining which tumors will be favorably affected by pregnancy and which may be deleteriously enhanced. This woman's 80% five-year survival prognosis must therefore be seen as a tentative assessment at best.

What are her chances with chemotherapy? The best evidence available, again derived from parallel clinical situations in non-pregnant women, suggested that her five-year disease-free survival probability would be slightly better than 85%.

What about administering chemotherapy during the pregnancy? The reason for recommending termination of the pregnancy in this case was concern for the possible teratogenic effects of potent chemotherapy on the fetus which would be exposed to high doses at 12 weeks and for the remaining duration of the pregnancy. However, allowing the pregnancy to continue and administering therapy concomitantly was also a possibility; but here again, research is lacking: few women receive chemotherapy during pregnancy and the effects on both mother and child are largely unknown, although recent experience suggests that some chemotherapy regimens can be administered safely during pregnancy.

A further factor to consider is the mother's firm desire to continue with this pregnancy. Psychological and emotional factors may be highly significant in affecting survival and recovery from serious illness; it is entirely possible that coercing this woman to abort against her very strong contrary desire may in fact materially decrease her survival chances to a degree that may more than offset any benefits of chemotherapy. The statistical weight of this component of the clinical equation is difficult to measure but must certainly be taken seriously.

The dilemma was put to Rabbi Eliashiv. He indicated that the mother should be allowed to continue with the pregnancy and undergo treatment after delivery. Her desire to do this is legitimate; the possibility of increasing her chances of survival from 80% to 85% is not compelling enough to press her to undergo chemotherapy and certainly not to abort this particularly significant pregnancy when there is every chance that forcing her to do so may induce serious remorse and depression which in themselves may harm her more than a 5% increase in actuarial survival.

Approach to Dangerous and Terminal Illness

Dangerous Illness

The obligation to save life – *pikuach nefesh* – stands close to the pinnacle of the halachic hierarchy of obligation; it supersedes virtually all other duties. A dangerously ill patient must be aggressively treated, desecrating the Sabbath and transgressing almost all other prohibitions if necessary.[1] Even where there is no known definitive therapy, whatever can be done for the patient must be done both to prolong life and improve its quality; and even where it is clear that no medical therapy will help, the patient must not be abandoned.[2]

Terminal Illness

From a halachic perspective, there are two categories of terminal illness: *chayei sha'a* and *goses*. Loosely translated, *chayei sha'a* refers to a terminal situation, where death is very likely in the near future; *goses* refers to an agonal situation, where death is almost certainly immediately imminent. These must be clearly distinguished as the halachos (laws) pertaining to patients in these two categories differ markedly.

---

[1] See Principles, p. 32.

[2] Even if only in order not to cause the despairing realization that the situation is hopeless – anguish, despair and pain are halachically regarded as real dangers to a very ill patient (Igr. Moshe Ch.M. 2:75). Even where a patient *must* be informed of a grim diagnosis (for example where consent and cooperation will be needed for treatment) the information must be conveyed gently and with a very clear message of hope (see p. 289 and notes 2 and 3 there).

A. Terminal Illness – *chayei sha'a* ("temporary life")

Terminal illness is generally defined in halacha as a medical condition that is clearly expected to be fatal[3] within one year[4] [5](as opposed to *chayei olam*, life that is under no such short-term threat). The derivation of this twelve-month period is not explicit in original sources; the suggestion that it derives from the period of survival associated with the category of *treifa* should be seen as setting up a general parallel more than a strict derivation.[6] Consequently it has been suggested that this period should not be seen as an absolute cut-off and that a more basic element of the definition of *chayei sha'a* is the presence of a lethal process or pathology that is presently inexorably threatening life in the relatively short-term; the exact duration of that short term is not necessarily fundamental to the definition. However, expected survival of less than a year has become the generally accepted criterion of *chayei sha'a*.

---

[3] A lethally dangerous but curable or definitively treatable condition does not render a patient *chayei sha'a* where the appropriate treatment is being given – an insulin-dependent diabetic on appropriate insulin therapy is not in the *chayei sha'a* category (and of course such patients must be aggressively treated).

[4] Igr. Moshe Ch.M. 2:75 and Y.D. 3:36; R. Shlomo Kluger, Sefer HaChaim. Hag. Chochm. Shlomo (155:1) gives a rationale for the period of 12 months; also quoted by Darchei Teshuva Y.D.155:1:6.

[5] Some secular jurisdictions adopt 6 months as the relevant period for a definition of terminal illness. A period of 6 months was chosen for current Israeli law with regard to possible withdrawal of treatment, after deliberations that included rabbinic advisors; it was decided to regard survival of more than 6 months as outside the terminal category to allow a margin of safety for diagnostic and prognostic uncertainty (Prof. A. Steinberg).

[6] Rabbi Feinstein (Igr. Moshe Ch.M. 2:75) indicates that since a survival of less than twelve months is relevant (although not definitive) in the category of *treifa* (one who is suffering from any of a set of pathologies that will generally not allow survival of 12 months) it can be applied to the category of *chayei sha'a* as the period that indicates loss of the normal assumption of life (*chezkat chaim*). Rabbi Feinstein emphatically states that where the medical consensus is that the patient will not live for *two* years, such a patient has no less claim to treatment than any other, not even where triage decisions must be made. In other words, patients who are expected to live for more than a year must not be regarded as "terminal" in any way that would deprive them of therapy or appropriate treatment priority.

Withholding and Withdrawing Therapy

In certain situations of terminal illness, treatment may be withheld (subject to stringent conditions – see below). There is an important distinction, however, between withholding and withdrawing therapy: while withholding therapy may be appropriate (and even obligatory) under certain specific conditions, withdrawing life-sustaining therapy that is already being administered is generally forbidden. More accurately (because "withholding" and "withdrawing" do not correspond exactly to the relevant halachic categories): while withholding therapy may be proper in certain situations, actively shortening life is not allowed.

(This is in clear opposition to a number of secular sources which make no distinction.[7] A strict utilitarian approach holds that the only issue of significance in such situations is the outcome: if the outcome is that the patient will not survive there is no real meaning to the distinction between acting to bring about that death or failing to act in such a way that death is allowed to occur. Some go further and assert that there is no moral difference between murder and failure to save;[8] in Judaism there is certainly a difference between these two forms of moral failure, with very different consequences.)

Three categories must be distinguished:

(a) Withholding: not starting a therapy that is not currently being administered;

(b) Withdrawing: stopping a current therapy in such a manner that death is a direct consequence;

(c) Withdrawing a therapy that is being administered intermittently by withdrawing it during an interval between administrations (stopping a therapy by not starting it after a regular break in its use). This may be seen in some sense as "intermediate" between (a) and (b).

Examples of category (a) would be: withholding chemotherapy (where such therapy has not yet begun) from a patient with widespread

---

[7] See Gillon R, Philosophical Medical Ethics (John Wiley, 1986), especially chapter 20: "Acts and omissions, killing and letting die;" and Hauser M, Moral Minds (Little, Brown, 2006), see for example the case on page xvi of the prologue and the discussion there. Beauchamp and Childress argue against distinguishing between the language of "killing" and "letting die."

[8] See Hauser (previous note) for exactly this assertion.

metastatic disease, or the decision not to operate on a patient who is a poor surgical risk.

Examples of (b) would be: withdrawing ventilation from a patient who is currently totally dependent on ventilation, or stopping an infusion of pressor agents that are currently being continuously infused to maintain adequate circulation.

Examples of (c) would be: the decision, implemented between dialysis sessions, to stop intermittent dialysis; or:

– stopping the long-term administration of a drug that is being given as a once-daily or weekly dose, or as a series of cycles such as chemotherapy;

– withdrawing demand cycle ventilation while the ventilator is inactive but attached ready to ventilate if respiratory function deteriorates below a set standard;

– inactivating cardiac pacing or defibrillation (by an implanted automatic device) during the inactive standby phase.

In general, category (a) is the most lenient of these categories in halacha; there are cases where such withholding may be allowed and even obliged (see below, pages 105-112).

Category (b) is forbidden in the context of dangerous illness; stopping a continuously needed life-sustaining therapy amounts to active euthanasia and is forbidden.[9]

(Distinctions between "withholding" and "withdrawing," or "active" and "passive" conduct may not cover all cases unequivocally;[10] mature halachic judgement is needed.)

Each case in category (c) raises the question of whether that particular treatment modality is seen as continuous or intermittent in halacha. Is a course of treatment comprising intermittent administrations deemed to be

---

[9] A life-sustaining therapy such as ventilation may not be stopped on a terminal patient even to save another patient who could be saved for the long term; the general rule is that one person may not be killed to save another. See Clinical Case 21, p. 191.

[10] See Clinical Case 20, p. 185 for discussion of a case that illustrates an aspect of this difficulty.

continuous in essence from a halachic perspective? That question must be answered specifically in each case independently.[11] [12]

The distinction is important because directly stopping a continuous life-sustaining therapy may well constitute a homicidal act; the perpetrator is terminating the patient's life by stopping a needed therapy, directly bringing about death – that is utterly forbidden in halacha. Distinct from that, however, is the withholding of a therapy that has not yet begun: in that case death results from the underlying pathology and the failure to prevent it – and there are situations in halacha where that may be permitted, as will be demonstrated below.

Withholding treatment in *chayei sha'a* situations

A number of sources indicate that certain categories of therapy may (and sometimes should) be withheld in some terminal situations. Although healing is a mitzva (commandment), there are conditions under which it does not apply. In certain situations, treatment that is extremely painful or that prolongs severe suffering falls into this category.[13]

---

[11] For a case that illustrates the problems that arise at this interface of categories, see Clinical Case 6, p. 130. That case raises the question of inactivating an implanted defibrillator that is permanently in place and performs a function of permanent surveillance, but that is expected to function only intermittently and perhaps not at all, in case of emergency need. Is such inactivation to be considered withholding (and if so, is that kind of withholding allowed?) or withdrawing in a way that is forbidden? See there for discussion.

[12] Other relevant distinctions can be drawn here too: is actively *removing* a device that will be needed soon while it is presently inactive worse than passively *failing to give* such a therapy when it falls due? Removing an implanted defibrillator may well be more problematic halachically than not implanting one in the first place (in situations of equal clinical need), or not giving the next dose of chemotherapy when it is due. The latter cases may be discretionary in halacha, the former may not.

[13] Kraina d'Igerta 190 states that one should not prolong the suffering of a *goses* (see p. 127) and probably not that of any terminal patient. Igr. Moshe Ch.M. 2:75 adds that one should ask the patient: if he prefers to live despite his suffering, one should certainly attempt to prolong his life. R. Eliashiv points out that life is of such inestimable value that one should ideally choose to live despite great suffering; unfortunately this is not universally recognized and that choice cannot be forced on an individual who does not want it. (What to decide for a newborn

The following introductory points should be borne in mind throughout this section:

A. This discussion concerns the parameters governing withholding treatment, as in category (a) above, not actively hastening death which is never allowed.

B. Withholding therapy does not include withholding staples such as adequate fluids, nutrition, oxygenation and other basic needs. Therapy that may be withheld in appropriate circumstances includes surgery, chemotherapy and other medical treatments and interventions that will increase or prolong suffering or add risk; basic and staple needs must always be provided. Perhaps more accurately, all modalities must be provided except those that will add significant danger or pain.[14] [15]

Treatment may be withheld when certain conditions apply. When all of the following conditions are satisfied, treatment may be withheld and indeed may be *forbidden*:[16]

1. The patient is in the category of *chayei sha'a,* terminally ill.

2.(a) The patient is suffering uncontrollably, or alternatively:

  (b) The patient is unconscious with no hope of ever recovering consciousness even for a moment.

3. The patient does not want continued treatment.[17]

---

may be more difficult – see p. 110-112.) The Chazon Ish too (quoted by R. Farbstein) stated that one is not required to prolong terminal suffering.

[14] The distinction between "ordinary" and "extraordinary" or "natural" and "artificial" has limited application in halacha; for detailed discussion of this point see R. JD Bleich, Bioethical Dilemmas Vol. I, pp. 72-74.

[15] For experimental therapy, see p. 203.

[16] Igr. Moshe Ch.M. 2:75 (also in R. M. Hershler, Halacha and Medicine Vol. 4, p.102); based on Ketubot 104 and Ran, Nedarim 40: when therapy can neither cure the underlying disease nor prevent extreme suffering in terminal situations but will only prolong that state of suffering, it is appropriate to withhold such therapy. Where this is clearly the case, although one may do nothing actively to shorten life, it may be appropriate to pray for the patient's demise. See also Tif. Yisrael (Yoma 8:7 Boaz 3) on this.

When *all three* of these conditions obtain, treatment should be withheld.

However, the details qualifying each of these criteria are critical:

1. *Chayei sha'a*

Chayei sha'a here means that the consensus of duly qualified opinion is that the patient will not survive a year. This judgment must be made by fully competent expert opinion based on the best medical information available in terms of the relevant particular disease process and its clinical stage, applied to the particular patient at hand.

If it is doubtful whether the patient has *chayei sha'a* or *chayei olam*, the stringent view must be adopted – that is, the patient is regarded as having *chayei olam* until the doubt is resolved. The general principle in *pikuach nefesh* (lifesaving) is that the default approach must be to regard life as potentially salvageable; the burden of proof always falls on the less optimistic opinion.

2. (a) Uncontrollable suffering

This may be physical or psychological.[18] Suffering should not be regarded as uncontrollable until all appropriate expert therapeutic options have been exhausted.[19] Pain that has been inadequately treated cannot be used as a rationale for justifying the withholding of lifesaving therapy.

Psychological suffering including depression secondary to somatic pain indicates failure to treat the pain; that must be done competently before intractable psychological suffering is diagnosed. Psychological and psychiatric problems that are not secondary to physical pain need treatment in their own right no less aggressively than somatic problems.

---

[17] R. Moshe Feinstein states that if a terminally ill patient in extreme suffering requests continued treatment due solely to a conviction that his religious duty requires him to do so, treatment should be withheld – there is no religious duty to prolong terminal life artificially at the cost of extreme suffering. If however the patient genuinely wants to continue therapy in the face of severe suffering, that wish should certainly be honored.

[18] Psychological suffering is no less real than physical suffering in the eyes of halacha – see Tosf., Shabbos 50b.

[19] See below, Analgesia in Dangerously or Terminally Ill Patients, p. 112.

The treatment of psychological issues such as depression and the sense of being a burden on family must be dealt with appropriately: treatment should not be limited to drug therapy – if practical arrangements are necessary to relieve suffering those must be made. Again, failure to relieve psychosocial, practical or financial issues that can be alleviated cannot be used as justification for withholding lifesaving therapy.

2. (b) Permanent unconsciousness

Despite the fact that the patient is not obviously suffering,[20][21] irreversible coma in a terminally ill patient may justify withholding treatment[22] (where the patient has clearly indicated such a wish – see point 3 below).

For the halachic status of brain stem death, see references on page 136.

---

[20] This point is the subject of dissension between R. S Z Auerbach and R. Y S Eliashiv regarding resuscitation (Prof A. Abraham). R. Eliashiv's view is that coma does not represent a state of suffering; R. Auerbach's view is that it may (that is, perhaps a deeply comatose patient suffers but is merely unable to demonstrate that due to inability to respond appropriately – absence of clinical signs in this situation may not represent absence of pain but only absence of the ability to respond to pain in a clinically recognizable way). R. Auerbach held that if the patient was in pain before becoming comatose it should be assumed that he may continue to suffer while comatose. According to this view, there is no reason to change a decision to withhold resuscitation that was appropriately taken while the patient was conscious; the reason for withholding resuscitation then was to avoid prolonging suffering, it is no different now. However, according to the view that coma does not involve suffering, perhaps that previous decision should be amended – now that the patient is no longer suffering, that reason for withholding resuscitation no longer applies. (Their respective rulings were made in the context of DNR decisions; presumably their views would apply to treatment decisions as well.) In practice, modern halachic authorities do not require changing treatment or resuscitation decisions for terminal patients who become comatose.

[21] A common error here is to confuse a family's suffering with that of the patient's. The family of a comatose patient with no hope of recovery may indeed be suffering greatly, but that is not what is meant by intractable suffering justifying consideration of the withholding of lifesaving treatment; it is the patient's suffering that is relevant here, not the family's.

[22] This goes further than both positions mentioned in note 20: according to this opinion therapy and resuscitation may be withheld without reference to suffering; irreversible coma itself would be reason enough. See Nishm. Avraham Vol. II, p. 323. See Meiri on Yoma 84 for possible rationale.

3. The patient does not want to continue

The patient's wish to allow a lethal condition to take its natural course is relevant only when:

(a) No safe curative therapy exists (that is, therapy that could prolong survival beyond *chayei sha'a*). Where safe and painless curative therapy exists it should be administered.[23] Where the effectiveness or safety of a therapy is subject to dispute among experts, the patient is not obliged to undertake it.[24]

(b) Therapy exists but is risky in its own right and the patient refuses such therapy on account of that risk.[25]

(c) Therapy exists but is painful or mutilating and the patient refuses it on that account; in some such cases coercion may not be allowed.[26]

(d) The patient is a fully informed mentally competent adult.[27]

(e) The patient is not refusing therapy due to inadequately treated pain, depression or other ameliorable suffering or any external coercive pressure.

Unconscious patients

Where the patient is unconscious and cannot express the wish to cease therapy:

1. If such a patient has previously unequivocally expressed the personal desire for cessation of therapy in such circumstances and there is no reason to think that that opinion may have subsequently changed, that

---

[23] See Coercion and Consent, p. 155. Where a more expert physician is expected, treatment should be continued (despite suffering) until that expert has seen the patient. This applies also to a physician who is not necessarily more expert but who may have a helpful opinion (Igr. Moshe Ch.M. 2:75.)

[24] See Mor u'Kzia O. Ch. 328 for other limits to obliging acceptance of therapy.

[25] However, such risks may be taken – see below, p. 118.

[26] The patient is however acting incorrectly in refusing safe lifesaving therapy and should be strongly encouraged to consent. See Coercion and Consent p. 155 for circumstances in which the patient may be treated against his will.

[27] See below for patients who are unable to express a preference: unconscious, incompetent or minor patients.

opinion would remain valid and may be applied as if given explicitly now.[28]

2. Where the patient is not known to have expressed a clear personal opinion but the family, knowing the patient well, can testify that the patient would have wished for cessation of therapy, such testimony can constitute valid proxy. More generally, even if the family does not know what the patient would have wanted they are entitled to decide on his behalf – most people rely on their close family to act in their best interests and this trust tacitly empowers family members as *de facto* proxies.[29] Of course, this can be accepted only where there is no reason to suspect that the family may be acting from inappropriate motives.

Minors and mentally incompetent patients

Where the patient is a minor[30] or is mentally incompetent:

The parents' opinion can substitute for the patient's in such cases; parents are the usual *apotropos* (guardians) here;[31] and again, this applies only where their motives are not questionable. (See below, page 112 and note 41 there concerning parents who abandon a child.)

In general, where it is not possible to ascertain a patient's wishes, it may be assumed that the patient would not want suffering prolonged when that suffering is so great that a clear majority of people would respond thus.[32]

Neonates and infants with short life expectancy

Principles for treating babies with short life expectancy (for example, a baby with Werdnig Hoffman disease):

---

[28] This should be established with the family – see next point.

[29] Igr. Moshe Ch. M. 2:74.

[30] That is under barmitzva age: 12 years for a girl and 13 for a boy.

[31] R.Y. Zilberstein. Igr. Moshe Ch.M. 2:74 includes close family (not necessarily only parents) when decisions must be made in a patient's best interest (since most people would rely on family in such situations). Where there is no family, the local Bet Din (halachic authority) should assume responsibility for such decisions.

[32] Prof. A. Avraham quoting R. S Z Auerbach; Igr. Moshe Ch. M. 2:73.

1. Even where there is only a small chance that the child will survive, for example where there is a 5% chance of surviving beyond 18 months, the child must be treated;[33] there is no reason to withhold lifesaving treatment because the patient is a baby. The child who is a *chayei sha'a* must receive all the treatment that an adult would receive.[34] The baby must be ventilated if necessary.

2. If the child will not survive and the ventilation or other therapy will be very painful, it should not be administered; oxygen should be given to ease respiratory difficulty. One is not obliged to cause serious suffering to prolong a terminal disease.[35]

3. Therapy to relieve suffering must be given,[36] even where this may prolong the terminal state.[37]

4. If ventilation or other lifesaving treatment modalities are limited and there is another child who can be salvaged in the long term who also needs the treatment, that child takes precedence.[38]

5. When the child is a *goses*[39] do not initiate ventilation; provide oxygen.[40]

---

[33] In general, if the child will survive for at least one year, all treatment should be given (R. Y. Zilberstein). Where survival will be for a few months only and involve suffering, it may be more difficult to decide about therapy such as major surgery. Major surgery with little chance of success which will impose much suffering with no appreciable chance of survival should be withheld.

[34] Mishna Yoma 8:6 and Bartenura there; Rambam Hilch. Shab. 2:18; Sh. Ar. O.C. 329:4. See also Meiri, Yoma 84b for a rationale behind this ruling where the patient is a conscious adult, and R. Eliyahu Baal Shem Tov, Sefer HaMitzv. where the patient is not conscious. See also Igr. Moshe. Ch. M. 2:71.

[35] Igr. Moshe Ch. M. 2:73.

[36] Igr. Moshe Ch. M. 2:73 discusses the obligation to give therapy to relieve suffering safely.

[37] Tif. Yisrael, Mishna Yoma 8:6, Boaz 3, demonstrates that it is preferable to lessen suffering in terminal situations even where such action will prolong the terminal state rather than allow a more rapid demise where that would be more painful.

[38] Igr. Moshe Ch. M. 2:73:2. See also Triage, p. 171.

[39] See p. 127.

[40] Igr. Moshe Ch. M. 2:73:3.

6. The above factors apply regardless of the opinions of the guardians of the child; no guardian is empowered to deprive a child of appropriate therapy. Where relevant decisions must be made, however, it is usually the parents who must make those decisions; but where the parents have abandoned the child and foster parents have stepped in, the foster parents are the proxies; that is, those who have taken upon themselves the mitzva of caring for the child, not those who have abandoned him.[41]

Analgesia in Dangerously or Terminally Ill Patients

In modern medicine, uncontrolled pain should be extremely rare – the modern medical and surgical armamentarium includes modalities capable of relieving even the most severe pain. Traditionally, pain relief has been poorly taught and practised (there have been major improvements in this field and pain relief is now a recognized area of specialization and expertise); it has been suggested that one reason for this failure was the fear that liberal administration of narcotics may depress respiration and hasten patients' demise.

To be sure, some of the analgesic and palliative modalities that may be needed to relieve severe pain carry significant risk; but such risk is acceptable in the treatment of severe pain in dangerously and terminally ill patients and in fact such risk *must* be taken, subject to certain principles of care, as detailed below.

In life-threatening circumstances risky analgesic interventions may be permitted even if they carry a risk that is more than moderate. This requires explanation: why is an intervention that poses a risk to life acceptable when it is directed at symptoms and not cure? Surely life should not be seriously endangered to deal with symptoms? High risk interventions are acceptable when they are undertaken in the attempt to cure potentially lethal conditions, but why in situations where the gain will be only symptomatic? Ordinarily, high risk can be undertaken only when life is at stake.

The halachic rationale is this: unavoidable significant risk accompanying analgesia is acceptable in life-threatening circumstances because in such situations *the pain is not innocuous* – it is an assumption of halacha that severe pain may be a real factor adding to the danger of an underlying

---

[41] Rabbi Y. Zilberstein, based on Maharam Shick and on Zecher Shlomo P. Lech Lecha regarding a child's obligation to honor parents who abandon the child.

primary pathology.[42] In situations of dangerous illness severe pain itself constitutes a real additive risk; it is a burden that increases the present risk to life.[43][44] A patient's will to live and battle illness is a real factor in that patient's healing and survival,[45] and relieving severe pain (and alleviating anguish, despair and depression) is therefore *not only humane but also therapeutic.*

Rabbi Feinstein reasons that since pain (and depression, hopelessness and mental anguish) are tangible additive lethal elements, a measure of risk is acceptable in the course of treating the pain just as it would be in treating the disease itself.

A common clinical application of this principle would be in the case of a terminally ill patient suffering severe pain due to a widespread malignancy. In such circumstances the physician may naturally hesitate to prescribe high doses of narcotic analgesics for fear of suppressing respiration in a very ill patient; however, according to Rabbi Feinstein such medication would be permitted and even obligatory because the patient's pain is part of the clinical problem no less than the underlying pathology.[46]

---

[42] Igr. M. Ch. M. 2:73. See also Palliation of Pain in R JD Bleich, Bioethical Dilemmas, Vol. II.

[43] Experienced physicians know that adequately addressing severe pain, anguish, despair, loneliness and depression may be critically important for healing and survival.

[44] In life-threatening situations halacha ascribes significance to factors that may be considered minor in other settings. One may desecrate the Sabbath for a critically ill patient to provide for the patient's needs including needs that may not appear to be directly lifesaving. Where satisfying such needs will help the patient emotionally (though physiologically unnecessary) they are mandated in halacha *(yishuvei daatei...).* Such needs are material enough to be considered lifesaving.

[45] A seriously ill patient must not be given bad news. Sh. Aruch Y.D. 337; Nishm. Avraham Vol. II, p. 294; Igr. Moshe Ch. M. 2:73.

[46] R. Feinstein rules that an ordinarily prohibited procedure may be performed for palliation even where there is no registered survival benefit: he allows orchidectomy for palliation of metastatic prostate carcinoma even where research may not have shown a statistically significant survival advantage. Rabbi Feinstein reasons that even if a survival difference is not recognized in terms of statistical significance, since it is known that severe pain may shorten survival in

A number of important limitations apply here, however:

1. The analgesic must be administered only with the intention of relieving pain, and not to terminate life or compromise it at all.[47] Narcotics must be titrated carefully and expertly against the pain to provide adequate analgesia with minimum danger; any dangerous unwanted effects due to the therapy must be treated appropriately.

2. Only the most qualified and experienced physician available may administer the therapy; this is a general principle in medical halacha[48] but is particularly relevant in situations of known danger involving very ill patients where therapeutic skill is likely to be critical.

Of course, it is the patient's pain that must form the indication for analgesia, not the family's suffering.[49]

Withholding Fluids, Nutrition and other Basic Needs

Even where therapy may be withheld, basic staple needs must always be provided.[50] A patient may never be starved or dehydrated to death, no matter what the clinical situation. Basics that must be given include adequate fluid and attention to electrolyte balance, adequate nutrition, oxygenation and anything else that the patient would have ordinarily needed: if the patient is taking insulin, it must be continued. The same applies to thyroid hormone replacement or any other therapy that is a

---

serious illness it stands to reason that alleviation of pain is likely to prolong survival *at least slightly* – and that is enough to allow it (Igr. Moshe Ch. M. 2:73 (also in R. M. Hershler, Halacha and Medicine Vol. 4, p. 114).

[47] See discussion on the "Principle of Double Effect," Part II, p. 228.

[48] See above, p. 27 and note 12 there.

[49] This error is not unknown. An experienced internist reports: "A terminally ill patient was coherent, lucid and not in pain. His family asked to have him on morphine as they could not deal with relating to him. I refused. During my leave, he was given morphine. On my return I found him heavily sedated. I gave him Narcan, his sedation was reversed and he sat up and hugged his wife (to her distress). Ongoing sedation was requested. There was a standoff and I was removed from his care."

[50] Nishm. Avraham Vol. II, pp. 319-325; Igr. Moshe Ch.M. 2:74. Rabbi Feinstein points out that food, unlike medications, is a constant and universal need for all living creatures; patients must be fed (see there for specific exceptions).

staple ongoing need for that patient. Whatever has been necessary over the long term may not be stopped when the patient becomes terminally ill; those needs are staple and ordinary for that patient, and there is no reason to stop them now. Withholding food or any life-sustaining need for long enough will certainly kill, regardless of the acute clinical situation, and that is never allowed.

In the modern context, in hospices and other settings, it is becoming common practice to withhold food and fluids from terminally ill patients.[51] The undoubted result is that in many such patients the specific cause of death is starvation or dehydration rather than the underlying pathology. This is absolutely unacceptable in Judaism; such action amounts to homicide.[52]

Fluids: maintaining fluid and electrolyte balance can be a serious clinical challenge in extremely ill patients; this must be skilfully managed. It is important to understand that the problem here is clinical, not ethical – whatever must be done to maintain fluid balance is obligatory; how that is handled medically may well be a clinical challenge, but that does not in any way allow less than full attention to this basic medical need. This includes intravenous fluid and electrolyte administration if oral intake is inadequate.[53]

Nutrition: feeding extremely ill patients is recognized as an area of clinical difficulty. Desperately ill and cachectic patients may absorb very poorly no matter what route is chosen for the administration of nutrition. But again, this is a clinical problem; appropriate medical expertise must be applied to the challenge. Despite the fact that it may appear almost impossible to nourish an extremely ill patient adequately, and indeed some forms of nutrition may entail risk and potential harm, withholding all food for long enough will certainly kill the patient.

---

[51] See below, Part II, and Appendix II: Modern Historical Overview of Euthanasia and Assisted Suicide in Western Countries.

[52] For the question of whether causing death by depriving the victim of a life-sustaining need is actionable in Jewish law, see Maimonides, Hilch. Rotzeach.

[53] Clinical expertise and experience may be needed. Proper hydration of a clinically unstable patient takes skill; on occasion complications of inadvertent excessive fluid administration such as pulmonary edema can be prevented by the use of a pediatric intravenous administration set – medical and nursing personnel must be adequately expert in all aspects of care when treating terminal patients.

In an imminently terminal situation where a patient will clearly die from the underlying disease process *sooner* than a lack of nutrition would cause any harm, food may be withheld.[54] Since food is not ordinarily needed from minute to minute or even hourly, where death is inevitable within a very short time there may be no benefit in attempting to feed a patient who is not absorbing and who indeed may be harmed by such efforts. (This is not the case with liquids where fluid balance may be unstable in the very short term.) For the management of a *goses* in general, see below.

Where oral feeding is impossible or dangerous, feeding by nasogastric or other route must be instituted. Where gastrostomy or jejunostomy would be the best clinical solution they must be performed. Where a patient is deemed too ill for such a procedure, some method of feeding must be found (except for situations of imminent demise as outlined in the previous paragraph) – no matter how clinically difficult; guaranteeing death by starvation is not a Jewish option.

Oxygenation: Breathing is perhaps the most basic of needs, and adequate oxygenation must be provided. Where nasal cannula or facemask administration is inadequate to prevent respiratory failure, mechanical ventilation must be used. Where mechanical ventilation has not been started, the patient is terminal, and is *not suffering from the inability to breathe*, it need not be started (where all the conditions for withholding therapy as discussed above have been satisfied) – not every dying patient needs mechanical ventilation. Where the patient is suffering from acute air hunger that suffering must be relieved;[55] if mechanical ventilation proves necessary for this it must be administered. Where mechanical ventilation has been started it may not be stopped while the patient is

---

[54] Nishm. Avraham Vol. II, p. 324 concerning a *goses* who does not want staples, where death will occur sooner than their lack will cause, writes in the name of R. S Z Auerbach that these may be withheld.

[55] Igr. Moshe Ch. M. 2:73. Rabbi Feinstein points out that this is a particularly severe form of suffering; it must certainly be treated. Morphine or sedatives must not be used to stop the struggle to breathe; that amounts to active euthanasia and is forbidden. (Where carefully titrated doses of appropriate drugs will allow the patient to relax and breathe more efficiently, however, thus avoiding the need for mechanical ventilation, that may be appropriate; but only where extreme care is exercised to ensure that the patient improves physiologically and remains stable. The goal must be to help the patient breathe; not to facilitate peaceful asphyxia.)

dependent on it. For withdrawal of ventilation in brain stem death, see Definition and Timing of Death, page 135.

Antibiotics, other drugs and blood products: The general rule is that antibiotics and blood products must be given (as a general rule, intercurrent infection in terminal patients must be treated). This rule applies to blood products and other drugs or agents that would be used if the patient were not terminal. Where a drug or other therapy will itself add a significant new danger, its use may be discretionary – for the relevant rules see pages 118-127 below. Drugs (such as pressors) need not be given to a patient in the final stages of the dying process where there is no hope of recovery and the drug will not change the overall clinical picture[56] (though a continuous infusion that is already running and that is maintaining life may not be actively stopped). For the administration of drugs to a *goses*, see page 127 below.

Nursing care: All standard care must be given to terminal patients including careful attention to movement for the prevention of pressure sores and all related therapy. For the question of moving a *goses*, see page 127.

Withholding and Withdrawing Ventilation, Dialysis, Cardiac Pacing

Subject to all the conditions outlined above (terminal illness, intractable suffering, the patient does not want this treatment) these modalities may be withheld if they have not been started but may not be stopped if they have. For cases of intermittent administration (where the therapy has been started but is not being given at the present moment), see page 103.

Ventilation: See "Oxygenation" above. Setting ventilator cut-off by timer: see pages 195-196 and note 26 there.

Dialysis: A patient in renal failure must be dialysed. A terminal patient who is dying from other (untreatable) causes and whose renal function deteriorates as part of the overall terminal process need not be dialysed (subject to all the provisos governing withholding therapy from terminal patients discussed above). Where renal failure is the specific clinical problem and is reversible it must be treated.

---

[56] Nishm. Avraham Vol. II, p. 327 quoting R. S Z Auerbach.

Cardiac pacing: Cardiac pacing that is sustaining life may not be stopped, whether the pacing is continuous or set to pace only on demand. In the latter case it is protecting life and that protection may not be withdrawn. An implanted defibrillator may not be inactivated; once implanted it is part of the patient's life-protecting functions and may therefore not be withdrawn.[57]

Risky Treatment in *chayei sha'a* Situations

Not uncommonly, therapy may be available for the treatment of a *chayei sha'a* condition, but only at the risk of worsening that *chayei sha'a* situation if it fails. Indeed, such therapy may be curative if successful and lethal if it fails. An example of this type of problem would be a hematological malignancy threatening to terminate life within a year, where long term remission may be achieved by marrow ablation and rescue grafting, but only with a significant risk of mortality from the procedure. Here, a procedure is available that will result in cure if successful but will foreshorten the patient's *chayei sha'a* if not. If successful, the weeks or months of survival that would be expected if the condition were untreated will be extended to years; but if unsuccessful those weeks or months will be sacrificed – the patient will die *sooner* than the natural *chayei sha'a* would have lasted.

A surgical example would be an enlarging aortic aneurysm that is expected to prove lethal within a year in a patient who is unfit for surgery. Surgery may be curative if successful but on the other hand may result in immediate death during the procedure.

What is the halacha in these situations? Is it preferable to preserve limited *chayei sha'a* or to choose a risky attempt to gain *chayei olam*?

The key source for this area of halacha is Avoda Zara 27b. The discussion there concerns the question of seeking medical attention that may itself prove lethal in a situation of grave danger to life, and offers as a Biblical source the case of four lepers who found themselves facing starvation outside the Jewish encampment during an enemy siege.[58] Their options were certain starvation, or entering the enemy camp where they

---

[57] Unless the patient is so distressed by its presence that the distress constitutes more of a threat than the absence of the device. See Clinical Case 6, p. 130.

[58] II Kings 7.

might either be saved or summarily executed. They chose to risk entering the enemy camp (where, as it happened, they survived). This incident suggests that in the equivalent medical dilemma it would be proper to risk immediate death for the chance of long-term survival.

The commentaries engage in extensive analysis of this source, variously construing its constituent parameters particularly with respect to the degree of the risks involved, and a range of halachic precedents is based on its various understandings. Rabbi Feinstein[59] raises a question that leads him to a principle in this area: these lepers were clearly spiritually negative individuals; why do we base halachic precedent on them? He concludes that this source demonstrates not necessarily a spiritually correct conduct so much as a logical and acceptable human choice; he therefore rules that in such situations the patient must choose between the immediate risk for long-term survival and the alternative short-term certain demise.[60]

It is thus clear that risk is permissible in these situations,[61] and even high risk according to many authorities.[62] The Shvut Yaakov[63] deals with a

---

[59] Igr. Moshe YD 3:36.

[60] The discretionary nature of this acceptance of risk appears to be agreed by the halachic authorities who deal with this question. Certainly where the risk of losing *chayei sha'a* is greater than 50%, those who allow such risk do so subject to the patient's choice.

[61] Other sources besides Av. Zara 27b corroborate the precedence of *chayei olam* over *chayei sha'a* in allowing such choices. B. Metzia 62a discusses the case of two stranded individuals one of whom possesses a flask of water sufficient to ensure the survival of only one. Two positions are presented: Ben Petura holds that the water should be shared allowing both to survive temporarily; Rabbi Akiva holds that the owner of the water should drink it and survive. Rabbi Akiva's opinion is halachically definitive here; *chayei olam* takes precedence over *chayei sha'a* – at least, one's own *chayei olam* takes precedence over another's *chayei sha'a*. The Chazon Ish (Hilch. Av. Koch. 69) states that if a *third party* were the source of the water, that third party would similarly be obliged to give it entirely to one, thereby saving one life in the long term rather than two in the short term (one *chayei olam* is preferable to two *chayei sha'a*). The Chazon Ish thus holds that *chayei olam* should take precedence over *chayei sha'a* quite apart from the obligation to save one's own life first.

[62] But not all; see Meiri (Av. Zara 27a – 28b) who mentions opinions that would not risk shortening temporary life; presumably this means only that high risk is unacceptable (since the gemara says explicitly that risks may be taken here). See also Tosf. Rid (Mahadura Kama Av. Zara 28a, para.10) who distinguishes

case in which a patient was faced with a disease that, untreated, would prove fatal within days, but had the option of taking a drug which might either cure or kill immediately; he allows taking the drug.

Rabbi Chaim Ozer Grodzensky[64] was presented with the case of a patient in Koenigsberg who was expected to survive for no more than six months without therapy. An operation was however possible that would prove curative if successful but fatal if not (the operation in this particular case had a greater than even chance of proving fatal). Rabbi Grodzensky allows the operation. He goes on to state that this applies even if the operation has only a "distant" chance of success since the language of the Talmud is "l'chayei sha'a lo chayshinan" – we are "not concerned" about temporary life in this type of situation and the Talmud makes no distinction between degrees of likelihood of success. In this he explicitly disagrees with Mishn. Chachamim who requires at least an equal chance of success to allow the surgery. (See below for discussion on the permissible limits of this risk.)

He mentions the requirement to have approval of the local halachic authority in each case and states that the physicians involved must be the most expert.[65]

Rabbi Moshe Feinstein[66] rules similarly that such a risky procedure is allowed, and that when a patient is faced with these options of *chayei sha'a* or risky therapy, the patient should be given the choice (as noted above); he agrees that the risky option is allowed even when the chances of its success are less than 50%. Where success is more likely than

---

between expert and non-expert practitioners in this context – his concern appears to be the relative levels of risk that these two confer.

[63] Shvut Yaakov 3:75 (quoted in Gilyon Maharsha Sh. Aruch Y.D. 155:1).

[64] Achiezer, Part 2, Y.D. 16:6, based on Av. Zara 27b and referring to Shv. Yaakov 75 brought in P. Teshuva Y.D. 339, Gilyon HaRashba 336, Binyan Tzion 200, Tif. Yisrael in Yoma (presumably Boaz 3 in Mishna 8:6) and Mishn. Chachamim 108.

[65] The Shv. Yaakov stipulates that the doctor must deliberate with particular caution, that he obtain other expert medical opinions and that they come to a clear majority decision (that is, a proportion of at least 2:1, according to Melamed L'Hoil's understanding of the Shv. Yaacov here) and in addition that the decision be approved by the local rabbinic authority.

[66] Igr. Moshe Y.D. 3:36.

failure, the patient should choose the therapy[67] (that choice would be halachically correct and preferable although the patient cannot be coerced); where it is less likely (that is, where the mortality of the therapy is greater than 50%) it is discretionary.[68] [69]

Rabbi Feinstein states that in this context the period to be considered the limit of *chayei sha'a* is twelve months[70] – he states that the Achiezer quoted above mentions six months only because that happened to be the period that was relevant in the case at hand; the general rule to be applied should be based on a period of twelve months. Where expected survival is longer than this, one should not undertake such risks; Rabbi Feinstein writes that if a patient has a condition that may allow survival for years although it could prove suddenly fatal at any time, it would be difficult to permit a dangerous procedure to attempt cure.

What choice should be made for a patient who cannot choose (a patient who is unconscious, incompetent or a minor)? This must be decided in each case by appropriate halachic consultation. The decision may depend on the degree of risk; if the risk is reasonable, the appropriate choice would be to attempt cure despite the risk. Some authorities hold that even where the chance of success is under 50% that chance should be taken where the alternative is certain death.[71] Where the mortality is less than 50% (that is, there is a majority chance of saving life for the long term)

---

[67] Rabbi Feinstein does not quote a textual source for this obligation; he states that it is "logical" or "reasonable."

[68] A risky therapy that has a greater than 50% chance of success is permissible even in *chayei olam* situations – see Risking Long Term Life for Longer Term Life, p. 126 and Clinical Case 9, p. 132.

[69] Rabbi Feinstein (Igr. Moshe Y.D. 3:36) allows risky therapy in *chayei sha'a* situations only where the therapy will remove the threat to life *completely* if successful; *chayei sha'a* should not be risked for longer term life that is constantly under threat of death. The risky therapy must be *curative* with respect to the threat to life (it may be used where the long term life gained will be of lower quality than previously, but not where the original pathology will linger, subjecting the patient to ongoing risk of death that could occur at any time).

[70] Igr. Moshe Ch.M. 2:75 and Y.D. 3:36; R. Shlomo Kluger in Sefer HaChaim.

[71] R. M. Sternbuch.

most would agree with Rabbi Feinstein that the choice to be preferred is the active attempt to save long term life.[72]

Does halacha empower or indeed oblige parents to choose for a child in this situation? Some authorities hold that only the patient can choose to actively undertake high risk; caregivers cannot impose high risk on incompetent wards. Rabbi Feinstein holds that parents can make this choice for a child.[73]

Limits of risk

In these *chayei sha'a* situations, how small must the chance of cure be to render the procedure forbidden? There is a range of opinion on this point: the Mishnas Chachamim quoted by the Achiezer (mentioned above) requires a success rate of at least 50% to allow the attempt.[74] The Achiezer does not give a figure but holds that even a "distant" chance of success in an otherwise hopeless situation is enough.[75]

---

[72] Rabbi Feinstein holds that this amounts to an obligation; presumably he would require it for an incompetent or minor patient.

[73] Igr. Moshe Ch. M. 2:74. This is the generally accepted view. See however Melamed L'Hoil (104; p.115) who states that where there is a clear majority of medical opinion (at least 2:1) in favor of a risky operation on a child where the alternative is certain death, parents have no right to refuse and that indeed parents never have a right to endanger their children.

[74] The logic behind this figure appears to be that a therapy that has a success rate of over 50% is properly considered a therapy; a procedure with a *mortality* of over 50% cannot be deemed to be "therapy" (R. Moshe Shapira). Tzitz Eliezer (10:25) similarly requires a 50% chance of success.

[75] The logic behind this opinion (and the others that find a chance of less than 50% acceptable) would seem to be that as long as the therapy is successful in a *significant minority* of cases it is worth attempting in otherwise hopeless circumstances; the Talmud states that the temporary life being risked is "of no concern" here. (The debate among these opinions is on the question of how small a minority should be considered significant in this particular context.)

Tosf. and others ask how the Talmud can hold that temporary life is "of no concern" when elsewhere (Yoma 85a) it mandates desecrating the Sabbath to excavate a person who is buried under rubble no matter how temporary the life gained will be; the saving of even moments of life obliges this. The answer is that in both cases we act for the patient's good: in the case of excavating a victim, if nothing is done he will certainly die, and in the case of lethal illness too, if nothing is done the patient will die. In both cases we choose the lifesaving

Rabbi Feinstein similarly holds that even a distant chance of success is adequate to make the risk permissible.[76]

Rabbi Eliashiv requires a chance of success of at least 30%.[77] [78]

Others hold that even one in a thousand may be adequate.[79] The Chatam Sofer would not sanction a "remote" chance but does not stipulate a specific probability.[80]

The range of opinion is thus wide;[81] this is an area for judgment by competent halachic authority.

Terminal life, therapy safe but efficacy doubtful

Where *chayei sha'a* can be treated with a therapy that is safe but of doubtful efficacy (that is where the therapy may or may not succeed in prolonging *chayei sha'a* into *chayei olam* but will certainly not shorten the *chayei sha'a*) it should be attempted.[82]

---

attempt (Tosf.) Put another way: in the case of excavation where the victim faces certain death or only temporary life, we act to save that temporary life. In the case of lethal illness where the patient faces certain death or the chance of cure, we risk temporary life for that chance of cure (Ritva; Tosf. R. Elchanan). Temporary life is "of no concern" *only* when long term life is the possible alternative.

[76] Ig. Moshe Y.D. 2:58.

[77] R. Y. Zilberstein.

[78] Rabbi Zilberstein would be unwilling to allow surgery for a neonate with congenital heart disease where the chances of surviving surgery are given as no more than 5-10%. Even where the prognosis without surgery is dismal (less than 1 year survival), such surgery is too risky to allow (based on R. Eliashiv; see above).

[79] Beit David 2:340

[80] Chatam Sofer, Y. D. 76.

[81] It appears that there are two broad issues here: firstly, there is a debate over whether more than 50% chance of success is required; as suggested (notes 74 and 75 above) the point at issue here may be whether a therapy that has a mortality of over 50% can properly be regarded as "therapy" or not. Secondly, among those who allow less than 50% chance of success there is a debate over how small the chance must be in order to be reckoned insignificant.

[82] Igr. Moshe Ch. M. 2:74.

Risking terminal life to prolong terminal life

There is a general obligation to prolong temporary life (except in the specific circumstances discussed above). This is so even when the extended period will remain in the temporary category, since any period of life, no matter how short, is of inestimable value,[83] and the patient should be counselled thus.

Is there such an obligation in the face of significant risk? If there is no obligation, is it permissible to risk terminal life for its temporary extension?

Where a risky therapy exists that will extend terminal life (but not long enough to constitute long-term life) if successful, but will shorten it if unsuccessful, the therapy should ordinarily not be given;[84] however, some authorities would allow a patient that choice, at least where the risk is low enough.[85] What is the limit to the risk that may be accepted in this circumstance? It seems that less than 50% risk may be acceptable, and that 50% risk or more would make the therapy prohibited.[86] Where patient choice is not an issue, the proper course of action is to avoid

---

[83] R. I. Jacobovitz, Jewish Medical Ethics p.152.

[84] Igr. Moshe Ch. M. 2:75. Rabbi Feinstein does not offer a primary source for this ruling but states that logic suggests it. In summary: where the dangerous therapy has only a 50% chance of prolonging life beyond 12 months, it is doubtful whether it should be given (but the patient may choose to take it); where the chance is over 50% it is certainly permitted (and should be chosen); where there is no chance of prolonging life beyond 12 months but only extending it somewhat at the cost of risk, this should not be done. Where it is clear that the therapy will extend temporary life with no risk, or at least will do no harm if unsuccessful, it should certainly be given (unless it will add or prolong unbearable suffering and the patient declines for that reason).

[85] R.Y. Zilberstein. Rabbi Feinstein appears to disagree; see next note.

[86] R. Feinstein states that high risk is acceptable in *chayei sha'a* situations only where a successful outcome will remove the threat to life *completely;* that is where the *chayei olam* gained will not be under constant threat of death due to ongoing pathology (see note 69 above). Thus it follows that Rabbi Feinstein would not allow high risk where the *chayei sha'a* status will not be removed at all. In fact, in Igr. Moshe Ch. M. 2:75 he states clearly that risk is not permissible to prolong *chayei sha'a;* there he appears to include any significant level of risk, and he makes no mention of allowing a choice (although it is possible that he does not mean to prohibit such a choice).

adding any significant degree of risk of precipitating death for the possible benefit of prolonging temporary life.[87]

Intercurrent and secondary problems in terminal illness

Intercurrent or secondary problems (such as an intercurrent pneumonia) in a terminally ill patient must be treated[88] (where treatment will not add risk or suffering, as outlined above).

Acute Intermittent Threats to Life; Chronic Disease with Acute Life-threatening Exacerbations

What is the halachic status of a patient who has a chronic threat to life due to acute events, or exacerbations of his chronic disease? Where patients typically survive for more than a year but there is an incidence of acute events that may be life-threatening occurring at any time, is such a patient in the *chayei sha'a* or the *chayei olam* category?

There are two broad groups of clinical conditions that raise this question:

1. Chronic conditions with acute exacerbations such as chronic obstructive pulmonary disease, where the patient has an ongoing illness that may worsen gradually over time but tends to be punctuated by acute exacerbations that may be life-threatening;

2. Conditions in which the patient is typically well but is subject to unpredictable acute events such as cardiac arrhythmias, as in intermittent atrial fibrillation without structural cardiac disease, or the Wolff-Parkinson-White syndrome.

Other conditions may be intermediate between these: for example, chronic conditions that smoulder in a low-grade or quiescent manner for long periods but may become active – some hematological malignancies that tend to be indolent but may become acute such as chronic lymphomas that may undergo unpredictable blastic transformation.

---

[87] An example of this type of situation would be a terminally ill cancer patient who develops massive gastro-intestinal bleeding and becomes severely unstable hemodynamically; if transfer to hospital for fluid resuscitation and transfusion is likely to involve significant risk of precipitating death because the patient is too ill to survive the transfer, it should not be attempted (see previous note). A risk of 10%-20% is probably sufficient to be considered significant here.

[88] Igr. Moshe Ch. M. 2:75 states that there is no reason to think otherwise.

In these categories, statistical survival figures are much less meaningful for the individual patient than in a gradually and uniformly progressive disorder. Actuarial survival for the group may be measured in years, but some individual patients will experience an acute threat to life in any given year, and it may be impossible to predict which individuals will experience such a threat sooner and which will experience it later or never.

Where the group survival is more than a year, these types of conditions are not considered *chayei sha'a*. Therefore, despite the fact that the individual with such a condition is under a certain degree of constant threat, it is difficult to allow a high-risk procedure or therapy in an attempt to lessen the risk of an acute episode.[89]

These same general considerations probably apply to patients who have life-threatening allergies triggered by particular antigens (such as foods or insect stings). Here, a statistic is even less meaningful – the danger depends on whether the patient is exposed to the particular trigger or not. Again, where the risk of exposure is low it would be difficult to allow a therapy that carries high risk.

Extreme Old Age

Age has no bearing on the obligation to treat. Even in extreme old age all available therapy must be given. Where an old patient requests no therapy in a dangerous situation claiming old age as a reason to be allowed to die, that is not a halachically acceptable reason to abandon the patient. Old age should not be invoked as a reason to give a patient lower priority even in triage decisions.[90]

Risking Long Term Life for Longer Term Life

May one risk long term life for longer term life (risking *chayei olam* for longer *chayei olam*)? Where the risk is low enough, this may be considered.[91]

---

[89] Igr. Moshe Y.D. 3:36. Rabbi Feinstein states that if a patient can live for years but could die at any moment, it is hard to permit a dangerous procedure.

[90] Igr. Moshe Ch.M. 2:75.

[91] See Clinical Case 9, p. 132 for details. See also Clinical Case 10, p. 133.

Prolonging Long Term Life with Severe Suffering

As discussed above, where terminal life can be prolonged only for the short term and at the cost of great suffering, there is no general obligation to do so. However, where a patient's life can be prolonged indefinitely (*chayei olam*) but only at the cost of severe permanent pain and suffering, it is more difficult to decide whether an obligation exists. In practice, Rabbi Feinstein rules that the decision should be left to the patient, or the patient's family in the case of a child.[92]

B. Terminal Illness – *goses*

It is important to distinguish *chayei sha'a* from the situation of a *goses*: a *goses* is agonal, that is, in the throes of death.[93] Understanding the distinction is vital because the halachos pertaining to a *goses* differ radically from those pertaining to a *chayei sha'a* who is not a *goses*.

A *goses* manifests certain signs, among them a characteristic gasping respiratory pattern or inability to clear respiratory secretions; the Talmud states that most *gosesim* do not survive for 72 hours (although this is not part of the definition of *goses*; a small majority do survive longer than this).[94]

A patient may become a *goses* in the final stages of disease, or due to injury.[95] At least one authority holds that brain stem death represents a possible *goses* status.[96]

---

[92] Igr. Moshe Ch.M. 2:74.

[93] Shabbat 151b; Shach Y.D. 339:5; Semachot 1:4; Rambam H. Avel 4:5.

[94] R. M. Feinstein suggests that although it is claimed that expertise in diagnosing the state of *gesisa* is rare nowadays, doctors can become familiar with the signs characterising this condition by observing patients *in extremis* in the clinical setting (in R. M. Hershler, Halacha and Medicine Vol. 4, p. 106).

[95] It is clear that R. M. Feinstein (Ch. M. 2:73; also in R. M. Hershler, Halacha and Medicine Vol. 4) regards an individual in the throes of death due to injury as a *goses* – Rabbi Feinstein is discussing the case of Rabbi Chanina ben Tradyon who was being burned to death.

[96] R. S Z Auerbach; see brain stem death pp. 135-138.

A *goses* may not be moved. The reason for this is that the *goses'* hold on life is so tenuous that any movement may snuff it out – a *goses* is likened to a candle flame at its last ebb; the slightest movement may extinguish it, and to do that would constitute taking life.[97]

Whether injecting fluids or drugs intravenously (into an existing intravenous line – that is, without moving the patient) is considered "movement" that is forbidden for fear of extinguishing life is debatable. There are authorities who hold that it is;[98] such injections should therefore be limited to fluids and drugs that are already being continuously infused, or material injected in an attempt to cure.

Although one may do nothing to shorten the life of a goses directly, one may remove an external impediment to the dying process[99] in order to avoid unduly prolonging the last moments of separation of body and soul.[100] If an external stimulus is responsible for maintaining the flickering *gesisa* status (such as a repeated loud noise that stimulates the patient to continue gasping respiration when respiration would otherwise cease), one may remove that stimulus (in this case, stop the noise).

Similarly, medical modalities that merely prolong the state of *gesisa* may be withheld – for example where repeated bolus doses of pressors are being infused to maintain blood pressure in an inevitably terminal *goses* situation these need not be continued indefinitely.[101]

A *goses* is considered alive in all respects. If there is a chance that treatment may reverse the *gesisa* situation and bring about recovery it

---

[97] Avel Rab.; Semach. 1:4; Shabb. 151b; Rambam H. Avel 4:5.

[98] R. S Z Auerbach was of the opinion that intravenous injection may in fact cause a more significant perturbation than external movement and is therefore more dangerous and hence certainly forbidden (Nishm. Avraham Vol. II ch. 32).

[99] Sefer Chasidim 723; Rema in Sh. Aruch Y.D. 339:1 and also in Darchei Moshe on Tur Y.D. 339:1. From these sources it is clear that only an extrinsic impediment to the dying process may be removed; no action may be done to the *goses* himself, not even mere movement, that may extinguish life. The distinction is this: one may not actively shorten life – that is homicide and utterly forbidden (regardless of the state of health of the victim); however, where a stimulus entirely external to the *goses* is preventing death, thus prolonging his suffering (see next note), one may stop it.

[100] This is understood to be a spiritually painful state (Igr. Moshe Ch. M. 2:74).

[101] See Nish. Avraham, Vol. II, p. 327, in the name of R. S Z Auerbach.

must be given. Where there is a chance of curing a *goses* but only at the risk of precipitating death, the halacha is no different than for any *chayei sha'a* (as discussed above); the treatment may be given (for that purpose the *goses* may be moved – the risk of precipitating death is acceptable where there is a real chance of cure).[102]

A *goses* may be moved indirectly – that is the bed on which he lies may be moved carefully for an essential need, for example to save another endangered patient.[103] Routine observations such as temperature and blood pressure measurement should generally not be performed where they require directly moving the patient and will not alter what is being done for the patient.[104]

---

[102] Beit Meir Y.D. 339; see there for details. See also Tzitz Eliezer 17:10.

[103] See Nishm. Avraham Vol. II, p. 318-319 for details and related extensive discussion regarding *goses*.

[104] See exceptions in Nishm. Avraham Vol. II, pp. 318-319.

Clinical Cases – Dangerous and Terminal Illness

Clinical Case 6: Withdrawing / Withholding Therapy

A man with an implanted defibrillator has widely metastatic cancer. The device is designed to defibrillate only: it is not functioning continually as a pacemaker. He requests that the defibrillator be inactivated – due to his terminal situation, in the event of a lethal arrhythmia he does not want to be resuscitated by the device. Does his request accord with halacha?

Analysis:

This case was presented to Rabbi Eliashiv, who approached it as follows: if the patient had refused implantation of a defibrillator in a situation of terminal illness, that would be an acceptable decision. He is not required to undergo its implantation if he has only *chayei sha'a*, temporary life, but may choose passively to remain without such a device.

However, since the device is now in place, it would not be proper to remove or inactivate it. (Perhaps it should now be regarded as an integral "part" of the patient – it would certainly be forbidden to remove or inactivate a native part of the body that is needed to avert lethal incidents, even if such lethal incidents were not inevitable.)

If, however, the patient is distressed by the presence of the active device to the point that his distress raises the concern of a real threat to his health, it would be permitted to inactivate it, but only if reasonable alternatives exist such as the availability of usual resuscitative measures. (For circumstances in which it would be permitted to withhold resuscitation altogether, see Resuscitation, page 143.) The reason for this is that one is not obliged to provide the highest level of care where an alternative lower level meets *rigorous standards of adequacy* (this is not in conflict with the halachic requirement that only the best physician available should treat; that standard too allows for the provision of treatment by those not at the highest level of qualification provided that the treating physician is *fully competent* and *adequately qualified*). [105]

Here, although inactivating the device and depending on less reliable interventions exposes the patient to a higher risk, this is acceptable since the patient is at risk of a real deterioration in his health due to his extreme distress, and those less effective means meet acceptable standards of care.

---

[105] See above, page 27 and note 12 there. For other circumstances in which the best level of care is not absolutely mandatory, see page 178 and note 17 there.

Clinical Case 7: Dangerous (but not Certainly Terminal) Illness

A 65 year old woman underwent excision of a left atrial mass, thought to be a myxoma, together with the mitral valve which was replaced with a prosthetic valve. The mass proved to be a pleomorphic sarcoma (a malignant condition which carries a risk of recurrence). Now, six weeks after surgery, the patient has developed heart failure; on ultrasound scanning a mass is seen just above the prosthetic valve. The differential diagnosis includes a vegetation due to infective endocarditis, thrombus, or recurrence of tumor. The patient is receiving appropriate medical treatment; her surgeons do not want to re-operate. The question of a biopsy arises; the risk of death or major complication due to the biopsy is estimated to be 20%. The chance of tumor recurrence at this stage is thought to be 3%. Should the biopsy be done?

Analysis:[106]

The biopsy should be avoided. The chance of recurrent tumor is relatively small (3%); the chance of a complication of biopsy is much larger (20%); therefore it is probably better to manage the patient without a biopsy if possible. (If the risk of recurrence were 20%, the biopsy should probably be done; at a risk of 10%, the proper course of action would be debatable.)

Clinical Case 8: Risky Procedure in *chayei sha'a*

A 50 year old man has hepatitis-C related chronic cirrhosis. He has declining liver function and is not expected to survive one year without liver transplantion. A live donor transplant is recommended; his chances of surviving the transplantation surgery are presently excellent but will decline significantly if it is delayed. The overall five-year survival rate for liver transplantation is currently over 75%; this particular patient's probability of five-year survival is thought to be closer to 85%. Should transplantation be performed, and if so, when?

Analysis

This patient's options are death within a year or transplantation. The procedure carries a risk of death or serious complication that is presently well under 50%; if surgery is delayed this figure will rise due to his progressive liver disease. A transplant is appropriate and permissible in

---

[106] R.Y. Zilberstein.

this situation (but the patient may not be coerced to undergo it). The optimal timing of the procedure would be to delay it for as long as possible without significantly compromising the chances of its success; when that point is reached it should not be delayed further. If expert surgical opinion is that the patient is fit for surgery but will soon lose that status, the procedure is indicated now.

It should be noted that many authorities mention *complete* cure when allowing risky therapy in *chayei sha'a* situations; a high risk of immediate death is not acceptable when the *chayei olam* that may be gained will be subject to constant threat by incompletely treated disease (see note 69 above). Now organ transplantation is not a complete cure; patients survive with some degree of permanent ongoing risk. Does this mean that it should not be allowed?

That is not the case. Although there may be ongoing risk, the primary pathology has been eliminated and survival for many years can be expected. The patient is no longer under constant threat from the original disease and although ongoing therapy may affect strength and general quality of life, that is not a reason to forbid the procedure. Therefore such procedures are not forbidden in *chayei sha'a* situations, particularly where the immediate risk of the procedure is well under 50%.

(This analysis relates only to issues concerning the organ recipient; for the permissibility of live organ donation, see page 81.)

Clinical Case 9: Risky Procedure in *chayei olam*

Two brothers aged 12 and 17 have chronic granulomatous disease (CGD). Survival in CGD is currently between 20 and 30 years (with wide variability). Hematopoietic stem cell transplantation (HSCT) is proposed; if successful it will be curative. The procedure has a 75% success rate and a 25% mortality. The boys and their parents do not want the procedure. Does halacha accord with their choice?

Analysis:[107]

Although the proposed HSCT has a greater than even chance of success, it is dangerous (25% mortality). This level of danger would be acceptable (and even obligatory, subject to the patient's consent) in *chayei sha'a* situations; however this is not a *chayei sha'a* situation – the boys are

---

[107] R Y. Zilberstein.

expected to live into their twenties and perhaps longer. In view of the patients' and their parents' unwillingness to undergo the therapy, it should be avoided for the present.

Rabbi Eliashiv was asked whether the procedure should be performed if the family wished to undergo it; his opinion was that even in that case it would be inappropriate, particularly in view of ongoing research that may provide safer options over the next few years.

Clinical Case 10: Serious Disease, Risky Procedure

A 30 year old mother of two children has CML (chronic myelogenous leukemia). There is a risk of transformation to AML (acute myelogenous leukemia) of approximately 25% per year; she is unlikely to survive more than a few months after AML develops. She is offered marrow ablation and rescue transplantation, a procedure with a mortality of 60 - 70%. Should she choose the 30 - 40% chance of cure and accept the high risk of the procedure?

Analysis:

Rabbi Zilberstein is of the opinion that one should not undergo a procedure with a 60% - 70% mortality despite the fact that an illness is present that is likely to threaten life over the next few years. If her life were in immediate danger (*chayei sha'a*) she would be free to choose such a desperate measure; and conversely, in her present situation, if the success rate of the marrow transplant were 60% - 70%, that would constitute an acceptable risk. Where a treatment has a greater than 50% chance of success it may be used in the attempt to prolong *chayei olam,* but where the risk of treatment is greater than 50% it is not appropriate.

Clinical Case 11: A Newborn with Multiple Abnormalities and a Poor Prognosis

A newborn suffers from a degenerative neurological disease; the child is blind and has multiple abnormalities including exomphalos. Around 95% of children with this syndrome do not survive for 18 months; death is usually due to failure of muscle function including swallowing and respiratory muscles. Should this newborn be treated? If the child encounters respiratory difficulties, is ventilation required?

Analysis:[108]

The child must be treated. A poor prognosis does not mean that a patient can be abandoned; the child requires surgical correction of treatable abnormalities and any other necessary therapy. Acute respiratory problems must be actively treated, including ventilation if necessary. Halachically, even short-term life must be prolonged where possible and this case should be no exception. However, if treatment will add or prolong unbearable suffering, such treatment should be withheld; multiple painful surgical interventions are not indicated if they will not be curative. If the child enters terminal respiratory failure, ventilation should be withheld if the child can be made comfortable without it.

Clinical Case 12: Futile and non-Futile Treatment

A 61 year old woman is admitted in acute-on-chronic renal failure. She had a primary breast carcinoma resected eight years previously; she now has secondaries in her spine which appear to be slowly progressive but no other evident spread of disease. She is independent and enjoys a relatively good quality of life; her bone pain is controlled on multiple analgesics (which may be related to her renal disease). She has recently refused chemotherapy after multiple cycles because her disease is no longer responding; she has not refused any other form of treatment, and she has not signed a DNR order. The hospital staff tell her family that treatment is futile and recommend palliative care only. How should she be treated?

Analysis:

This patient needs full and aggressive treatment of her renal failure, including dialysis if necessary. This is not at all a situation of futile treatment: any reversible element of her renal disease requires treatment; if treatment is successful she can be expected to return to her previous reasonable quality of life. Her prognosis is unclear but even without chemotherapy she may be expected to survive for months and quite possibly for more than a year; there is therefore no reason to withhold therapy for her acute problem, and indeed there is a full obligation to treat. In order to withhold therapy it would be necessary to demonstrate that her disease has become terminal and irreversible and that ongoing therapy would only cause or prolong unbearable suffering; in that situation she would be free to opt for no definitive treatment.

---

[108] R. Y. Zilberstein.

Definition and Timing of Death

Defining the moment of death is important for many reasons. Apart from perhaps the most obvious question of knowing when it is permissible to desist from therapy, a number of other consequences depend on it including medical, civil, criminal and religious questions.

A partial list of issues with major halachic and legal consequences that depend on accurate timing of death would include:

1. Stopping life-support: it is important to know when one may stop ventilation and other treatment for a number of reasons.

   (i) In a non-Jewish medical system that may require the cessation of ventilation or the vacating of an ICU place sooner than halacha would allow (for example, due to a definition of death that is not halachically valid) it is important to know the point beyond which one need not come into conflict with that system.

   (ii) Treatment can be expensive and resource-intensive: even brief unnecessary continuation of treatment can significantly deplete payer's resources.

   (iii) Triage: the ventilator, ICU place or other treatment modalities may be needed for others; this can be a matter of life and death.

2. Harvesting of organs for transplantation: where transplantation is halachically allowed and organs must be harvested as soon after death as possible, determining the time of the donor's death is critical.[1]

3. Laws of mourning.

4. Laws of inheritance.

---

[1] But see The "Circulatory Death" Debate, page 139, concerning problems of organ donation after circulatory death.

5. Marital status of a spouse.

6. Legal status of contracts, documents and legal instruments that are time or date sensitive and that hinge on the status of a principal.

7. Criminal matters such as murder and homicide: bringing about the death of a patient obviously requires that the patient be alive at the time of commission of that crime; knowing the moment of death in this setting can be a matter of life and death for both victim and perpetrator.

Although "brain stem death" has become accepted in many jurisdictions, it is not the correct standard according to a majority of senior halachic authorities; the halachic standard is complete and irreversible cardio-respiratory cessation. Although this issue has generated debate over the past few decades, most leading halachic authorities hold that a patient in irreversible coma who fulfils the secular criteria for "brain stem death" is fully alive. Rabbi S Z Auerbach held that such a patient is either a *goses* or dead (and therefore following his opinion it may be appropriate to detach the ventilator in some circumstances as this would amount to no more than "removing the impediment" to death discussed above (page 128). This subject has been thoroughly examined elsewhere.[2]

In the secular world, despite the widely accepted legal definition of death that relies on brain stem function, the matter is not settled beyond the narrow confines of the law.[3] In the medical ethical literature and in the popular mind it is far from clear that brain stem death represents a meaningful standard. Many ethicists have pointed out that the brain stem criterion was chosen to facilitate transplantation surgery (particularly heart transplantation), not because it is natural or appears intrinsically correct.[4] Many remain uncomfortable with it for this reason, and because

---

[2] Details of the debate on this issue and relevant rulings can be found in Nishm. Avraham; Steinberg A, Encyclopedia of Jewish Medical Ethics and the references given in those works, and in Bleich R. JD, Time of Death in Jewish Law (Z. Berman, 1991) and Bleich R. JD, Contemporary Halachic Problems Vol. I ch. XVI; Vol. III ch. XIII.

[3] See: Brain Death – Well Settled Yet Still Unresolved, New Engl J Med Editorial, 2001; 344:1246.

[4] This origin of the brain stem definition of death has led to accusations of the medical profession's "gerrymandering the definition of death" – see note 10 below.

"brain dead" patients manifest so many signs of life[5] – apart from ongoing heartbeat and perfusion, there is also brain activity, such as appropriate hypothalamic and posterior pituitary function.

It seems that even those who have no trouble accepting the legal definition do not regard it as "real" – a Pennsylvania judge writes that "[W]hen the life-supporting measures were suspended, death ensued [although the person] was legally dead even before heroic life support procedures were discontinued."[6] Here a judge, of all people one who surely understands exactly what the law means, distinguishes between legal death and "real" death.

Among doctors too, the legal definition of death may be accepted, but it is questionable how real that definition seems from the perspective of clinical appearances. Doctors may have accepted the legal definition, but their medical intuition is often at variance with it – a case report in a leading medical journal included this passage describing the final sequence of events in the case of a woman declared dead while on life-support: "The patient was declared brain-dead." And then, subsequently: "She died after life-support measures were terminated."[7]

For these reasons, some leading ethicists have responded by urging a rethinking of the issue. Among these, there are two approaches: some feel that since brain stem death is neither an accurate nor an honest[8] definition of death, using it to harvest organs contravenes the "dead donor rule," the

---

[5] A New England Journal of Medicine editorial (see note 3 above) recommends that "Doctors should avoid terms such as "brain death" and allow families time to understand the basis of a diagnosis of death that is not self-evident when the respirator-supported body of their loved one manifests many outward signs of life."

[6] In Commonwealth vs Kostra, 502 A.2d 1287,1291 (Pa. Super Ct 1985).

[7] Case Records of the Massachusetts General Hospital (Case 32-1997). N Engl J Med 1997;337:1149-1156. This revealing description was criticised in correspondence: "We were surprised by the description of a patient's demise at the end of the presentation of Case 32-1997... which concluded: 'The patient was declared brain-dead. She died after life-support measures were terminated.'... If the patient was truly declared brain-dead, then death was determined at the time of that declaration, not when life-support measures were later terminated." (Letters to the Editor, April 30, 1998; followed by an apology).

[8] See Moral Debate and Semantic Sleight of Hand in R. JD Bleich, Bioethical Dilemmas Vol. II.

widely agreed basic rule that prohibits removing organs from a still-living donor. Doing so kills the patient, and that is unacceptable. In the opinion of these thinkers, death must be defined in terms of more traditional criteria such as irreversible cessation of cardiorespiratory function, and organs must not be removed until those criteria obtain.[9]

There has also been a diametrically opposite response: some ethicists urge revising the law to acknowledge openly that brain death is not death, but to allow the removal of organs anyway.[10] They advocate going back to the conclusion of the original Harvard committee that investigated brain stem death criteria in search of a new definition of death: that brain stem death represents a state of "irreversible coma," not death; but they argue that this should be adequate to allow cessation of life support and removal of organs under certain conditions. For these ethicists the relevant issue is not death at all but donor consent or societal consent – if society finds it acceptable to allow termination of life where there is no hope of recovery for the purpose of transplantation that should be in order.

This latter approach, of course, would abandon the "dead donor rule" altogether.[11] Needless to say, this is anathema in Jewish thinking. If the patient is still alive it is no less than fully culpable homicide to terminate that life in the process of removing organs.

---

[9] See below, The "Circulatory Death" Debate, p.139.

[10] "[I]t appears that reliance on the dead donor rule has greater potential to undermine trust in the transplantation enterprise than to preserve it. At worst, this ongoing reliance suggests that the medical profession has been gerrymandering the definition of death to carefully conform with conditions that are most favorable for transplantation. At best, the rule has provided misleading ethical cover that cannot withstand careful scrutiny. A better approach... would be to emphasize the importance of obtaining... consent for organ donation... before the withdrawal of life-sustaining treatment in situations of devastating and irreversible neurologic injury." (Truog, RD; Miller FG. New Engl J Med 2008; 359:674-675).

These authors state explicitly: "[W]e argue that it is time both to face honestly the fact that our current practices of vital organ donation violate the dead donor rule, and to provide a coherent alternative ethical account of these practices that does not depend on this norm." (Hastings Center Report 12/02/2008).

[11] On this debate, see Arnold RM, Younger SJ. The dead donor rule: should we stretch it, bend it, or abandon it? Kennedy Inst Ethics J 1993;3:263-78.

The "Circulatory Death" Debate

A separate debate has arisen concerning harvesting organs after cardiorespiratory death ("circulatory death," previously referred to as "non-heart-beating donation"). The idea here is to use circulatory death criteria for organ donation to avoid the more controversial brain death standard.

Using this protocol,[12] a donor, typically a patient with major neurological damage (but who does not fulfil criteria for "brain death") on life support is prepared for donation while alive. This may involve insertion of lines for vascular access and administration of heparin and other drugs to ensure that donor organs will remain viable after removal. Life support is withdrawn. Death is then awaited; cessation of heartbeat usually ensues within minutes.[13] A short period is then allowed to elapse before harvesting of organs begins.

This short waiting period is critical: it must be long enough to ensure that the heart will not spontaneously re-start ("auto-resuscitation") but short enough to ensure minimum ischemic damage to donor organs. Early protocols used a two minute waiting period; this has now been reduced to 75 seconds. The logic for this period is that spontaneous recovery of heartbeat is thought not to occur after 60 seconds;[14] therefore waiting any longer is unnecessary and will only harm the quality of harvested organs.

Many objections have been raised against this solution to the problem of avoiding harvesting organs from donors who are not yet dead. Firstly, if the donor heart begins beating in the recipient, it must be viable – this suggests that it would have begun beating in the donor too had external

---

[12] For details of the process and the attendant debate, see the report of heart transplantation after declaration of cardiocirculatory death, the Editorial and three Perspective articles in the New England Journal of Medicine, August 14, 2008. In this series, newborns with severe neurological damage were used as donors. (N Engl J Med 2008;359.)

[13] Less than 30 minutes is considered suitable for purposes of donation; in this series the period ranged from 11.5 to 27.5 seconds.

[14] The US Institute of Medicine recommends a waiting period of 5 minutes after asystole in cases of withdrawal of life support to ensure that a heart rhythm sufficient to generate a pulse does not resume; but because that period is too long to render organs viable for transplantation and because it is thought that a shorter period is probably enough to ensure that a rhythm will not spontaneously begin, it was decided to shorten the waiting period to 75 seconds in these donors.

resuscitative measures been instituted. But that would defeat the validity of this definition of death: death must be defined as an *irreversible* cessation of circulation; this heart had clearly not irreversibly stopped. (And if a longer period is allowed to elapse after cessation of heartbeat, say, five minutes, to ensure real irreversibility, the heart will be useless – it will certainly not start in the recipient.)

So the point of this exercise, namely to use a clear and universally acceptable definition of death, has not been achieved. On the contrary, objectors point out that if donor circulation has not irreversibly ceased when surgical harvesting of organs begins, those organs are being harvested from a living donor and that surgery is the cause of death of the donor.

Secondly, serious objections have been raised against the practice of invasive manipulations of the donor's body before death for the sake of the recipient. Many have pointed out that it is not ethical to administer drugs and otherwise interfere with the donor in preparation for organ harvesting when that interference is not for the benefit of the one on whom it is being done.

These objections have stimulated a number of responses. Two recent ones are:

1. Since it is immoral to take organs from a living donor, change the definition of death: define death as the cessation of higher brain functions instead of the cessation of brain stem function. This so-called higher-brain definition would require loss of the brain functions that are responsible for consciousness but no more than that. This solution would respect the "dead donor rule" by simply redefining death.[15][16]

2. Change the law to allow removal of organs from donors while they are still alive. This solution proposes doing away with the "dead donor rule" altogether.[17]

---

[15] It has been pointed out that this definition would mean that permanently unconscious patients would also be "dead."

[16] Veatch, RM, in N Engl J Med 2008;359:672.

[17] Truog RD and Miller FG, in N Engl J Med 2008;359:674. See above, page 138 and note 10 there.

Halachic objections

These proposals would be halachically unacceptable for many reasons, and in fact use of "circulatory death" as presently understood and practised would transgress more severe halachic prohibitions than the use of brain stem death criteria.

Firstly, removal of life support that leads directly to death is considered homicidal in halacha (and certainly according to all opinions when the patient does not meet even brain death criteria).

Secondly, after spontaneous circulatory cessation, the halacha requires a waiting period before the body is moved; this period is typically 20 to 30 minutes or more (depending on the local custom of various Jewish communities). No halachic authority would allow interference in less than five minutes.[18]

Thirdly, where the potential donor is a *goses*,[19] he may not be moved for fear of extinguishing life; it is certainly forbidden to perform invasive procedures and intravenous manipulations, and all the more when those procedures are not for his benefit.

Both of the above proposed responses are invalid halachically: changing the definition of death to "higher-brain death" would be far worse than using the present brain stem death standard (in addition, from a general ethical point of view there is something clearly odious in changing a definition to suit a need, and nowhere more than in the case of a change to a definition that affects life and death and proposes nothing less than simply exonerating homicide by semantic device).

The second suggestion, that of changing the law to allow removal of organs from living donors thereby bringing about their deaths is obviously no halachic solution. In halacha, handling life and death questions requires more than a change of laws or definitions.[20]

---

[18] R. M. Sternbuch.

[19] See definition and laws pertaining to a *goses*, p. 127.

[20] Examining outcomes in isolation may also be halachically inadequate. Commenting on this series of transplants, the journal editorial referred to above (note 12) ends with this: "[O]ne conclusion is clear. As a result of their investigational protocol, three babies are now alive; had the procedures not been performed, it is virtually certain that all six babies would be dead." That is undisputed; the point at issue however, is whether three babies were killed in the process.

Time of Death

Quite apart from the issue of brain stem death, a number of situations raise the question of how to determine the moment of death. These include:

1. Operations that rely on cardiopulmonary bypass in those instances where the procedure ends with failure to re-establish a natural heartbeat and circulation and the patient must be declared dead. A similar problem arises when a heart transplant recipient dies during the transplant procedure. In these situations, which is the moment of death – is it when the heart was initially stopped and bypass began, or is it when bypass and attempts to re-start the heart are finally abandoned? In a failed transplant, is the moment of death when the native heart is removed, or is it when the implanted donor heart fails to re-start and the procedure is abandoned?[21]

2. When a cardiopulmonary resuscitation (CPR) attempt fails, is death deemed to occur at the moment of initial pulseless collapse or at the moment when the resuscitation attempt is abandoned and all externally generated circulation ceases?

In the cases of bypass and transplantation, there is debate (generated by both technical and halachic considerations) about fixing the moment of death.[22] In the case of CPR, the consensus is that death occurs when the situation of cardiopulmonary arrest becomes irreversible; if there is no response during the resuscitation attempt the moment of collapse is deemed the moment of death.[23]

---

[21] See above, Resuscitation, p. 143 and note 1 there.

[22] See Nishm. Avraham Vol. II, pp. 58-59 for discussion.

[23] See Resuscitation, p. 143 for a more detailed discussion.

Resuscitation

Before considering the practical halacha regarding resuscitation, a theoretical point must be clarified: is resuscitation to be regarded as an act of *pikuach nefesh* (lifesaving) or an act of resurrection of the dead? On the one hand, if all the signs of cardiorespiratory collapse that are necessary for a definition of death are present and life is therefore to be regarded as ended, a successful resuscitation attempt must be seen as resurrection. But on the other hand, perhaps a successful resuscitation should be regarded as a demonstration that death had not in fact occurred, despite the absence of circulation and respiration.[1]

The consequences of this distinction are far reaching. If resuscitation is in fact a lifesaving act, it would be obligatory, and even against the patient's wishes.[2] Sabbath laws would be set aside for an attempt to resuscitate, as would the laws of priestly sanctity. The attempt would be mandatory even where the chances of success are slight, and all the stringencies of *pikuach nefesh* would apply.

---

[1] A similar question arises in situations of controlled cardiac arrest during heart surgery, and even more sharply during transplant surgery when the recipient's heart is removed but has not yet been replaced by the donor organ. For wider discussion of this and related issues see R. JD Bleich, Contemporary Halachic Problems Vol. III, Artificial Heart Implantation. See also above, Time of Death, p. 135.

[2] See below for limits to this obligation.

If however resuscitation is to be regarded as an act of resurrection, the obligation is much less clear (there may in fact be no halachic obligation to resurrect the dead at all). In addition, if the patient is to be regarded as dead in the moments between collapse and successful resuscitation, all the halachic consequences of death must be assumed to have occurred: his wife is a widow, the laws of levirate marriage are effected, his children have inherited his estate, and indeed his very status as a living individual after resuscitation will need to be clarified, as well as other seemingly bizarre consequences.[3]

In addition, this distinction may be relevant to such issues as accurately determining the time of death (a consideration of potentially major halachic and legal import) in the event of an unsuccessful resuscitation attempt.[4]

In fact, this matter is the subject of halachic discussion. According to the Chida in Birchei Yosef,[5] in cases of apparent death and subsequent re-animation the patient has not died despite temporarily manifesting the definitive criteria of total cardiorespiratory collapse. Put differently, *reversible* cardiorespiratory cessation is not definitive of death; death can be said to occur only when its usual defining features become irreversible.[6] The consequences of this approach are clear – the patient is to be regarded as alive until it becomes unequivocal that his inanimate state is irreversible: all efforts must be made to revive him, the Sabbath must be set aside in the attempt, and none of the consequences of death are applicable in the interim. Although others disagree, it seems clear that the stringent view should be accepted, certainly with regard to the full obligation to resuscitate. (Even according to the dissenting view, namely that resuscitation represents a revival from a state of death, it is doubtful that the legal sequelae of death, such as change of marital status and inheritance, are to be applied.)[7]

---

[3] See R. JD Bleich (note 1 above), esp. pages 165-170.

[4] See above, Definition and Timing of Death, p. 135.

[5] Birchei Yosef, Even HaEzer 17:1.

[6] This is the opinion of R. SZ Auerbach cited in HaMa'ayan, Tishrei 5729, p. 20, and R. M. Sternbuch, *Kuntres ba'ayot ha'zman b'hashkafat ha'Torah,* 1; p. 9.

[7] Cf. R. Elchanan Wasserman, Kovetz Shiurim II:29; R. Chaim Kanievsky, Siach haSadeh, Kuntres haLikkutim 4. See R. JD Bleich (note 1 above) for a discussion of this point.

Time of Death in Failed Resuscitation Attempt

With regard to fixing the time of death, it would follow that the time of death will be the moment that the patient's status becomes irreversible. In practice this will be measured as the moment that all signs of life or response cease before or during the resuscitation attempt – if the resuscitation succeeds, the patient was always alive; if a full and adequate resuscitation attempt fails, the patient's lifeless status is thereby demonstrated to have been irreversible.

When is Resuscitation Obligatory?

In practice, resuscitation is obligatory no less than any other lifesaving medical intervention. When is the attempt to resuscitate contraindicated? The general principle to be applied is that where there is an obligation to treat, there is an obligation to resuscitate. Conversely, where there is an obligation to desist from treatment (as outlined in the discussion on withholding therapy),[8] there is no obligation to resuscitate and such action would in fact be forbidden. When a terminally ill patient who is suffering severely has chosen to forego therapy that may prolong life only at the cost of prolonging that state of suffering (as permitted in halacha), just as it would be forbidden to force such therapy on the patient it is forbidden to perform resuscitation against the patient's will.[9] Put simply: where there is an obligation to save life prior to collapse, there is an obligation to resuscitate; where there is no such obligation to save life, there is no obligation to resuscitate.

Adequate Duration of Resuscitation Attempt

A resuscitation attempt must continue until it becomes futile; that is, until the chance of success is vanishingly small. How long is that? This is essentially a technical question, and the halacha will follow the medical answer to that question.[10] Since the issue here is lifesaving, the decision

---

[8] Above, page 103.

[9] This follows from R. M. Feinstein's opinion regarding withholding therapy.

[10] It is generally accepted that resuscitation attempts are unlikely to be successful after 30 minutes of full resuscitation including defibrillation with no response. This excludes situations such as cold water immersion or other forms of hypothermia in which patients have been successfully resuscitated after much longer periods. Similarly, this period is irrelevant where the patient may have

must not be based on majorities – the attempt must continue until there is no real minority that would survive[11] (the general halachic principle of majorities is not applicable in lifesaving).[12] The fear of salvaging a patient with a "low quality of life" due to a prolonged or inadequate resuscitation attempt, while a real concern, is not a reason to stop the attempt prematurely (since quality of life is not an overriding criterion in lifesaving in halacha). [13]

Advance Directives and "Do Not Resuscitate" (DNR) Orders

A DNR order is valid only where the halacha regards resuscitation as genuinely discretionary, as outlined above. Only in such cases is the patient free to forego resuscitation; in other situations it is mandatory. An inevitably terminal patient should not be resuscitated only to experience ongoing intractable pain where the patient has clearly and freely made that choice. A clear indication that expresses that choice prospectively would be valid in halacha provided there is no reason to assume that the patient may have come to desire a different option in the interim. However, the common modern application of a DNR order in which a patient prospectively refuses resuscitation as an expression of the principle of autonomy has no place in halacha; one may not forego a

---

circulating drugs or toxins that preclude successful resuscitation. In such situations it is imperative that resuscitation continue until all possible reversible factors have been excluded or corrected.

In general, any limit that is chosen will be adequate only if it can be shown that not even a small minority survive when resuscitation continues beyond that limit.

[11] A British study of in-hospital resuscitation identified variables affecting probability of success (apart from time elapsed to start of resuscitation): age, precipitating event (whether cardiac or respiratory), type of cardiac arrhythmia present, and whether there was any return of spontaneous circulation within 15 minutes of resuscitation effort. Of the survivors, 62% were resuscitated in less than 14 minutes with 20% surviving if the resuscitation lasted more than 15 minutes. For example, for an 80 year old patient with no return of spontaneous circulation after 15 minutes of resuscitation effort, the chance of success with continued resuscitation was 5%. This is certainly not negligible. (Cooper S, Evans C. Emerg Med J 2003;20:6-9).

[12] See above, Principles, pp. 34-35.

[13] See above, Principles, p. 24.

lifesaving intervention except in the specific circumstances outlined above.[14]

Even where a DNR order would have halachic validity, there is a secondary concern of major importance. It is common experience in clinical practice that a "Do Not Resuscitate" order is often perceived as a tacit "Do Not Treat" order. Although these two are quite clearly distinct in meaning, in effect the patient who refuses resuscitation may be perceived as not wanting to live. In fact a patient who does not want to be resuscitated when the time comes may very much want to be treated actively until such time; but the subliminal message that is projected by a large and clear "DNR" on the chart seems almost unavoidably to suggest a desire for life to end sooner rather than later. The deeply worrying concern is that such a patient may receive less aggressive treatment than would otherwise have been the case. Senior physicians testify that despite repeated instructions not to treat patients who have signed DNR orders any less conscientiously or aggressively, such patients are less likely to be admitted to an ICU or investigated and treated as thoroughly (say, for intercurrent infections) as those who have no such order.[15] Inevitably, since DNR says "I do not want to live" in at least one set of circumstances, it is difficult not to perceive that as "I do not want to live" more generally.[16] This concern is good reason to discourage DNR orders in general.

---

[14] See also p. 103.

[15] This is a registered problem. The Presidential Commission on Deciding to Forego Life-Sustaining Treatment (1983) found it necessary to emphasize that DNR does not mean "do not treat."

See Beach MC et al: The effect of do-not-resuscitate orders on physician decision-making. J Am Geriatr Soc 50:2057, 2002. This study found that physicians are less likely to transfuse, transfer to ICU, order diagnostic studies, utilize critical care monitoring and procedures, and perform intubation on DNR patients.

See Keenan CH et al: The influence of do-not-resuscitate orders on care provided for patients in the surgical intensive care unit of a cancer center. Crit Care Nurs Clin North Am 12:385, 2000. This study found that a DNR order resulted in fewer medical interventions and chart documentation in a surgical ICU.

[16] For example: In his book about the Katrina Hurricane ("Code Blue: a Katrina physician's memoir." Deichmann RE. Bloomington, Rooftop Publishing, 2007) when describing the predicament of hospitalized patients trapped by the flood,

This problem goes further. Apart from unwarranted assumptions that DNR orders may evoke, the term "DNR" itself is variably defined in various contexts – although its narrow and specific meaning refers to resuscitation in the situation of cardiovascular collapse, it is often taken to refer to treatment in general in desperate or terminal situations.[17] This dangerous ambiguity invites confusion at best, and lethal mismanagement at worst.

The ambiguity in "DNR" may stem at least in part from the fact that the term "resuscitation" itself has variable meanings in medicine. Although it specifically denotes the attempt to reverse acute and total cardiovascular collapse by CPR (cardio-pulmonary resuscitation involving external cardiac massage and ventilation), it can also mean the treatment of life-threatening hypovolemic shock, for example, a process totally distinct from CPR.[18]

With regard to resuscitation in the case of comatose patients, see above, page 108 and note 20 there.

"Do Not Hospitalize" (DNH) and "Allow Natural Death" (AND) Orders

A number of directives and terminologies have recently come into use such as "Do Not Hospitalize" (DNH) orders in the case of frail and elderly nursing home residents, and Allow Natural Death (AND) orders

---

Dr Deichmann writes that the incident commander asked him whether euthanasia should be considered for some patients with DNR orders.

Now why should patients with DNR orders be considered for euthanasia? DNR does not mean "I want to die" (and it most certainly does not mean "Kill me"); it means "Do not resuscitate me in the event of cardiovascular collapse" and not more than that. Here it can clearly be seen that a DNR order is interpreted as a far broader message than the specific request not to be resuscitated in the event of terminal collapse.

[17] Beauchamp and Childress (p.123) state: "Hospital staffs, as well as patients or their families, are often unclear about what, if anything, DNR orders imply about other levels of care and other technologies. For example, some patients with DNR orders still receive chemotherapy, surgery, and admission to the intensive care unit, whereas others do not." There is clearly unacceptably broad latitude in the interpretation of "DNR."

[18] See Clinical Case 13, p. 150.

designed to facilitate withdrawal of therapy and avoid the starker language of "Do Not Resuscitate." It has been proposed that replacing the terminology of "Do Not Resuscitate" with "Allow Natural Death" will ease acceptance of these orders because some patients and families may perceive "Do Not Resuscitate" as overly harsh and negative whereas "Allow Natural Death" has a more beneficent tone. For the possible dangers of this trend, see Part II.

Clinical Cases

Clinical Case 13: "DNR" and "Do Not Treat" Confusion

The following case was reported in AHRQ WebM&M (an Agency for Healthcare Research and Quality online journal produced by an editorial team at the University of California, San Francisco):

The Wrongful Resuscitation

(AHRQ WebM&M. Joan M. Teno, MD, MS. April 2008.)

The Case:

An 80-year-old man with diabetes, peripheral vascular disease, bilateral below-the-knee amputations, and poor quality of life had previously been resuscitated from sudden death. After his recovery, he completed a DNR (do not resuscitate) form signifying his desire to avoid such treatment in the future.

The patient presented to the emergency department in extreme pain and was found to have a ruptured abdominal aortic aneurysm. Although his DNR form was with him, neither the emergency department staff nor the consulting surgeon looked at it. The patient was rushed to the operating room, where his aneurysm was repaired.

Postoperatively, an internist came upon the DNR form in the patient's chart and discussed resuscitation preferences with the patient and the family. The patient reconfirmed his desire to avoid resuscitation and heroic procedures, expressing anger that he had been taken to the operating room for the aneurysm repair. The family agreed with the patient's choice. The internist wrote a DNR order in the chart, but the surgeon... was furious, changing the code status back to "full code." Ultimately, the internist consulted with the hospital ethicist, who convinced the surgeon to honor the patient's and family's wishes. The DNR order was reinstated, and the patient later died of a cardiac arrest during the hospitalization.

[From] The Commentary:

[T]he actions of the surgeon in this case raise important concerns... A critically ill nursing home resident is transferred to the emergency department with severe abdominal pain and hypotension. In the midst of crisis, the physician did not realize that the patient was DNR and successfully resuscitated this elderly patient. This is an important error.

[S]hould that physician be sanctioned for making a decision that flagrantly ignored a patient's preference? I believe that such behavior should receive the same scrutiny as operating on the wrong side of the brain – each is a bodily assault that provides harmful care to which the patient did not consent. Such a case should be reported to the appropriate state authorities, and the resulting sanctions and corrective actions should ensure that informed preferences by future patients are honored.

Analysis:

This case report demonstrates a serious confusion: the surgeon in this case is being criticized for operating to repair the aneurysm – *"In the midst of crisis, the physician did not realize that the patient was DNR and successfully resuscitated this elderly patient."* But that was not a "resuscitation" in the sense usually meant in a DNR order – that was a lifesaving operation. DNR means do not apply CPR when the patient suffers sudden cardiorespiratory collapse; it does not mean "do not treat" when the patient is desperately ill. That would require a "do not treat me if my aneurysm bleeds" order, not a DNR. This represents a dangerous conflation of two usages of the word "resuscitation," namely, CPR-type resuscitation in cases of sudden collapse, and the resuscitation familiar to surgeons attempting to prepare hypovolemic patients for emergency surgery which consists of volume replacement and other appropriate measures, including surgery itself. These are entirely different exercises, yet in this case report it is confidently assumed that a DNR order intends not only avoidance of CPR in the event of terminal collapse, but also desisting from lifesaving surgery in the event of a treatable surgical emergency. This is a very serious confusion in a matter of life and death.

If the patient had *specified* in his DNR that his intention included the avoidance of surgery (in which case the order would more properly be a "Do Not Treat" order), there is room to debate whether such a DNR would be halachically valid – where the surgery is likely to add significant extra risk or severe and prolonged suffering to a terminal situation, the patient may indeed be free to refuse such therapy. But to extend "DNR" to "Do Not Treat" in the absence of such specification is unacceptable and criminally derelict in Jewish law.

It is true that the patient in this case is reported post-operatively as responding angrily at having been saved, indicating that he may well have intended to refuse treatment; but unless the original DNR had clearly documented such an intention, the surgeon acted entirely properly. (We are told about the original DNR only that after being previously *"resuscitated from sudden death"* the patient had signified *"his desire to avoid such treatment in the future."*) On the contrary, in Jewish law the surgeon would be deemed criminally negligent had he allowed his patient to bleed to death with no attempt to save him. Even the patient's present rejection of "heroic procedures" needs careful analysis: abdominal aortic aneurysm repair, despite its high mortality when performed in an emergency setting, is not necessarily to be construed as the kind of "heroic procedure" that the patient would reject – at least not without specification.

The discussant goes on to state: *"[S]uch behavior should receive the same scrutiny as operating on the wrong side of the brain – each is a bodily assault... Such a case should be reported to the appropriate state authorities..."* In this discussant's opinion it as actionably derelict to save life wrongly as to operate on the wrong side of the brain – mistakenly saving a patient's life is an "assault" to be deplored and punished in the same vein as the performing of a disastrously inappropriate operation. This is hardly the halachic position.

In summary, this report fails to distinguish between resuscitation in the sense of reviving a patient with acute cardiorespiratory collapse (referred to here as "sudden death") and the sense of operating on a desperately ill patient in the attempt to save life. It is possible that the failure to distinguish between these totally variant usages derives at root from the current focus on quality of life: if this "low-quality" life is not worth reviving, it is not worth prolonging, and therefore distinguishing between the various meanings of "resuscitation" in this setting becomes merely academic. This view is not valid in halacha.

Euthanasia, Suicide and Assisted Suicide

These subjects have been extensively treated elsewhere.[1] See Part II for aspects of the contrast between halacha and modern medical ethics and practice in this field.

Euthanasia

Active euthanasia is never allowed in halacha. The solution to the problem of unbearable suffering is to provide relief, not to kill the patient. If adequate relief can be obtained only at the cost of risk, such risk is acceptable.[2] Killing a person who is only moments away from inevitable death is murder in Jewish law; whether such a deed is actionable in a human court depends on the specific pathological status of the victim immediately prior to death, but in any event it is certainly murder.

A patient's request for euthanasia does not change this; Jewish law does not recognize a proprietary right to one's body or life.[3] The secular value of autonomy is not applicable here.[4]

---

[1] A. Steinberg, Encyclopedia of Jewish Medical Ethics Vol. III p. 1024; Nishm. Avraham Vol.II ch. 35; R. Bleich, Bioethical Dilemmas Vol. I, p. 113.

[2] See Analgesia in Dangerously or Terminally Ill Patients, p. 112.

[3] Radbaz on M. Torah Sanhedrin 18:6; Sh. Aruch HaRav Hilch. Nizkei HaGuf 4; Sefer Chasidim 723; Rivash 484; Chazon Ish, Nezikin 19:5; Igr. Moshe, 2:174.

See also R. SY Zevin, L'Ohr HaHalacha 2nd ed. (Tel Aviv, 5717) pp. 318-335 for an extended discussion of Antonio's contract with Shylock obliging him to pay a pound of flesh in the event of a loan default. This contract is null in Jewish law – just as Antonio cannot pledge assets that he does not own, he cannot create such a pledge on his body; he does not own it.

[4] See Autonomy, p. 219.

Refraining from painful lifesaving therapy or from therapy that will prolong great suffering in terminal illness may be appropriate under a specific set of conditions.[5] Where a patient is halachically advised to continue therapy in such circumstances but chooses not to, such a choice, although improper, is not considered suicide.[6]

An impediment to the dying process may be removed in the case of a moribund patient who fulfils certain specific criteria.[7]

Suicide and Assisted Suicide

Suicide is forbidden, it is forbidden to assist a suicide, and there is an obligation to prevent a suicide.[8] [9]

---

[5] See Withholding and Withdrawing Therapy, p. 103.

[6] R. Eliashiv; see above, p. 62, note 7. Refusing safe and painless lifesaving therapy where suffering is not a factor, however, is another matter. See R. Bleich, Bioethical Dilemmas Vol. I, note 12, pp. 98-100 for discussion on whether refusing such therapy is considered suicidal in halacha.

[7] See *Goses,* p. 127.

[8] See also Part II, p. 237.

[9] Concerning preventing suicide, see above, Lifesaving Interventions, p. 61 and note 65 there.

Coercion and Consent

There is an important distinction between treating without consent and treating against a patient's wishes. The former includes cases where consent is simply absent (where for example it cannot be obtained, such as in the case of unconscious or incompetent patients) but where there is no reason to assume that there would be any objection to treatment. Where halacha sanctions treatment in such cases it is not usually in conflict with secular ethical or legal norms. The logic and legal reasoning mandating treatment in such cases is presumed consent, sometimes expressed as the presumption that the patient will (or would) retroactively agree that what was done was correct (or more accurately, that what was done accords with what that patient would have chosen).

Treatment against a patient's wishes is another matter entirely. In the current ethos of Western medical ethics the default position is that such treatment is improper and may in fact invite legal action.[1] [2] In halacha however, there are certain circumstances where therapy can be administered even against a patient's wishes.[3]

---

[1] See Autonomy, p. 219.

[2] Current Israeli law permits a competent patient to be treated against his or her expressed will if the legally constituted hospital ethics committee is convinced that there is "reason to believe that after receiving the treatment, the patient will give… retroactive consent." (Patient's Rights Law, 1996:327).

[3] See Informed Consent in A. Steinberg, Encyclopedia of Jewish Medical Ethics, Vol. I, pp. 554-560 for references to coerced therapy in halacha.

Principles of Coercion and Consent in Halacha

The following categories indicate where consent is necessary and relevant (for therapy or diagnostic investigations):

1. Treatment obligatory

Where danger (to life or to a limb or organ) is clear and immediate,[4] and a particular therapy is clearly indicated, appropriate and safe, it should be administered. The patient's refusal here is inappropriate; consent is not required if it cannot be obtained and indeed one should administer therapy against the patient's will if necessary.[5]

In cases of danger to life, where the therapy is painful or mutilating (for example, a lifesaving amputation): if the threat to life is immediate, such therapy is obligatory.[6][7]

---

[4] The Chazon Ish Y.D. 208:7 writes that the laws of *pikuach nefesh* (dangers to life that allow and oblige extreme and otherwise forbidden responses) do not apply to dangers that lie in the distant future. To override Torah prohibitions (or a patient's wishes) a real and present danger is required. See Principles, p. 34.

[5] Tosefta, Shekalim 1:2, quoted by Rambam, states that a lifesaving amputation must be performed if necessary even if the patient must be constrained. Magen Avraham O.C. 328:6, quoting the Radbaz, similarly states that the amputation should be performed despite the patient's refusal, and that the Sabbath must be desecrated to save life even if the patient resists this. See Sh. Aruch Ch. M. 420:3; also M. Berurah 618:5; Maharam MiRotenberg 39. Mor u'Ktzia O. Ch. 328 states that one must do whatever is necessary to save life, based on the injunction of "Do not stand idly by your fellow's blood."

One of the elements that form the basis for this approach is the fact that in the Torah view one does not own one's body and life in the sense that they may be disposed of at will; rather, they are entrusted to the individual to care for and use appropriately for as long as that trusteeship is granted. See p. 153 and note 3 there.

[6] Igr. Moshe Ch. M. 2:74 states that the patient should be treated against his will in such a situation in order to save his life unless applying the necessary force is likely to cause serious harm (such as major psychiatric decompensation).

[7] To impose risky treatment, the danger indicating that treatment must be immediate, not a long-term danger where relevant parameters may change before the need for treatment becomes critical (R. Y. Zilberstein). See note 4 above.

In cases of serious illness without danger to life, where the treatment is safe and painless, one is obliged to attempt to convince the patient to accept treatment, but it may be administered despite refusal if necessary.[8]

Rabbi Moshe Feinstein[9] states that in general, where a patient's refusal (of treatment or investigations) is unreasonable – for example where the patient is concerned with the anticipated short-term discomfort of a treatment or procedure; and where all available medical opinion concurs that the procedure is necessary; and where every effort has been made to accommodate the patient's wishes (such as obtaining the services of a particular physician or hospital of the patient's choice) and no further such accommodations can be made, the patient should be coerced to accept the treatment or investigation. Similarly, where the patient's refusal is due to depression[10] or an inappropriate emotional response despite the knowledge that the proposed therapy will be curative, such refusal is inappropriate and treatment should be given. However, of course this must not be done where the patient will react to the coercion in such an extreme manner that his reaction itself will constitute a danger as great or greater than omission of the relevant procedure.[11]

---

[8] Tzitz Eliezer 15:40 and 17:2.

[9] Igr. Moshe Ch. M. 2:74; also in R. M. Hershler, Halacha and Medicine Vol.4, p.111.

[10] Note that in modern secular ethics, even severe depression is not a reason to override patient autonomy unless the depression is affecting the patient's mental competence. This is sharply at variance with the halachic view. See throughout Part II, for example, p. 253.

[11] With regard to the imposition of lifesaving therapy, Rabbi Yaakov Emden (Mor u'Kzia O.Ch.328) writes: "In the case of an illness or wound... about which the physician has certain knowledge and clear recognition and with a proven medication, we impose therapy on a patient who refuses in the face of such danger... even to amputate a limb, in order to rescue the individual from death... We ignore his will if he... prefers death to life... and we do all that is necessary for the saving of life... He does not have the right to commit suicide."

But he sets clear limitations to this obligation to impose therapy (in addition to requiring the physician's "certain knowledge" and "clear recognition"):

"We impose therapy only if he wishes to avoid a proven treatment suggested by an expert... but if he refuses treatment because he does not regard the treatment as effective, even in his own personal opinion and certainly if he has support by a single other physician, we do not impose treatment. If he is afraid that the

2. Treatment forbidden

Where it is not clear whether the patient will live or die if untreated, and therapy will cure if successful but will kill if not, it is forbidden to treat (this applies even if the patient consents to the treatment – the problem here is not one of consent).[12]

3. Treatment discretionary

Where the benefit of the treatment is not clear, the therapy is not standard or not agreed upon by experts, and the patient objects, the treatment should not be administered. In such circumstances consent is essential.

Where the danger is not clearly present and the appropriate therapy entails great suffering, the patient cannot be coerced to accept therapy.

Where coercion itself will harm the patient, even where the patient is wrongly refusing treatment such coercion must not be applied.[13]

If the treatment is inherently dangerous, even where that danger is materially less than the danger of the underlying disease, the patient should not be forced.[14]

Where death is certain in the short term if no treatment is given and a dangerous therapy will cure if successful but may kill instead, the patient must choose. Such dangerous therapy may legitimately be chosen, even where the majority probability is that the therapy will kill.[15]

---

treatment that is recommended by the physician may harm him, one may not impose therapy..."

Rabbi Feinstein similarly expresses reservations about forcing a patient to accept therapy that the patient feels will be harmful, including forced feeding where the patient feels that the food will harm him. Rabbi Feinstein points out that therapy may be ineffective or worse where a patient is convinced that it will be harmful. In such cases force should ordinarily not be used. Where a patient refuses to eat altogether and will die of starvation, however, force must be used if necessary.

[12] See Unknown Benefit, Unknown Harm in Principles, p. 37.

[13] Igr. Moshe Ch. M. 2:74.

[14] Igr. Moshe Ch. M. 2:74.

[15] See above, p. 118.

Where the patient cannot choose, such as a child or an unconscious or incompetent adult, the family should decide.[16]

In cases of illness without danger where treatment will be painful, the patient's consent is required.[17]

For cosmetic procedures or the treatment of non-serious illness in general, the patient must be informed about any dangers of therapy and treatment cannot be forced.

Even in cases of danger to life, where more than one treatment option exists the patient must be informed and his choice of a particular option is required. This applies to serious illness that is not life-threatening as well. If the patient cannot choose, a valid proxy (*apotropos*) must be informed and the proxy must choose.

Consent is essential in research and situations involving experimental therapy.[18]

Treatment Against Patient's Wishes – Summary of Principles

A. Life threatening illness:

1. Safe, painless therapy: treat despite refusal.

2. Safe, painful therapy: treat despite refusal.

3. Risky therapy: consent required; even high risk therapy allowed where patient consents.[19]

4. Efficacy of therapy not established, experts disagree on therapy, therapy experimental or of unknown efficacy, alternative therapies exist, patient has reason to believe the therapy may be harmful: consent required.

B. Serious non-life threatening illness:

1. Safe, painless therapy: treat despite refusal.

2. Safe, painful therapy: treat despite refusal.

---

[16] See p. 110 and note 31 there.

[17] Where an illness may have serious consequences (even without danger to life), this may change.

[18] See below, p. 203.

[19] See above, p. 118.

3. Risky therapy: consent required; permitted risk of therapy limited even where patient consents.[20]

4. Efficacy of therapy not established, experts disagree on therapy, therapy experimental or of unknown efficacy, alternative therapies exist, patient has reason to believe the therapy may be harmful: consent required.

Rabbi Feinstein gives the general principles for administering therapy (in dangerous illness where the illness is more dangerous than the therapy) as follows:[21] [22]

1. The therapy must be known to be safe *in the relevant clinical situation* and not by theoretical extrapolation from dissimilar situations such as from experience with patients who are younger, healthier or at different stages of the relevant disease condition.

2. The therapy must be known to be beneficial in a majority of cases – over 50%; or else only a very small number of previous patients have been endangered by this therapy.

3. The therapy must be appropriate according to a consensus of senior physicians.

4. Where the therapy has a risk, even if that risk is much less than the risk of the disease and the therapy is commonly used in that disease, nevertheless it must not be given without the patient's consent.

Obligation to Disclose Risk

Concerning the requirement to inform the patient about the danger of a therapy: what level of danger is necessary such that failure to disclose that danger would constitute negligence?

1. Danger to life:

In cases of life-threatening illness, if the danger of the intervention is less than 1%, failure to inform the patient of that danger would not constitute

---

[20] Igr. Moshe Ch. M. 2:74. Risk of serious harm must be less than 50%; therapy must have likelihood of success of more than 50%.

[21] Igr. Moshe Ch. M. 2:73.

[22] In *chayei sha'a* (terminal) situations, other rules apply; see p. 118.

actionable negligence because even if the patient refused therapy there is an obligation to treat against the patient's wishes.[23] Where the risk of the intervention is greater, the patient must certainly be informed because consent becomes essential where risk is significant.[24]

2. Serious illness without danger to life:

As discussed in the section on risk,[25] certain risks are acceptable in the pursuit of a livelihood and other genuine needs. As noted there, Rabbi Feinstein rules that participating in a professional sport is acceptable where the danger of serious (life-threatening) injury is one in some thousands.[26] (Rabbi Feinstein points out that the danger of causing injury to others must also be considered – where those others enter the relevant situation knowingly such danger may be permitted at the same low level of probability as that which permits exposing oneself to risk.) According to Rabbi Zilberstein, Rabbi Feinstein would allow a danger of 1 in 1,000; he mentions "one in a few thousand" only because that was the figure presented to him in the specific question.

The figure of 1 in 1,000 is corroborated by R Akiva Eiger[27] and the Magen Avraham.[28] Shem Aryeh[29] mentions the Sefer Chassidim who expresses concern about dangers that are 1 in 1,000 and explains that the Sefer Chassidim is setting a limit beyond what is strictly required.

The need to treat serious (even non-life threatening) illness justifies such low risk, and therefore in view of these sources, in Rabbi Zilberstein's opinion one in a thousand can be disregarded, and if a patient is not informed about a danger that is less than one in a thousand such failure to inform would not be materially negligent.

---

[23] As discussed above.

[24] See below, and p.118.

[25] Approach to Risk in Halacha, p. 45.

[26] Ig. M., Ch. M. 1:104 based on B.M. 112 and Noda B'Yehuda.

[27] R. Akiva Eiger, Resp. 60.

[28] Mag. Avraham O.C. 316:23.

[29] Shem Aryeh 27.

3. Where therapy will not endanger life but may result in significant harm:

One per hundred is not significant – Rabbi Eliashiv assumes that people in general would not regard 1% danger of harm as serious enough to prohibit therapy in cases of serious illness. If that is the case, the halacha follows such a generally accepted standard.[30] Failure to disclose a danger that is less probable than this would not constitute culpable negligence.

Summary

Failure to inform a patient of the following levels of risk would not constitute culpable negligence:

(i) Life threatening illness, when therapy has a danger to life of less than 1 in 100;

(ii) Serious illness where therapy has a danger to life of less than 1 in 1,000;

(iii) Serious illness when therapy will not endanger life but has a risk of causing harm that is less than 1 in 100.

---

[30] A more formal source for this approximate figure has been suggested by Rabbi Y. Zilberstein: Mishk. Yaakov Y.D 17 rules that 1 in 10 is a significant minority (in the context of the kosher status of animals) – such a minority cannot be ignored. Rabbi Eliashiv holds that in general, 1 in 20 would be an insignificant minority. A possible source for Rabbi Eliashiv's opinion (according to Rabbi Zilberstein) that 1 in 100 is certainly insignificant is the Rashba (Responsa 2:371), in the context of inheritance law, who says that "We do not have to be concerned with the possibility of a twin pregnancy at all" (where a woman is pregnant and the child she is carrying will affect the inheritance of other, already extant, children). We assume that she is pregnant with a single child because that is the majority case. Now the general probability of a twin pregnancy is approximately 1 in 80, so it would seem that the Rashba is saying that 1 in 100 would certainly be considered insignificant. (Note however that the Rashba may be referring only to the probability of twins where both are male, since that is the case that would be relevant to the specific question under consideration; if so, the probability is less than 1 in 80 since that figure includes cases of twins where at least one of the twins is female. If this is the intention of the Rashba we would not have a proof from his words that 1 in 100 is insignificant.)

Clinical Cases – Coercion and Consent

Clinical Case 14: Treatment Without Consent

A 37 year old woman with primary infertility has had three pregnancies following in-vitro fertilization. The first terminated spontaneously at an early stage; the second was an ectopic pregnancy requiring salpingectomy. The third resulted in a cesarian section for the delivery of twins, performed under general anesthesia. At operation, the single remaining fallopian tube was noted to contain a 3-centimeter mass in its mid-portion. The doctor performing the cesarian was undecided whether to resect the mass leaving the rest of the tube for later attempted reconstruction or to resect the entire tube. After consultation with a senior colleague he elected to resect the tube.

Did he act correctly in resecting the patient's single fallopian tube without her consent?

Analysis:

General guidelines for approaching this case would be as follows (leaving aside the separate halachic question of female sterilization):[31] What are the chances of a future natural pregnancy if the tube is preserved, and what are the risks of a future ectopic pregnancy in the tube? If the probability of natural pregnancy were less than 5% and the risk of ectopic pregnancy greater than 10%, the doctor's action should be seen as reasonable (and particularly if he had cause to be concerned that the tubal mass may be malignant); these levels of chance and risk suggest that his action was in the patient's best interest and her consent could reasonably be assumed.[32]

If however the chance of a future pregnancy were greater than 10%, he would be better advised to wait and ascertain the patient's preference, even though this may mean another operation with its attendant risks. (R.Y. Zilberstein).

In the case of a correctly indicated hysterectomy, would it be permitted to perform bilateral oophorectomy without the patient's permission? Rabbi

---

[31] See Nishm. Avraham Vol. III, p. 51; Steinberg, Encyclopedia Vol. I, p. 128.

[32] Less than 5% is generally considered insignificant, more than 10% significant in many halachic contexts. See Risk, pp. 52-53 and notes there.

Feinstein states that where there is a 5% risk of malignancy developing that can be averted by the procedure, it would be in order (where a hysterectomy has been performed, there is no longer a question of sterilization due to the added oophorectomy) and the patient's consent is probably not needed. Even if a 5% risk is judged to be too small to justify the risk of an operation *ab initio* where the risk of the operation will be significant, where the operation is already being done and the extra procedure adds virtually no risk or discomfort, the reduction of 5% risk of malignancy is certainly to be regarded as major. Unless there is reason to believe that the patient may object (because of hormonal benefits and the like), the oophorectomy would not be inappropriate and the patient's consent could be assumed.

Clinical Case 15: Treating a Child Against Parents' Wishes

A three year old child has pneumonia. When seen by a pediatrician, the child is acutely ill and in respiratory difficulty. The pediatrician urges immediate admission and intravenous antibiotic therapy but the parents refuse, citing their belief that the child is improving and their preference for holistic and alternative medicine. They also express the opinion that antibiotics are harmful and will predispose the child to other illnesses, and their fear that the child may contract additional infections in the hospital. The pediatrician insists on admission and threatens to call for police assistance if the parents refuse; the child is admitted and treated despite the parents' ongoing protestations.

1. Are the pediatrician's actions correct?

2. Should the child be forcibly removed from the parents' care to prevent subsequent similar episodes?

Analysis:

Normally, parents are the natural guardians and their status as such is endorsed by halacha; they must make the relevant decisions. Parents may choose among various therapeutic options just as individuals may choose for themselves, but legitimate choices extend only to those therapies that would be approved by local halachic authority, or in the modern context, that are registered and approved by standard medical practice supported by standard medical accreditation and licensing.[33]

---

[33] Aruch HaShulchan, Y.D. 336.

Guardians may not act to the detriment of their wards; parents are not authorized to make decisions that are objectively harmful for their children. In this case, the child's life was clearly in danger and the parents' actions were obstructive. Forced hospitalization and treatment was correct and necessary.

Removing the child from the parents' care would however probably be incorrect; while the child is in danger now and needs treatment against the parents' wishes, future danger is uncertain and does not clearly justify the trauma of forcible removal from the family. (R.Y. Zilberstein).

Clinical Case 16: Treatment Without Consent and Against Parents' Wishes

A 41 year old Down's syndrome patient has diverticulitis. He is treated conservatively and recovers. His surgeons then recommend partial colonic resection for prevention of another acute episode, giving the chance of recurrence as 30%. His parents refuse the procedure.

Should the operation be performed against the parents' wishes?

Analysis:

The procedure cannot be forced. If the danger of an illness is less than 50%, an invasive procedure cannot be performed without consent. Since the majority chance is that there will not be a recurrence, coercion is inappropriate.

If the recurrence rate were over 50%, would coercion be correct?

Normally, a majority probability has significance in halacha. At first glance, therefore, it may seem that surgery would be indicated (and even against the parents' wishes) where the statistical risk is greater than even. But here a question arises that requires an understanding of the halachic approach to majorities in order to decide whether this type of majority has significance.

An important point (elucidated by the Chazon Ish)[34] has major consequences for situations in which the halachic effects of a majority can be applied: a majority has significance only where the group constituting that majority has characteristics that make it a natural group.

---

[34] The Chazon Ish explains this concept in detail in E. HaEzer Ishus 31:2 and 31:5 with reference to Gittin 28a.

Where the group is formed only by external, unrelated events, that group is not subject to the halachic consequences of a majority. For example, elderly people form a group by virtue of a common element: namely, old age; however, this has no halachic significance with respect to a particular outcome for any given individual, for example death due to old age. There will be no halachic assumption that a particular elderly person has died within a certain period of time, even when it is known that most people of similar age have died during that period. That majority is not relevant halachically: since each elderly individual who dies does so as the result of a specific and individual pathology, the group of those who die is considered a group by virtue of *events* (specific pathological events), not as a *natural* group. Since the members of such a group are not bound into a unit by a *common event* they are to be seen as individuals from a halachic perspective.

A statistic relevant to individuals in such a group may be valid and useful, but it will not have the force of a halachic majority. Such statistics may be used for general diagnostic and prognostic purposes but they do not have the power to mandate or permit invasive interventions.

The Chazon Ish shows that the group must be bound by an element that is truly common for it to be considered a group with halachic significance: if a ship sinks with many people on board and most do not survive, then for certain halachic purposes, any particular individual on that ship may be assumed to have succumbed – he is part of a group and the majority assumption may be applied to him. But if ten ships sail from port and nine sink in unrelated incidents, we can say nothing about the tenth based on majorities. Each ship has its own separate destiny and no common element can be invoked with halachic significance that can tell us anything predictive about the unknown tenth. (If however, all ten ships were subject to a common circumstance, for example if they all sailed through a minefield in convoy and nine were sunk, we can indeed posit a consequence for the missing tenth. In that case they became a group subject to a common effect, and that is enough to bind them in a commonality with halachic significance.)

Where the nominal group is affected by disparate events, that is, where each of its members may be affected by a different event, the fact that the majority of its members share a common outcome has no halachic significance, at least so far as halachic majorities are concerned.

Is an acute exacerbation of diverticulitis an intrinsic event, or is it triggered by an external stimulus, for example a particular dietary burden or insult? In the case of a disease that has an intrinsic pattern, where the natural history of the disease is progressive and does not depend on external precipitating events, it may be appropriate to apply the statistical probabilities relevant to that disease in management decisions and in addition these probabilities may have halachic consequences. But where a disease state confers a vulnerability to extrinsic triggers and will not manifest in the absence of such triggers, such a situation is not amenable to the halachic application of majority.

So, for example, surgery for a tumor that behaves in a certain characteristic way may be guided by majority; we may consider operating where there is a majority probability that a particular pathological event will occur in such a case because the group of patients who have that condition constitute a real group in halachic terms. Where the group is subject to danger we will apply the rule of majority and operate on the individual to avert that statistical danger, and without consent if necessary (such as in the case of a child or mentally incompetent individual). But where a medical condition threatens danger *only when externally triggered*, then even when the majority of patients with that condition are likely to encounter the relevant trigger, we may not be able to apply the concept of majority to perform an invasive procedure on any individual patient without consent. In such a case there is no halachic majority that tells us that the particular danger we hope to avert is real and present; in each individual case it will depend on the relevant particular external trigger (which may never occur) and that makes each case subject to individual assessment and not part of a natural group.

This approach would lead to the conclusion that surgery should not be forced on a patient without consent in such a case. Whether diverticulitis falls into the category of a condition with a progressive natural history, or rather into the category of susceptibility to external triggers that cause acute inflammatory episodes may be legitimately argued, but that is essentially a medical debate rather than a halachic one; the halacha will follow the medical consensus.

In summary, not every statistical majority has the halachic power of majority. The natural history of a condition is known by observation of many instances of that condition; that information undoubtedly has statistical value. However, when applied to a particular patient, that information remains a probability and no more, and not every measure of probability invokes the unique power of halachic majority.

Clinical Case 17: Obliging One Person to Save Another

A teenage girl agreed to donate bone marrow to a woman suffering from acute leukemia. After the recipient had undergone marrow ablation chemotherapy in preparation for the transplant, the donor refused to continue (she had felt unwell during testing and become afraid). At this stage, the recipient's life depends entirely on receiving the donated marrow; she proceeded with her own marrow ablation only because she had been assured that the donation would be forthcoming.

Can the donor be forced to go through with the donation?

Analysis:

Although she is seriously derelict in refusing at this stage and is in flagrant transgression of the obligation to save life ("Do not stand idly by the blood of your fellow"), and indeed is the indirect cause of the recipient's immediate danger, she cannot be legally obliged. Although she will be the indirect cause of the patient's death, she cannot be physically forced to undergo the donation procedure; however, every effort should be made to induce her to continue, including an offer of financial compensation (it is entirely in order to compensate a donor financially in such a case).

It is true that there are Talmudic cases in which one party can extract payment from another where the second party has spent money on the assurance of the first; one must make good a loss incurred by an assurance that one would fulfil an obligation which in fact he fails to fulfil. Where one is the cause of a loss to another, one must make good that loss. Money can be extracted forcibly when one person has spent it on the assurance of another, but not bone marrow. In the case of donation of a body part or tissue, there is no obligation parallel to a financial obligation; the obligation here remains in the category of "Do not stand idly by..." (Rabbi Y. S. Eliashiv)[35]

---

[35] See McFall v. Shimp, no. 78-1771 in Equity (C.P. Allegheny County, Pa., July 26, 1978) in which a man began compatibility testing for marrow donation to his cousin who was dying from aplastic anemia but subsequently refused to continue with testing and donation. Despite the patient's claim that he had suffered critical harm due to the delay occasioned by his cousin's conduct, the court upheld the donor's right to refuse donation. The judge ruled that he had not violated any legal obligation but concluded that his conduct was "morally indefensible."

Clinical Case 18: Unreasonable Refusal of Therapy

A 35 year old single man with early stage uncomplicated localized colonic cancer refuses surgery because he does not want a colostomy as it may interfere with his marriage prospects. His disease has an excellent prognosis with surgery and a disastrous prognosis without it.

Should his refusal be respected?

Analysis:

This man's refusal to accept lifesaving therapy is unreasonable. Every effort must be made to convince him to agree to surgery, even if he will require a long-term colostomy. If he continues to refuse, some method must be found to induce him to undergo the procedure; allowing his disease to spread with no attempt at cure is halachically irresponsible and unacceptable.

Triage

Distribution of scarce resources is a problem that pervades modern medicine. Almost every medical action involves an element of prioritising: treatment given to one patient very often means less given to another; less time and attention or less availability of a scarce technology.

The problem has a wide reach: triage is practised not only at the immediate clinical level in the emergency room or at the roadside scene of an accident, but throughout the system – when a hospital administrator apportions a budget, triage decisions must be made. Is it appropriate to fund a clinic that practises pediatric preventive medicine in the face of a lack of intensive care beds? Should broad screening programs be funded while there are immediate acute needs that are unserved? It is axiomatic in medicine that "prevention is better than cure" – but is it acceptable to channel resources to the prevention of future disease in the face of present suffering that demands alleviation?

Indeed, at the broadest political level similar questions arise: may a society fund its parks and museums in the face of competing national defence or health needs? How are immediate lifesaving needs at the societal level to be balanced against broad economic needs that in the long run also affect life in a real way?

The Talmud[1] discusses the situation of a town with a water source that is sufficient for the town and others beyond, but only if the locals drink and do not wash laundry. If the locals drink and wash, there will be insufficient water for the more distant population. May the locals wash or are they constrained by halacha to drink only so that there will be water for the distant population to drink too? Although at first glance it may seem obvious that they should drink only, the Talmud records an opinion that holds that they may in fact wash as well. The reason is that if they do not maintain adequate hygiene there will be spread of disease among them that will present danger, and although that danger may not be quite as acute as the danger presented by immediate thirst, it may be taken into account. Although there are dissenting opinions in this scenario, it is apparent that broader considerations than the immediate and most obvious may be relevant to a community facing life and health risks.[2]

Some years ago, a couple suffering from long-standing infertility was assisted in conceiving and giving birth to a child by a hospital in Israel. The grateful father made a substantial donation to the hospital, stipulating that his money should be used by the hospital's fertility unit to assist other couples in similar circumstances. The hospital's director, however, declined the gift on the grounds that saving life ought to take priority over fertility treatment – surely, he argued, it cannot be right to spend limited funds in bringing children into the world when there are people already in existence whose lives are threatened by disease; those already-extant individuals should be treated first. The donor stood his ground and refused to make his contribution unless it were to be used for fertility treatment, and Rabbi Eliashiv was asked to adjudicate.

Rabbi Eliashiv ruled that the man was entitled to have his funds used for fertility purposes. When asked why that should take priority over lifesaving needs, Rabbi Eliashiv stated that a country needs a normal spread of facilities; if one allows only emergency needs, one risks developing an embattled mentality that may lower morale in a real way, and that too is a threat to a community. One cannot require this individual to contribute to a particular cause against his will; he may fund the service of his choice.[3]

---

[1] Nedarim 80b.

[2] Issues of priority setting on the societal level are discussed at length in A. Steinberg, Encyclopedia of Jewish Medical Ethics, Vol. III, pp. 848-860.

[3] Related by Rabbi Y. Zilberstein.

Triage in the Acute Setting

Who takes priority in saving life when choices must be made among individuals?[4] Various selection criteria are relevant in halacha; the following are the main ones (where there is dissension, the majority view is presented; references are provided for minority views and further discussion).

There are two levels that require study here, namely, the criteria themselves and their organization in a hierarchy – each triage criterion assigns priorities, but beyond that, the criteria need to be ordered. Which criteria are to be applied first, or put differently, which priorities take priority? Building a hierarchy of priorities is a complex exercise; in the list that follows it will be pointed out where an element is decisive and where it may be equal or secondary to another, but it must be remembered that nuances of each scenario can affect the decision and mature halachic judgment is needed.

Unless indicated otherwise, each of the following criteria applies where it is the only consideration (each is subject to circumstances that may require it to be overridden).

Proximity *(ein ma'avirin)*

One of the most basic criteria in halachic triage is given by the principle of *ein ma'avirin al hamitzvot* – one may not bypass a mitzva, or put another way, when all else is equal, obligations are to be discharged in their order of proximity.[5] This principle can be superseded by a number of others (see below for examples), but it is a basic starting point. The principle states that when more than one mitzva require fulfilment, the one that is closer takes priority: if two patients need attention, the doctor must treat the patient who is physically closer to him – he may not bypass that obligation for an equal but more distant one. All else being equal, one does not bypass a mitzva.

---

[4] See below, Appendix VI: Current Selection Criteria for Renal Dialysis and Transplantation for comparison with secular criteria.

[5] Igr. Moshe Ch. M. 2:75 as applied to seeing patients – the patient who calls first (or the patient closest to the doctor when there is no prior call) should be seen first.

In Hadassa hospital around 60 years ago, at the start of the modern antibiotic era, eight children with meningitis required treatment. There was unfortunately only enough penicillin for two children, and the doctors approached Chief Rabbi Herzog for his opinion on how to decide which two children should be treated. Bacterial meningitis has a high mortality and at that time penicillin offered a very good chance of cure; this was certainly a life-and-death question. Rabbi Herzog called Rabbi Moshe Feinstein in New York and they discussed the dilemma. Rabbi Feinstein indicated that the doctors should enter the children's ward and give the medication to the first two children they encountered. The first child should receive treatment – that child may not be bypassed; thereafter a similar consideration would apply to the second (the next closest) child; thereafter there would unfortunately be no medication left.[6]

Relatives

One is obligated to treat one's own family members before others (this is not specifically a medical obligation – one should also give charity and other assistance to one's relatives first).[7]

This criterion may be inappropriate in the usual hospital setting where applying a personal priority such as this may in fact constitute an infraction of the rules – in such circumstances a doctor would not be entitled to give priority to his own relatives.

Where this obligation does apply however, it will take precedence over the previously listed prohibition of not bypassing a duty; that is, all else being equal, one would have to bypass a stranger to treat one's own close relative.[8]

---

[6] Rabbi Feinstein was of the opinion that the Mishna (Horiyos 13a) concerning a particular set of selection criteria was not relevant in this case. Rabbi Feinstein (Igr. Moshe Ch. M. 2:75) states that even where those criteria are relevant, proximity (or a prior call to see a patient) takes priority. Tzitz Eliezer (18:1) too relegates those criteria to limited circumstances.

[7] Deuteronomy 15:7 and Isaiah 58:7. For discussion of further priority criteria, see Ch. Sofer Ch. M. 127. For extensive discussion in English, see R. S. Taub, The Laws of Tzedaka and Maaser (ArtScroll, 2001) pp. 49-57 and note 1, pp. 50-51 for original sources.

[8] The halachic derivation of this point is beyond the scope of this work (the student of halacha will find it an instructive exercise).

Definite vs doubtful danger

A definite danger takes priority over a doubtful danger; treatment must be given to the patient who is in certain danger before one who is only possibly in danger.[9] As a corollary to this, if both are in equal danger but an available medication will certainly help one and only doubtfully help the other, it must be given to the one who will certainly benefit.[10]

This criterion may be set aside when the definite danger to a few is offset by a doubtful danger to many – depending on the degree of doubt and the numbers of people involved; see the next item.

Many vs. few

When many are in danger efforts to save them must take priority over efforts to save fewer; resources must be applied such that they benefit as many as possible.

Several subcategories can be distinguished here:

(i) Saving many with possible harm to few:

When saving many depends on *possible harm* to a few (that is, where there is a chance that attempts to save the many will actively harm others) more caution is needed although in principle such action may be undertaken with extreme attempts to avoid such harm. In the collapse of a building where emergency excavation is undertaken to save many who are buried in the rubble, but necessarily at the cost of the chance of injuring some in the process, it may be acceptable to proceed. Here, the decision must be based on the relative likelihood of saving many and the chance of actively injuring the few; work should proceed as far as possible in layers to give the maximum chance of rescuing those in more superficial layers before going deeper to reach others with the attendant risk of harming those still undiscovered in the upper layers.

(ii) Many doubtful vs few certain:

When a choice must be made between saving a few who are in definite need or many who may only possibly be in need, the relative probabilities become relevant, and the relative proximities will also modify the decision.

---

[9] Pri Megadim 328; 7:1.

[10] R. M. Hershler, Halacha and Medicine Vol 4, p. 84.

A few examples will clarify this. A terrorist shot the guard at the entrance to a settlement and ran on into the settlement. A bystander was faced with the choice of stopping to help the guard who was seriously wounded or pursuing the attacker in an attempt to prevent many residents from becoming victims of a suicide attack. Rabbi Eliashiv was later asked what the correct choice would have been; his opinion was that under the circumstances described, pursuing the attacker would be the preferred option. Where there is almost certain to be an attack on many that could very possibly be thwarted, one should make that attempt.

However, a similar situation that occurred at around the same time elicited a different response. On that occasion, a terrorist injured an individual on the outskirts of Jerusalem and proceeded in the direction of the city. A doctor who arrived on the scene was placed in the dilemma of having to choose between helping the victim or pursuing the perpetrator who had disappeared by the time the doctor arrived. In this case, Rabbi Eliashiv's opinion was that the immediately threatened victim should be treated. Here there are many elements of doubt regarding subsequent events: there is no certainty that the terrorist will reach the city and achieve his aim – he may be stopped by others or fail to detonate his explosives; and in addition there is no assurance that the pursuers will find him or in fact be able to stop him. In such a scenario treating the definitely endangered victim who is here now takes precedence.

The general approach is that these scenarios need individual assessment: in each case the risks and benefits on both sides of the equation need to be weighed in order to reach an appropriate decision. The default position is that the definite takes precedence over the doubtful in halacha, even when the definite are few in number and the doubtful are many. However, when the odds are clearly in favor of benefit to the many the default must be altered; and the numbers of people in danger on both sides of the question are also relevant – the balance will shift if very many people are endangered.

Another example to illustrate this point: the victim of a road traffic accident needs attention, but there is an obstruction in the road threatening to cause further serious accidents. The rescuer must choose between attending to the injured victim or removing the obstruction. The correct choice here depends on the relative probabilities as assessed by the rescuer at the scene – if it is close to certain that further serious accidents are imminent, it would be proper to remove the obstruction first. If it is not clear that this is the case, the victim must be stabilized first and only then the danger averted.[11] The default rule in halacha is to prioritise the definite and the immediate; where overwhelming danger exists to many however, even when that danger is not as immediate, this default may shift.

Where treatment has already begun

A patient who is being treated acquires a certain "right" to continued treatment;[12] where a patient has already begun receiving treatment one may not abandon that patient to treat another. Even where abandoning the patient involves adding no active element of harm this would not be allowed; it is certainly forbidden where the act of abandoning the patient would cause harm – where, for example, the patient will react to being abandoned with a sense of panic or hopelessness (such emotions are halachically considered real elements of danger to a seriously ill patient).[13]

This stricture applies even to abandoning a patient whose chance of salvage is doubtful for another who can certainly be saved, abandoning one who is terminal for another who could be salvaged in the long term, and abandoning one patient to treat many.[14] In all these situations, the patient who has already been admitted to an ICU (intensive care unit) or other treatment facility may not be moved out due to his poor prognosis in order to admit a patient with a better prognosis; once treatment has begun the patient has a right to its continuation.[15]

Where treatment has not yet begun, one may bypass a non-salvageable patient to treat a salvageable one, and bypass one to save many (the

---

[11] Rabbi Y. Zilberstein.

[12] Igr. Moshe Ch.M. 2:73.

[13] Igr. Moshe Ch.M. 2:73 and 2:75.

[14] At a mass disaster scene, one may not leave one patient who needs lifesaving attention once treatment has begun to move on to assess others (this may conflict with some current triage protocols; see below, p. 184).

[15] This applies even where the first patient was improperly admitted, whether deliberately or in error. In addition, the first patient, once admitted, has no obligation to make way for the second even where the first patient's prognosis is poor and the second's is good; indeed, he may be forbidden to do so (Igr. Moshe Ch.M. 2:73). See Salvageable vs non-Salvageable Patients, p. 178.

principle of *ein ma'avirin* is set aside in these circumstances), provided that the act of bypassing causes no active harm.[16]

However, it is permissible to move one patient from an ICU to a lower care ward if that would facilitate the treatment of many, but only where the lower care ward offers a *fully adequate* level of care. One does not always have to provide the highest level of care as long as the care offered always meets rigorous objective standards.[17]

Healthy vs ill

Where two are in danger and only one can be saved, the healthier patient should be saved;[18] for example, when only one can be saved from a fire or other danger.[19]

However, if saving the sicker patient will enable *both* to survive, of course that must be done. In an emergency evacuation situation, where evacuating the sickest first will result in saving maximum lives (because the healthier will survive while the more fragile are being evacuated) that is what should be done. But when it is apparent that moving the sicker patients out first will leave the healthier ones to die, the priority becomes to save the healthier (this has been termed "reverse triage.")[20]

Salvageable vs non-salvageable patients

Salvageable patients *(chayei olam)* are given priority over the non-salvageable *(chayei sha'a)*.[21] One may bypass the non-salvageable to

---

[16] For example, where the patient being bypassed will become anguished or panic-stricken at the realization that he is being abandoned due to the hopeless nature of his condition (Igr. Moshe Ch.M. 2:73). See p. 180 for details.

[17] This is not necessarily in conflict with the statement of the Birchei Yosef (336) who says that a patient must request the services of the most expert physician available – as the Tzitz Eliezer explains (Ramat Rachel 5:22), that condition is probably mandatory only in situations where no objective standard of medical practitioners' qualifications exists; however, where all available physicians are stringently required to meet certain minimum standards (as with modern accreditation requirements), this would not be necessary.

[18] Yaavetz, Migdal Oz; Otzar Hatov 91.

[19] M. Berurah 334:68.

[20] See Anatomy of a Disaster, p. 271.

[21] See Clinical Case 21, p. 191 for derivation of this priority.

reach the salvageable[22] (provided no harm, physical or emotional, is done to the non-salvageable in the process; see below).

Rabbi Moshe Feinstein was asked about the following situation. Two patients require treatment; one is a *chayei sha'a*, terminally ill, and the other is a *chayei olam*, salvageable in the long term. Both need immediate ICU care: the former to prolong his temporary situation, the latter for observation and prevention of a sudden dangerous event (for example, a life-threatening cardiac arrhythmia), and although he may survive without ICU monitoring (he may not experience the event), if he does there will not be adequate time to get him into the ICU and he will die. (This can be summarised as a "certain *chayei sha'a*" against a "doubtful *chayei olam*.") Who takes precedence?

Rabbi Feinstein writes that if both cannot be admitted to the ICU, the long-term salvageable patient should be given priority. However, if the one who is expected to survive only for the short term *has already been admitted* to the ICU, it is forbidden to move him.[23] Once he has begun to receive treatment, that treatment is now being appropriately given; since the hospital's mandate is to treat all those in their care, each patient in his own right, he may not be set aside for another. This applies even if the first patient was wrongly admitted, whether in error or deliberately; once he is there, the place is "his." In addition, this applies whether the patient already receiving treatment is paying or not; if that particular healthcare system delivers therapy to all patients equally, irrespective of payment (that is, if the system is ordinarily obliged to treat such a patient where no more salvageable patient happens to be present), even if that patient is indigent he is fully entitled to the therapy he is now receiving and financial considerations may not be used to "sideline" him in favor of another.

Furthermore, the patient who is now receiving priority has no obligation to sacrifice his place for another patient even when that other patient has a better chance of long-term survival. Indeed, such sacrifice may be forbidden.

---

[22] The principle of prioritising *chayei olam* over *chayei sha'a* takes precedence over the principle of not bypassing a mitzva. The derivation of this precedence is beyond the present scope; see also p. 174 and note 8 there.

[23] Igr. Moshe Ch.M. 2:73.

Rabbi Feinstein points out that all this applies only if the less salvageable patient has *already been admitted* and his treatment commenced. If however treatment has not begun; for example where the patient has not yet been admitted to the ICU, and the more salvageable patient arrives subsequently, the second should be given priority. Although the less salvageable patient arrived first (so long as he has not yet been admitted to the unit), he is set aside in order to save the one who can be saved in the long term.

But this has an important exception: if the first patient is *conscious and aware that he is being set aside*, that may not be done – Rabbi Feinstein states that in such a case the first patient is likely to perceive his situation as hopeless ("I am being abandoned; I am probably incurable...") and that anguish and despair constitute real additive lethal effects in situations of desperate illness. (In halacha, since pain, anguish, depression and hopelessness are regarded as material factors affecting survival, the physician who ignores the significance of such factors may be guilty of adding to his patient's lethal burden.)[24]

What is the default assumption in such situations? Rabbi Feinstein is of the opinion that one should generally assume that a patient who perceives that he is being set aside for another patient who arrived later will panic or experience a dangerous feeling of hopelessness; therefore unless it is clear that the second patient can be advanced ahead of the first with no compromise of the emotional condition of the first, the default handling of such situations is to treat patients in order of arrival – "first come, first served." This avoids the possibility of causing dangerous anguish to an abandoned patient.

Note that in selecting a *chayei olam* over a *chayei sha'a*, nothing may be done that actively shortens the life of the *chayei sha'a*.

One salvageable vs. two non-salvageable patients

The Chazon Ish was of the opinion that one person's *chayei olam* should take precedence over two people who have only *chayei sha'a*. He demonstrates this based on the Talmudic discussion[25] of two people

---

[24] One may not inform a terminal patient of the gravity of his situation where that knowledge may cause anguish or despair (Igr. Moshe Ch. M. 2:73).

[25] B. Metzia 62.

threatened by thirst where one is in possession of enough water for only one to survive. There the question is whether the owner of the water should drink it and survive or share it with the other person to give both an extended but only temporary prolongation of life. The definitive conclusion is that the owner of the water should use it to save his own life. The Chazon Ish points out that in effect this ruling is teaching that a person is obliged to save one (himself, in this case) for *chayei olam* rather than enable two to survive for only a short while; based on this the Chazon Ish rules that if the water is in the hands of an outside third party, that third party should likewise give it to only one of the two to enable one to survive in the long term (ownership of the water, in the opinion of the Chazon Ish, is not the deciding factor in the original scenario). In other words, one *chayei olam* takes precedence over two *chayei sha'a*.[26]

First come, first served

Patients should be seen in the order in which they arrive when other factors (such as urgency) are equal.[27] The source for this is the general Torah obligation of fairness and decency.[28] [29] Since a physician is obliged to respond to a patient when called, a patient who calls first should be seen first (unless a subsequent call is to attend to a more urgent case).[30]

Men or women first

Although lifesaving priorities are given in the Code of Jewish Law (in the context of redeeming hostages)[31] among one's mother, father, Torah teacher and others, much of this is not relevant in medical triage.[32]

---

[26] Chazon Ish, Ch. Mishpat, Likutim 20.

[27] See Nishm. Avraham Vol. II, p. 181-185 for details and numerous exceptions.

[28] "And you shall do the straight and the good..." (Deut. 6:18).

[29] R. Y. Zilberstein.

[30] Igr. Moshe Ch. M. 2:74.

[31] Sh. Aruch YD 252:8:9.

[32] Igr. Moshe Ch. M. 2:74 and 2:75 indicates that those criteria are subservient to others and hard to apply. See also Minch. Shlomo Tinyana 86:1 and Tzitz Eliezer 18:1.

With regard to gender, Yaavetz discusses the question of whether a boy or a girl takes priority; he quotes Maharam Katz and disagrees with him.[33] This debate does not have major medical application;[34] however in certain circumstances such as assigning priority in the case of a cosmetic procedure, there may be a gender preference.[35]

In the case of fetal reduction[36] too, no priority is given to either gender (even if priorities were established according to the criteria discussed in Horiyos 13, these are not relevant to fetuses).[37]

Age

Old age is not a valid criterion for assigning a patient lower triage priority.[38] (Even extremely old patients must be treated fully and aggressively, and even where a patient himself claims advanced age as a reason to be allowed to die, such a claim is not valid.)

Other factors – marital status

Other issues may raise triage questions too: during the 1948 war in Israel, a volunteer was needed for an extremely dangerous mission. The commander responsible for selecting the volunteer sent an urgent question to the Chazon Ish: who should be sent – a married or an unmarried man? The Chazon Ish indicated that it is preferable to send a man who has children – one who has already fulfilled the mitzva of procreation rather than a single man who has no progeny.

---

[33] Sh. Yaavetz 68 and 69. See Yaavetz Migdal Oz; Otzar Hatov 91 for a list of triage priorities, including the issues of younger or older, adult or child, old or ill, and various others.

[34] See note 32 above.

[35] Rabbi Zilberstein gives priority to a girl over a boy in the case of cosmetic surgery for a facial deformity.

[36] See Fetal Reduction, p. 93.

[37] Rabbi Eliashiv states that the criteria of Horiyos 13 are not applicable to fetuses because (among other reasons) they are not yet obligated in mitzvot (and the hierarchy of precedence in Horiyos is based on relative levels of mitzva obligation).

[38] Igr. Moshe Ch.M. 2:75. But see note 33 above.

Military triage

Military situations are predicated on a different calculus with respect to a number of the criteria listed here.[39] In terms of the two principles of definite vs doubtful danger and many vs few, the following example provides an illustration.

A senior military medical officer was sent into Lebanon with a group of soldiers during the conflict there. He was the only doctor accompanying the group, although he was assisted by a military medic trained in basic medical skills. Soon after crossing the border one of the soldiers in the group was injured, and the doctor assessed his condition as so serious that if he arranged a helicopter evacuation to hospital in Haifa the man would probably survive, but only if he accompanied him personally; sending him with the medic would mean almost certain death for the injured man. But in order to accompany the soldier he would have to leave the rest of the soldiers in the field without a doctor, and he found himself in an acute dilemma. What was his primary duty – to the injured man, or to provide the medical cover for the group that was necessary to facilitate their mission?

(In the event, the decision was taken out of his hands: a large helicopter arrived and evacuated the entire group.) The doctor subsequently sought halachic insight into his dilemma, however, and Rabbi Eliashiv was consulted. Rabbi Eliashiv stated that in the equivalent civilian situation, there is no question that the proper course of action for the doctor would be to accompany the injured man personally. The reason is clear: a definite danger takes priority over a doubtful one – this man is *certainly* in danger now, while there is only the *possibility* that others may be injured later. However, said Rabbi Eliashiv, in the military situation, that consideration does not apply: the doctor must stay with his men.[40]

---

[39] See also p. 59.

[40] This case also raises the issue of the *certain few* vs the *doubtful many* discussed above: one man was definitely in danger, but there existed the possibility of many being injured later. (Although that is certainly relevant in military situations, it may not be the overriding deciding factor.) Detailed analysis of the halacha in wartime is beyond our present scope; see Preemptive War in Jewish Law in R. JD Bleich, Contemporary Halachic Problems Vol. III, especially pp. 275-278.

Conflict with Secular Protocols

Some established principles of modern triage may not accord with halacha.[41] For example, where a triage protocol calls for assessment of all the injured at a disaster scene before definitive treatment is given to any particular patient,[42] this may mean passing over a seriously injured patient who needs immediate treatment in favor of assessing the remaining victims. The logic for this system is to facilitate finding as many of the seriously injured as possible; this would be hindered by stopping the triage effort to treat an individual definitively. However, in halacha this may not be correct: if, during a triage effort, an individual is encountered who needs immediate care and will die if the triage doctor moves on, the doctor may not leave that patient, not even in the effort to find others who may be equally in need. This definite patient takes priority over the other possible ones. Generally, the patient who is clearly in immediate need of lifesaving treatment may not be abandoned to continue the triage assessment; this is certainly true where the patient in immediate need has already begun receiving at least some form of treatment so that moving on would constitute an act of abandonment with lethal consequences.

---

[41] See below, Appendix VI: Current Selection Criteria for Renal Dialysis and Transplantation.

[42] See for example: Hogan, DE, Burstein JL. Disaster Medicine, 2nd ed. (Lippincott, Williams and Wilkins, 2007); chapter 2. In mass disaster triage, rapid initial assessment of each victim typically takes 15 to 60 seconds.

Clinical Cases – Triage

Clinical Case 19: Triage: Many vs Few and Definite vs Doubtful

An ambulance is despatched to attend to an injured child. En route the ambulance crew receives a call to proceed to the scene of an accident in which five adults have been injured; the extent and severity of their injuries is unknown.

Should the ambulance continue to the child or divert to the injured group?

Analysis:

The answer to this type of question depends on the relative likelihood of the various options in the best judgment of the personnel involved. Factors to use in deciding should include: (1) relative numbers of injured – all else being equal the greater number should be given priority; (2) relative severity of injuries as far as can be determined; (3) where these are doubtful: proximity – whichever need is the closer. In this case, where the severity of injuries is unknown, the ambulance should probably continue its journey to the child if that is the closer destination.

See "Many doubtful vs few certain" (page 175) for comparison with other cases with differing relative variables.

Clinical Case 20: Disaster Scene Triage

A young lady doctor found herself applying lifesaving pressure to a severed artery in the neck of a child at the scene of a terrorist attack. It was clear to her that if she abandoned the child she would almost certainly be able to save others. Should she abandon this single individual in order to save many, or is she forbidden to abandon him since that would directly bring about (or at the very least, allow) his death?

Analysis:

A question that must be answered here is whether desisting from applying pressure to a bleeding vessel is to be considered actively causing death or passively allowing it to occur – is the removal of a finger in that situation an act of killing or merely the discontinuation of saving? If it is the former it is clearly forbidden in halacha; if the latter, would it perhaps be proper where there are multiple other lives to be saved?

And further, even if the removal of a finger from a bleeding artery is sufficiently homicidal to render it forbidden when it is an isolated act, is that true where the finger is being removed in the very act of saving another life? The Chazon Ish was asked about the case of a car careening down a mountain road with failed brakes, heading towards a group of people. The driver had the option of steering the car to one side, but unfortunately only to a place where an individual was standing. Should he passively allow his car to continue into the group or actively turn and run down the individual?

In the course of discussing this case[43] the Chazon Ish makes the point that while one may not hand over an (innocent) individual to murderers to be killed[44] even in order to save many, it is possible that one may be permitted to deflect an arrow that is about to kill many away from them towards a single individual. The difference is that in the former case one is committing an intrinsically cruel act with a murderous result (of course only in order to save the many, but such an act nonetheless), while in the latter one is primarily performing an act of salvation – the primary act is that of deflecting the arrow away from its imminent victims, and that is an act of saving. Perhaps turning a car away from a group of people in its path is likewise an act of salvation (even when the consequence is that an individual will now be in the vehicle's path). Against this consideration, however, is the fact that deflecting an arrow (or turning a car) towards an individual is an act that will kill; handing an individual over to murderers is not a direct act of killing. The Chazon Ish does not come to a definitive conclusion on this aspect of the question. It seems however, that the Chazon Ish would agree to an act that saves a group while endangering a lone individual where that act of salvation is not one that *directly* kills the individual.[45]

---

[43] Chazon Ish, Sanhedrin 25.

[44] See p. 189 and note 4 there.

[45] Perhaps changing the points on a railway line to deflect a train away from a track on which a number of people are standing onto a track where only one is standing may be an example – deflecting the train is an act of salvation, but it is questionable whether that act ought to be considered also the direct killing of the single individual. It would seem that deflecting an arrow directly towards a person is a more direct action than setting points that lead to a train's changing course.

In our case, where the intention is likewise to save the many, how should the action be construed? Should we see the primary act as the removal of the hand from the child's neck and therefore necessarily a forbidden act of abandonment (or worse), or should we see the primary act as the movement of the hand *towards* the many it will save and its withdrawal from the child no worse (and possibly better) than the act of deflecting the arrow towards the individual, and therefore ought to be allowed because its primary nature is an act of saving the many?

It seems that the former view is definitive here: releasing the pressure that is preventing catastrophic hemorrhage is forbidden, even when that act is also the beginning of a movement to save others.

There is another aspect to this question too. Rabbi Moshe Feinstein rules that a patient who has begun to receive treatment has a right to continue receiving that treatment, even where another patient would have taken priority were a choice to have been made before treatment began.[46] If two patients who both need intensive care arrive simultaneously at a unit that has only one available bed, the patient who is salvageable (*chayei olam*) should be treated rather than the one who is unsalvageable (*chayei sha'a*). However if the unsalvageable patient has *already been admitted*, he must not be removed – once his treatment has begun he has acquired the right to that treatment, even if he were improperly selected in the first place.

In light of this, it seems that the doctor would not be allowed to release the hemostatic pressure that is saving the child's life because since that treatment has begun the child has "acquired a right" to its continuation, quite apart from the fact that such an act may be considered homicidal in itself in the eyes of halacha. The presence of many others who could be saved (who should ordinarily be given priority) does not break that right; the doctor must not move. The doctor is therefore forbidden to abandon the patient who is currently receiving lifesaving treatment, even in the attempt to save others.

---

[46] See above, p. 179.

Destroying Life to Save Life

Ohe life may not be set aside for another: *ein dochin nefesh mipnei nefesh.*[1] One may not actively hasten the death of one patient to save another; not even when the life to be shortened is *chayei sha'a* (terminal) and the life to be saved is *chayei olam* (long term life). A ventilator may not be disconnected from a terminally ill or moribund patient who is dependent on it even to save a non-terminally ill patient.

One may not kill even to save one's own life[2] (apart from killing an aggressor in self-defence).[3]

Sacrificing One to Save Many

The lives of many take precedence over the lives of few; however it is forbidden to abandon one to save many where that act of abandonment will cause the death of the individual.[4]

---

[1] Mishna, Ohalot 7:6.

[2] There is a minority opinion that one may injure another to save one's own life – Hag. Mordechai, Sanhedrin sec. 718 states that one may cut off the limb of another to save one's own life.

[3] Sanhedrin 73a.

[4] An individual may not be chosen to be given to captors to be killed in order to save many (Jerusalem Talmud, Terumot 8:10). However, where the captors have made the selection (they demand a particular individual), there is a debate over whether this may be done. One position holds that this is allowed; another holds that the individual may be given over to be killed only if he has been designated and in addition is guilty of a capital offence. The default ruling accords with the latter view (Ran, Yoma 82b, Rosh and others rule that designation is enough; Maimonides, Hil. Yesodei HaTorah 5:5 rules that it is not; Rema, Y.D. 157:1 leaves the matter undecided); in practice, designation alone is not enough to

A medical application of this principle would be the removal of a lifesaving therapy or technology from an individual patient where that therapy could be used to save more than one patient. Where removing the therapy leads directly to the death of the individual, this is forbidden. Despite the fact that many could be saved, this may not be done at the cost of actively killing one.

Fetal Reduction

This form of destroying one (or a few) to save many is generally permitted where none of the fetuses would otherwise survive,[5] unlike the previous case involving adults where one may not be destroyed to save many; fetuses are subject to different rules in halacha.

Abortion

Where a pregnancy must be terminated to save the mother's life, this is allowed. This subject has been reviewed in detail elsewhere.[6]

Conjoined Twins

In the case of conjoined twins where both will die unless one is sacrificed, this may be allowed subject to certain conditions. This subject has been reviewed in detail.[7]

Killing a *goses*, *treifa* or *chayei sha'a* to save a *chayei olam*

It is forbidden to kill a *goses*,[8] a *treifa* [9] or a *chayei sha'a* to save a *chayei olam*.[10]

---

permit the sacrifice of an individual by the group in order to save the rest of the group. (An individual may, however, sacrifice his own life to save many.)

[5] See Fetal Reduction, p. 93.

[6] See Abortion in Halachic Literature in R. JD Bleich, Contemporary Halachic Problems Vol. I, p. 325.

[7] See Conjoined Twins in R. JD Bleich, Bioethical Dilemmas Vol.I and The Case of the British Conjoined Twins in Vol. II. See R. BD Povarsky, Bad Kodesh 4:52. See also this author's "The Twins Decision" in the Glatter Series "Medical Halacha" audio recordings for an extended discussion.

Clinical Cases – Triage; Destroying Life to Save Life

Clinical Case 21: Triage; Killing One to Save Another

A young surgeon training in emergency surgery in Johannesburg found himself in the following situation. The hospital's trauma unit had acquired a sophisticated new ventilator for use on severely injured patients; however, the hospital had issued strict instructions allowing its use only for patients thought to be salvageable. Any patient assessed as unlikely to survive was to be treated with older technology; the new machine was to be held in reserve only for those who might be saved in the long term. (The concern was that if a non-salvageable patient were ventilated using the new machine, a patient with a better prognosis arriving subsequently would receive inferior care because the ventilator is committed to the first patient.) In addition, this unit is so busy that the dilemma is inevitable – whenever a non-salvageable patient is given the ventilator, a salvageable patient is sure to be admitted during the time the first patient is using it and therefore be denied its use.

Is the hospital's rule correct? According to halacha, must the surgeon obey it (and consequently be able to save the second, salvageable, patient) or must he defy the rule and use the machine on any non-salvageable patient who happens to be admitted (and inevitably lose the subsequent salvageable patient because he has already committed the machine to the first)?[11]

---

[8] See p. 127 for definition of a *goses*.

[9] A *treifa* is an individual suffering from one of a number of lethal pathologies; for detailed discussion of factors that may render a human *treifa*, see Igr. Moshe Ch. M. 2:73. See also Achiezer part 1; E.H. 12:5 for consideration of the *treifa* status unique to humans.

[10] See Clinical Case 10 above.

[11] This question is analysed in detail in Tzitz Eliezer 17:10 and 17:72. The analysis assumes a case where the non-salvageable patient must be ventilated (this is not always necessary – see above, Withholding Therapy p. 103). It also assumes that there will certainly (or almost certainly) be a subsequent salvageable patient; if that is in doubt the halachic ruling would favor the first patient because a certainty generally overrides a doubt in halacha (see pp. 175-177).

Analysis:

This case presents an unusual triage dilemma: the need to choose between a *chayei sha'a* (temporary life) who is here now and a *chayei olam* (long term life) who is not yet present but will arrive shortly. There are two main issues to clarify:

A. May one kill a *treifa* (mortally injured patient) to save a *chayei olam*? That is, may one actively detach the ventilator from the first patient who is so severely injured that he is beyond all hope of survival in order to attach it to the second who is likely to survive thereby? If this were allowed, the solution would be to use the machine on any patient despite a dismal prognosis and then remove it from such a patient when the second arrives in order to save the second. This action would result in the immediate death of the first but would save the second. Is that allowed?

B. May one (or indeed, is one obliged) to select the *chayei olam* over the *treifa* or *chayei sha'a* in this situation? That is, if the answer to question (A) above is negative, may one hold the machine back from the first patient in order to use it on the second who will arrive later?

A. In analysing this part of the question, two component issues are relevant:

(i) Is detaching or switching off a ventilator considered killing in halacha?

(ii) If it is, may one do that to a *treifa* or a *chayei sha'a* to save a *chayei olam*?

With regard to (i), an action that results directly and immediately in death is considered homicidal in halacha even where that action is not in the nature of a direct blow to the body of the victim. The Talmud[12] considers this issue; the commentaries[13] elucidate in detail the borderline between sufficiently direct action to be culpable as homicide (and therefore legally actionable) and those actions that are sufficiently removed to escape such capital culpability, at least as far as human courts are concerned (actions leading indirectly to death that are beyond human legal redress are

---

[12] Sanhedrin 87.

[13] See Yad Rama there.

nevertheless fully culpable in spiritual terms – *chayav bi'ydei shamayim*). The act of switching off a ventilator that results in immediate asphyxiation is certainly homicidal.

(It is possible that if the action and its result are sufficiently widely separated, for example if deactivation of the ventilator were done indirectly or the patient were to die much later of gradually worsening respiratory failure, producing such a result may escape capital status in terms of human justice; nevertheless such actions remain murderous in nature.)

With regard to (ii): may one perform such a homicidal act on a *treifa* to save a *chayei olam*? Tzitz Eliezer demonstrates that this is categorically forbidden.[14]

It should be noted that a *chayei sha'a* who is not a *treifa* has a more severe status with regard to termination of life support than one who is a *treifa* – it is a more severe offence to kill a *chayei sha'a* than a *treifa*.

B. Having established that it would be unacceptable to detach the ventilator from the first, moribund, patient even for the purpose of saving the second, would it be correct to desist from its use entirely on the first so that it will be available for the second? May one pass over the first to save the second?

In the case of two patients who are both present, where one has a hopeless prognosis and the other can be saved, it is clear that the salvageable patient should be prioritised. The derivation for this precedence is given in the Talmudic discussion of individuals facing death in the relatively short term who chose the chance of long-term survival at the cost of the chance of immediate death.[15] This case is the classic source for allowing an individual to choose risky therapy in the face of otherwise inevitable death; however it also suggests that a salvageable patient should be given precedence over a non-salvageable one: if even a small chance of long-term life is preferable over certain short-term death for one individual, it can be concluded that long-term life for one individual should take precedence over short-term life for another where all else is equal.

---

[14] Tzitz Eliezer quotes Tif. Yisrael who opines that this would be allowed; Tzitz Eliezer strongly disagrees and proceeds to disprove that contrary opinion.

[15] See p. 118 for detailed discussion of this source.

In our case only the moribund patient is present; the salvageable patient will certainly be here soon, but he is not yet present. Does the guarantee that the second patient will arrive justify withholding the ventilator for his arrival? In other words, although it is clear that a *chayei olam* takes precedence over a *chayei sha'a* when both are present, does that rule apply even when one is present and one is not?

In order to understand this issue, it is necessary to recall another triage principle. A *chayei olam* takes precedence over a *chayei sha'a*, and it is ordinarily forbidden to bypass a duty (*ein ma'avirin*).[16] When these two principles conflict, the former takes precedence: one must bypass a closer *chayei sha'a* to reach a more distant *chayei olam*.[17]

However, wherever bypassing a duty for the purpose of saving life is being considered, a critical halachic condition must be met: *the life to be saved must be present*. The Noda B'Yehuda[18] makes this point in a responsum sent to London doctors who had asked him whether a post-mortem dissection might be allowed on a patient who had died of complications of urological disease – they were anxious to derive surgical and pathological information that they believed could be used to avert similar deaths in the future. Although post-mortem dissection contravenes a number of Torah prohibitions, these may certainly be set aside for the purpose of saving life,[19] but the point made by the Nodah B'Yehuda is that the life to be saved justifies setting aside those prohibitions only where it is real and present. To transgress Torah law to save life, a *choleh lefaneinu* is required – a patient "in front of us."[20] In the course of his discussion the Nodah B'Yehuda clarifies the parameters and limitations of the concept of *lefaneinu*; it is clear that the concept is not limited to

---

[16] See above, p. 173.

[17] See above, pp. 173-174 and pp. 178-181 for details and limitations to this precedence.

[18] Noda B'Yehuda 2, YD 210; see also Ch. Sofer YD 336.

[19] See above, p. 32.

[20] Note that the statistical degree of danger to that life can be small: majorities are not relevant in lifesaving in halacha. In addition, the likelihood of rescue or cure is also not a consideration – even a small chance of saving life has full halachic force. See above, pp. 33-36 for these points in more detail.

immediate geographical proximity but rather to the existence of a specific and identifiable patient whose life is in danger.[21]

Now the question in our case is this: does the assurance that a patient will arrive in the near future constitute a *lefaneinu* situation? Can that patient be deemed in front of us now? If so, it will be justified to hold the ventilator in readiness; the first (hopeless) patient may be passed over in favor of the second because a *chayei sha'a* is bypassed to save a *chayei olam* when the *chayei olam* is present, and the guarantee that a *chayei olam* will appear satisfies the requirement of *lefaneinu*.[22]

If however we do not accept the inevitable arrival of a salvageable patient as tantamount to that patient's already being present, it will be obligatory to use the ventilator on the first patient.

The Tzitz Eliezer rules that if there is a sufficiently high probability that a second patient will arrive who will be saved if the machine remains available, it should be held back for that purpose. The doctor should obey the hospital's instruction as according with Jewish law in this case.[23]

Another suggested approach[24] offers a unique solution: the ventilator could be fitted with a timed cut-off and a warning signal – the first patient would be ventilated immediately and ventilation would proceed until the automatic cut-off trips the ventilator at which point it is immediately re-started. This continues until the second patient arrives; the ventilator is

---

[21] Similarly, a real and present danger to identifiable individuals constitutes a *"lefaneinu"* situation – as-yet uninfected individuals in a life-threatening epidemic are permitted to set aside prohibitions to safeguard their lives. Also, a situation that is very likely to develop may be considered "in front of us;" emergencies that occur very frequently in a particular setting may fall into this category.

[22] In more depth: a typical *lefaneinu* situation usually conflates two issues – the physical presence of a patient whose life is in danger, and the assurance of saving that life. In this particular case, only the second is present: no patient is here yet (in fact no patient exists: the relevant injury has not yet taken place); but on the other hand one will certainly appear – we do have the assurance of saving a life in the near future. The question is this: are both necessary or is the chance of saving a life the only real operative halachic concern?

[23] This question has been put to other halachic authorities; not all have agreed. The degree of likelihood necessary to approximate *lefaneinu* status is a matter of judgment.

[24] R. Y. Zilberstein.

then allowed to trip but is re-started on the second patient instead of the first. The automatic stoppage avoids the prohibition of directly stopping the machine, and although there is ordinarily an obligation to re-start ventilation when it stops, there is now a second patient who has priority for that ventilation; it is therefore started on the second rather than re-started on the first.

More general application of this suggestion is currently being examined in both the halachic and secular worlds. Some (secular) institutions are considering this method for deploying ICU ventilators to avoid the problem of improperly withholding ventilation from patients who are judged too ill to ventilate for fear that they may be impossible to wean.[25] This device would allow all patients to be ventilated; those who prove impossible to wean where a decision is made to stop therapy would simply not have their ventilators re-started after automatic cut-off. Needless to say such an application would raise major halachic problems.[26]

---

[25] The dilemma currently faced by major hospitals is this: some patients who might benefit from ventilation are denied even a trial of ventilation – there is a reluctance to allow a liberal policy for ventilating very ill patients for fear of arriving at a situation in which ventilation resources are taken up by patients who cannot be weaned from ventilation thereby depriving others who could have been saved because these resources are scarce. Since prognostic tools for predicting which patients will recover are inaccurate, policies tend to reserve ventilation opportunities for those who are clearly good candidates for recovery. Such policies inevitably doom at least some patients who might have been saved. Therefore a system that would allow more patients a trial of therapy without leading to ventilators being taken up indefinitely by patients who will not recover is sorely needed.

[26] See Halperin M. Clinical experiment in secured systems that transform ventilation into discrete treatment – ethical introduction. Report submitted to Israeli Ministry of Health by the officer of medical ethics [in Hebrew]. Ministry of Health, Jerusalem 2002; Section A3.

Cosmetic Surgery

Cosmetic surgery presents a number of issues of potential halachic concern in addition to the question of risk and danger.[1]

1. Manipulating the natural

What is the Torah attitude to changing a natural feature? This question applies broadly: is it acceptable to change geographical features? Is it acceptable to change or manipulate biological organisms in general? Genetic modification in the plant and animal kingdoms is common today; are these allowed?

There is no general Torah prohibition in this area.[2] On the contrary, the world was given into human dominion and it is permitted to exert whatever control over the natural world is necessary for the benefit of mankind. There are certain specific Torah prohibitions concerning grafting of plant species and animal interbreeding, but there is no general constraint on altering features of the natural world.

Cosmetic surgery therefore does not infringe any specific Torah prohibition in this area.

---

[1] For reviews and references see: Nishm. Avraham Vol. II p. 60; A. Steinberg, Encyclopedia of Jewish Medical Ethics, Vol. III p. 1036.

[2] See Genetic Engineering in R. JD Bleich, Bioethical Dilemmas Vol. II, p.133 for a general review of this question. Cf. however Tzitz Eliezer 11:41 in the context of cosmetic surgery.

2. Injury

There is a Torah prohibition involved in causing injury. One may not inflict a wound or allow a wound to be inflicted on oneself. Surgery, no matter how minor, constitutes wounding and raises the question of this prohibition.

However, Rabbi Feinstein[3] makes it clear that this is not a relevant concern. The reason is that in codifying the laws of wounding, the Rambam[4] states that a wound that is caused *"b'derech nitzayon"* (in a malicious or aggressive manner) or according to an alternative edition *"b'derech bizayon"* (in a humiliating manner) is the type of wound that is forbidden. This clearly indicates that only a wound inflicted with malicious or harmful intent is forbidden; in fact the Torah source for this prohibition is in the context of an injury inflicted with clear intention to harm. Therefore, states Rabbi Feinstein, there is no prohibition involved in causing a surgical wound whose intention is entirely positive. Appropriately indicated surgery would therefore not invoke any problem in this category of Torah constraint.

3. Male cross-dressing

The Torah prohibits both male and female cross-dressing.[5] However, the prohibition for a male to wear female clothing goes further than disallowing only female garments; it includes any attention to beauty that is generally practised by women such as the wearing of cosmetics or shaving the legs or underarms or other such feminine beautifications relevant in a particular community. Now the question is this: when a man undertakes a cosmetic operation, is he committing a transgression in this category? Does a face-lift or hair transplant performed on a man breach this Torah stricture? This question has a long reach: if there is a prohibition here it may apply to cosmetic dentistry and numerous other categories of appearance-enhancing therapy.

The general approach of halachic decisors in this area has been lenient. Where a man requires a procedure to improve his appearance for a valid reason such as the correction of a scar or deformity that is the cause of

---

[3] Igr. Moshe, Ch.M. 2:66.

[4] Rambam, Hil. Chovel u'Mazik 5:5.

[5] Deut. 22:5.

distress, this should not be seen as a feminine concern that ought to raise the question of wearing women's garments. The suffering caused by physical deformity is real; the shame engendered by a bodily feature that makes human interaction awkward is at least as great a suffering as pain due to physical causes[6] and it is entirely legitimate to attempt correction of such pathologies.

Of course, the frivolous desire to improve appearance where such improvement is unnecessary is inappropriate and may well contravene the prohibition of female-type beautification for a male. In fact such a procedure may be prohibited for other reasons too, such as the risk involved (see below); such prohibitions apply to men no more or less than to women who wish to undertake inappropriate surgical procedures. The line dividing the frivolous desire for unnecessary beautification and a genuine need for modification of an unsightly feature may be fine; there is a large subjective component in this area. Objective factors may play a part too: a man who appears in public in the course of his professional activities may have a greater need for correction of a deformity than one who does not.

The general principle to be applied here (for both males and females) is to decide whether a cosmetic procedure is genuinely indicated for the correction of an unsightly feature that is causing real suffering. Where there is a genuine reticence to interact socially, and certainly where there is difficulty in finding employment or a suitable marriage partner due to the blemish, there is no reason to prohibit its surgical correction.

4. Tattooing

Modern cosmetic surgery occasionally involves tattooing. Probably the commonest application of this technique is in fashioning the nipple-areola complex during breast reconstruction[7] (both male and female; approximately 1% of breast cancers occur in males). Older techniques used skin grafting from a darker area of the body to achieve a normal-looking areola; this approach has significant drawbacks: a donor-site scar is created, infection is a possibility, and it may be difficult to achieve a

---

[6] Tosf., Shabbat 50b.

[7] Spear SL; Arias J; Long-term experience with nipple-areola tattooing. Annals of Plastic Surgery, 1995; 35:3, pp. 232-236. (This approach is not entirely free of complications; there is a small incidence of infection, rash and sloughing.)

natural appearance due to contraction of the grafted skin. It is also difficult to achieve a near-exact replica of the contralateral breast. A newer approach employs tattooing pigment into the skin to give the appearance of areolar pigmentation; the results can be near-perfect.

There is however a Torah prohibition of tattooing.[8] May this be done in the course of a cosmetic procedure? Rabbi Eliashiv's opinion in a particular case of breast reconstruction (involving both a Jewish patient and a Jewish surgeon) was that it would be preferable for a non-Jewish assistant to perform the tattooing.[9]

5. Risk

All medical interventions carry risk; in cosmetic surgery risk is undertaken for a benefit that is not lifesaving.[10] To permit a cosmetic procedure the risk must be relatively low and the benefit must be significant enough to warrant the intervention.[11] As noted above, psychological suffering is at least as great as physical suffering (as far as such categories can be compared) so that mental anguish is a real indication permitting the acceptance of risk in halacha.

---

[8] Leviticus 19:28; Rambam Hilch. Av. Zara 12:11; Sh. Aruch Y.D. 180:1. Tattooing was done as a religious statement; the tattoo typically depicted a religious symbol or writing and represented a branding indicating permanent dedication to a pagan deity.

[9] See: R. S. Wosner, Shevet HaLevi 10:137; R. N. Gestetner, Teshuvot Lehorot Natan 10:64; R. E. Basri, Techumin 10:282-287; R. S. Schneebalg, Teshuvot Shraga HaMeir 8:44 and 45. There are extensive discussions among the halachic authorities concerning cosmetic tattooing: a central question is whether the Torah prohibition relates only to the tattooing of writing or symbols of a religious nature; a second question concerns whether there is a rabbinic prohibition that extends to forms of tattooing that do not feature words or symbols and whether this may be relaxed in cases of medical need.

[10] Many cosmetic procedures are performed under local or regional anesthesia; however these techniques are not entirely free of risk. Where the option exists, local anesthesia should be preferred over general. Some halachic authorities hold that modern anesthetics (and many modern surgical procedures) are safe enough and sufficiently widely accepted that they are covered by the general halachic dispensation of *"shomer p'taim Hashem* – God protects the simple" (R. S Z Auerbach quoted in Nishm. Avraham vol. II p. 59). See Low Risk, p. 45.

[11] See above, Approach to Risk in Halacha, p. 45 for an extended discussion.

Therefore, cosmetic procedures that fall into the moderate risk category are allowed where good reason exists. A cosmetic procedure that enables a person to find employment, marry or simply to feel able to mix with others without shame would be allowed where the procedure does not entail excessively high risk.

In summary, where the risks are reasonable, a genuine indication exists and surgery is likely to alleviate the problem, cosmetic procedures are allowed.

Valid Indications for Cosmetic Procedures

Genuine indications include disfigurements causing embarrassment and physical features that limit employment or marriage opportunities. Promoting and maintaining marital harmony occupies a particularly privileged place in the hierarchy of Jewish values; therefore cosmetic procedures that are likely to enhance the quality of the husband-wife relationship are given special consideration. An example of this would be a situation in which a woman has a physical blemish or feature that obstructs her relationship with her husband due to his sensitivity to that particular feature. Where she is willing to undergo surgery and it is clear that the surgery is likely to eliminate the problem, then provided the risk is reasonable, surgery would be permitted even if the blemish in question is of a nature that most men would not find offensive. Despite the fact that the blemish is a subjective problem for this particular husband, since it is a real problem in this marriage and surgery is likely to solve it, surgery would be permitted.

Of course as a practical matter care must be taken to ensure that the medical indications for surgery are valid; plastic surgeons are well aware that many personality and relationship problems present as requests for surgery where surgery is unlikely to solve the problem. Great care must be exercised in this area; this is as much a problem of good medical practice as it is a halachic problem – medical halacha always demands good medicine.

Experimental Therapy and Research

Experimental and non-Established Therapies

There are significant halachic constraints on what may be done to research subjects.[1] In order to understand these, it is necessary to have a grasp of the underlying Torah philosophy (*hashkafa* or worldview). In the Torah view, healing is seen as emanating from the Creator. However, humans have an obligation to act in the natural world and not rely passively on Divine intervention. This obligation raises the question of finding the correct balance between responsible human action and the humility that must be manifest by the appropriate restraint of that action.[2] Too much assertion of human control represents a lack of faith; too little human effort represents a failure to act responsibly in the natural world as required by halacha. One must not act to the degree that would generate a false sense of human independence from the Divine, and yet one may not assume passively that Divine intervention, miraculous or otherwise, will supervene.[3]

Applied to the practice of medicine, this balance means acting with professional responsibility of the highest standard and yet acknowledging that the healing results not directly from the physician's actions but from a higher Source. It also means that the therapeutic modalities chosen must meet the standard of best accepted practice, but that there is no obligation to apply therapies that are untested and not established. Grasping at therapeutic straws in desperate situations is not appropriate; if all the best

---

[1] See Minch. Yitzchak 1:27-28; 6.99; Nishm. Avraham, Vol. II p. 11; R. G. Rabinowitz in R. M. Hershler, Halacha and Medicine, Vol. 3, p. 115.

[2] See Chazon Ish, Letters Vol. I, no. 136.

[3] Ramban, Leviticus 26:11, referring to previous generations; and in T. HaAdam. See Rambam, Mishna Pesachim 4:10 and Mishna Nedarim 4:4; Birchei Yosef Y.D. 336:2; Tzitz Eliezer 5, Ramat Rachel 1, 20, 21 and 10:25:30.

standard therapeutics do not result in a favorable clinical response there is no reason to apply unknown and untried methods. Since any healing that may be forthcoming will come from the Source of all healing, that Source does not require the help of outlandish efforts. This does not mean that experimental therapy and clinical research are never appropriate; but it does mean that there are clear restraints on what may be done in research, and it means that experimental therapies are certainly not obligatory in the sense that standard therapies are.

This is one reason for halacha's conservative approach to unestablished therapies, even in frustrating or desperate medical situations. While it may be true that desperate situations demand desperate means, even those desperate means should be ones that have established efficacy.

Any, and if necessary all, established modalities must be used to treat illness, whether life-threatening or not; but there is no obligation to apply potential therapies that have no record of effectiveness and certainly not where they are likely to add danger.

What are the criteria for attempting an experimental therapy? The therapy should be one that would be approved by experts in the field; all possible theoretical and laboratory background work must have been done; the therapy is not known to be unduly dangerous; and the patient consents to the therapy (a patient is not halachically obliged to undergo experimental therapy – it is discretionary). When initial research was being performed on implantable defibrillators, Rabbi Feinstein was asked when it might be appropriate to carry out a human trial. He answered that it would not be acceptable to endanger a human subject until all the relevant research had been completed.

Research and Clinical Trials

The criteria for carrying out a controlled trial of a new therapy in human subjects include the following:[4]

1. Possible risk or harm to participants is expected to be very small, in both the short and the long term (a very rough rule for a researcher's deciding whether the risk is small enough would be to determine whether he would subject his own closest family members to that risk);

---

[4] Rabbi Y. Zilberstein, quoting Rabbi Eliashiv on a number of points.

2. Real evidence exists to suggest that the therapy on trial is likely to be beneficial;

3. Participants' ongoing treatment will not be compromised in any way by stopping their regular therapy or by delaying the start of needed therapy (Rabbi Eliashiv is of the opinion that a trial should not be performed if participants must stop regular effective treatment during the trial of an agent of unknown effectiveness);

4. Informed consent is obtained; this means that all dangers are explained. Risks of over one per thousand must be explicit (a risk of death that is less than 1 in 1,000 or a risk of harm that is less than 1 in 100 need not necessarily be explained);[5]

5. No direct or indirect pressure may be applied to subjects; subjects must not be in any compromised situation that might constitute pressure or impede judgment;

6. Subjects will exit the trial if any untoward effect occurs, or as soon as the trial (or another) shows that the therapy on trial is ineffective or harmful;

7. Placebo is not used when the control should be standard therapy and not placebo (although the use of a placebo is not intrinsically forbidden);

8. The trial is authorized by recognized medical and ethical bodies with no vested interest;

9. Subjects may be compensated for participating;[6]

10. Investigators may be salaried if pay will not generate a problem of vested interest and thereby risk the safety of participants (or risk distorting the results of the trial);

11. Proxy carers may give consent where patients cannot; the most senior responsible proxy must do so.

---

[5] See Coercion and Consent, pp. 160-162 for discussion of this point.

[6] See Nidda 47.

Screening and Prevention

It is a medical truism that "prevention is better than cure." There are many sources indicating that prevention of harm in general and disease in particular are halachic obligations.[1] To what extent are modern screening and prevention strategies obligatory?

Screening

It is halachically acceptable to participate in screening programs for the detection of early stage disease or susceptibility.[2] Where a screening practice is standard, such as testing of newborns for treatable inborn errors of metabolism and other congenital conditions, or junior school hearing and vision testing, such screening is probably halachically obliged and failure to screen would be negligent. Where a screening test is available but not widespread and standard, although undergoing such tests is allowed, it is not obligatory.[3]

---

[1] Rambam, Hilch. Deot.

[2] See detailed reviews in Nishm. Avraham Vol. III, p. 318 and A. Steinberg, Encyclopedia of Jewish Medical Ethics Vol. III, p. 825.

[3] Screening programs of dubious effectiveness should be avoided. See Brink S. For the Busy Exec, a $2000 physical. Los Angeles Times, February 18, 2008.

A journal editorial comments: "In corporate boardrooms throughout the United States, executives are wrestling with the management of health care costs [and] demanding health care services that are effective and evidence-based... There's some irony, then, in the fact that many of these executives leave these

The general principle is that a technical standard that is accepted throughout society defines a norm in halachic terms. This applies to medicine no less than to other areas, and to the detection and prevention of illness in particular. Screening tests that are demonstrably effective but not yet standard in practice are not obligatory – one is not obliged to seek out and undertake every possible action that may yield benefit (in any field of human effort); one should follow a balanced and normal path exercising those options that are accepted and standard and not obsessively seeking every possible option. However, when a clear norm is defined in broad practice, that norm represents the balanced and normal path that ought to be followed, and in some cases refraining from such activities is considered halachically improper.[4]

Some screening programs have become widespread: newborn screening, cervical cytological screening, mammography for women over the age of 50 years and blood pressure monitoring for adults are all widely practised. Prostate-specific antigen (PSA) tests for men,[5] occult blood

---

boardrooms for days at a time to take part in one of modern medicine's most expensive and least proven approaches to care: the executive physical... Most involve a... day or two during which the executive undergoes an extensive and comprehensive battery of in-depth medical tests and evaluations, with results made available immediately... Most cost thousands of dollars..." Rank B. Executive Physicals — Bad Medicine on Three Counts. N Engl J Med 2008; 359:1424-1425. See the subsequent correspondence in N Engl J Med 2009; 360:421-423. See also Boulware LE, Marinopoulos S, Phillips KA, et al. Systematic review: the value of the periodic health evaluation. Ann Intern Med 2007;146:289-300.

[4] There is room for some flexibility here; since the balance between responsible action and trusting to Divine protection with less active effort is a personal one that should depend on the individual's stage of spiritual development, determining exactly how much effort to make in any area of life requires personal assessment; see above, p. 203 and notes 2 and 3 there.

[5] "In the United States, most men over the age of 50 years have had a prostate-specific-antigen (PSA) test, despite the absence of evidence from large, randomized trials of a net benefit. Moreover, about 95% of male urologists and 78% of primary care physicians who are 50 years of age or older report that they have had a PSA test themselves..." Barry, MJ. Screening for Prostate Cancer – the Controversy That Refuses to Die. New Engl J Med 2009;360:1351.

See the two large US and European studies in this NEJM issue examining the question of effectiveness of screening for prostate disease.

screening and routine colonoscopies[6] are becoming standard. Pre-marital genetic screening is available and is more or less standard in some communities.[7] Good antenatal care includes careful monitoring of a number of maternal and fetal parameters during pregnancy; these are directly relevant clinically and are certainly standard. Failure to monitor a pregnancy as required by modern obstetrical standards is therefore both medically and halachically negligent.[8] Screening for various diseases among families with strong histories of those diseases is widely recommended and in many cases certainly forms the standard of responsible care.

Prevention

The concerns and halachic considerations that apply to screening apply similarly to preventive strategies. Many preventive maneuvers are standard in modern medicine: in many institutions newborns receive antiseptic eyedrops and vitamin K, mothers receive oxytocics during the second stage of labor and surgical patients receive prophylactic anticoagulation designed to prevent venous thrombosis. Children undergo an extensive regimen of immunizations.[9] Lifestyle modifications with attention to diet, exercise, the avoidance of smoking and excessive sun exposure are recognized as standard. Society in general pays attention to sanitation, food and water supply quality, air pollution prevention, road safety and community health education. Here again, what has become standard defines the halachic norm.

Risks

What is the halacha when screening or prevention involves risk? Certain childhood immunizations will almost certainly result in rare instances of harm; are these allowed?[10] Mammography will detect a known proportion

---

[6] Rabbi Eliashiv is of the opinion that routine colonoscopy is a good practice but does not amount to an absolute obligation.

[7] See Genetic Screening in R JD Bleich, Bioethical Dilemmas Vol. II, p. 99.

[8] See Interventions in Pregnancy, p. 89 for tests that should be avoided and further details.

[9] See above, pp. 46-48.

[10] Halachic authorities debate the question of imposing a risk to avert a danger that is not yet active – may a risky intervention be used to prevent a future

of early stage breast disease; however exposure to mammography radiation will also induce a small number of tumors over time. In all these cases, screening and prevention programs attempt to maximize benefit for minimum risk (mammography for women aged 40 to 50 has generally been abandoned because the risk of the extra years of radiation exposure was judged to be too high for the benefit of the number of growths detected in that age cohort); but there is always some risk.

The general principle here is that the small risk involved in modern screening and prevention strategies is acceptable where the tests or preventive maneuvers are standard; one need not fear danger when one is behaving according to a sensible and broadly practised norm. Judgment may be required in specific instances: has a particular test or immunization become standard or not? Specific situations may require scrutiny, but the principle is clear. Similarly, individuals faced with questions of prophylactic surgery, for example in the case of familial conditions where significant danger may be averted at the cost of relatively major surgery, will have to seek halachic guidance (which will be based on the level of risks, personal perceptions of those risks and personal preferences, and current professional recommendations).[11]

---

threat? See Minch. Avraham 42 and Achiezer 2:72 who rule that future danger can be regarded as active (thus, in a case where abortion is allowed because of danger to the mother's life, the fetus can be aborted before labor begins if it will cause danger during labor); but see Seridei Eish II, p. 320.

See Tif. Yisrael Mishna Yoma 8:7 Boaz 3 who allows smallpox vaccination with a mortality of 1 in 1,000 where the mortality of the disease is higher than this; and Minch. Shlomo 2:29:4. See Tzitz Eliezer, 15:70 for underlying principles.

[11] See Clinical Case 22, p. 211.

Clinical Cases – Prevention

Clinical Case 22: Prophylactic Surgery

A 37 year old mother of two (a boy and a girl) underwent resection of a breast malignancy and chemotherapy one year ago; it is not clear whether the chemotherapy has affected her fertility. On genetic testing she is found have the BRCA gene; her mother died of ovarian cancer at a young age. Her doctors recommend that she undergo prophylactic bilateral mastectomy and oophorectomy. She is willing to undergo both procedures with immediate breast reconstruction following the mastectomies.

Background facts:

1. Ovarian cancer is usually diagnosed late; in many cases the disease has spread by the time of diagnosis.

2. There is a three-fold risk of breast or ovarian cancer in women who have an affected first-degree relative.

3. The BRCA gene gives a risk of breast cancer of 60-80%. The risk in the general population is approximately 10%. Mastectomy reduces the risk to 5% (but not to 0%).

4. The BRCA gene gives a risk of ovarian cancer of 20-40%. The risk in the general population is approximately 1%. Oophorectomy reduces the risk to 4% (but not to 0%).

5. Current recommendations for women who are BRCA carriers include prophylactic bilateral mastectomy and oophorectomy at age 35-40 or at the age at which the youngest affected family member was diagnosed.

Questions:

This woman has a number of risk factors for developing another malignancy: she has already had breast cancer, her mother was affected at a young age, and she carries the BRCA gene. In this setting, what is the correct halachic approach with regard to the following questions:

A. Surgery:

1. Is mastectomy obligatory in these circumstances?

2. Is oophorectomy permitted? (Female sterilization is generally halachically prohibited.) Is it obligatory?

3. May the patient decline oophorectomy if she wishes to have more children despite the risk? If she wishes to undergo the procedure, does her husband have a right to object on the grounds that he wants more children?

4. May she refuse mastectomy due to intimate marital concerns despite the risk? Is her husband's opinion halachically relevant?

B. Other issues:

1. Is a woman who is BRCA positive obliged to divulge that fact to a prospective spouse before marriage?

2. Is this woman's daughter obliged to undergo genetic testing to ascertain whether she has inherited the BRCA gene? If so, at what age?

3. Are all women obliged to undergo screening for BRCA status? (At present it is not clear that close follow-up of BRCA positive women alters their prognosis.)

Analysis:[12]

A. Surgery:

1. Due to the high risk to her life, the mastectomies should be performed.

2. Despite the prohibition of sterilization,[13] the oophorectomies should be performed.[14] Danger to life takes precedence over this prohibition.

---

[12] R. Y. Zilberstein.

[13] Analysis of this prohibition is beyond the present scope. See Sh. Aruch E.H. 5:11 and commentary of the Vilna Gaon there (sub. sec. 25). See Igr. Moshe E.H. 1:13 for further discussion in circumstances where alternatives to sterilization exist.

[14] Practical aspects of the surgery that should be given attention in order to minimize the prohibition are beyond the present scope.

3. The patient should not risk her life in order to have more children when the risks are high.[15] This is particularly true where the hormonal changes of pregnancy may increase the risk of malignancy. However, if the patient wishes to delay her oophorectomy for a year or two in order to have another child, this would be halachically acceptable (subject to medical opinion confirming that neither the delay nor the pregnancy itself will significantly increase her risk).

Her husband has no right to object to surgery; his wife's health and safety are paramount concerns.

May the husband insist on divorce after his wife's oophorectomy so that he can marry again in order to have children? A married woman who refuses to become pregnant on the grounds of abnormal pain and discomfort (in cases where her suffering will be severe) may do so;[16] in such a case she must agree to a divorce in order to allow her husband to remarry and produce offspring if he so desires. But that is true only where there is no danger to her life, and her husband has not yet fulfilled the commandment to have children; in our case the woman's life is in danger and the husband has already fulfilled his obligation – in such a case she is not required to agree to a divorce.[17] Due to circumstances entirely beyond her control she needs to undergo a procedure (oophorectomy) that will render her sterile; this is halachically analogous to the situation of a couple where it transpires after marriage that the wife is unable to conceive – in such a case she is not required to consent to divorce. Since she has done nothing to cause the problem, she is not required to agree.

4. Mastectomy: she should not refuse the procedure in view of the high risk. The husband has no right to obstruct her (particularly in view of the availability of modern breast reconstruction techniques); protecting her health is his obligation.

---

[15] It is essential to realize that these halachic responses apply to this particular case, where the risks are high and the couple have children. Where risks are lower or where a couple is childless, different responses may be appropriate. See Igr. Moshe E.H. 4:73 (3) concerning fertility therapy for couples who have children.

[16] See Ch. Sofer, E.H. 1:20.

[17] R. Y. Sh. Eliashiv. See Me'il Tzedaka (33), quoted in P. Teshuva (E.H. 154:26), who states that a husband whose wife has borne him one child (either a son or a daughter) may not divorce her against her will to allow him to remarry and father more children (since he has at least procreated).

B. Other issues:

1. A woman is required to divulge that she is a BRCA carrier to a prospective spouse at some time before marriage.

2. The daughter should undergo genetic testing; this should be done before the age at which she may be expected to develop disease, or before she reaches the age of marriage if that will be earlier.

3. There is no general obligation for all women to undergo BRCA screening; on the contrary, there may be grounds for avoiding this.

PART TWO

LIFE AND DEATH ISSUES IN JEWISH MEDICAL ETHICS AND THE MODERN WORLD

Life and Death Issues in Jewish Medical Ethics and the Modern World

Jewish doctors in the West find themselves practising in a medical and cultural milieu that reflects modern Western values. It is important to know and understand this context and to recognize where it intersects the world of Torah values and practice. At present, in a number of areas current norms are sharply at variance with those of Torah, and the gap appears to be widening.

The following chapters aim to identify some of the areas of divergence between these two worldviews, mainly by means of considering items from the current mainstream medical and general literature in order to trace the development of modern values that affect life and death decision making in clinical medicine and their steepening trajectory away from Jewish (and traditional) values.

Before considering specific applications, however, it is useful to identify the general principles of modern medical ethics and to note the differences between these as understood in the secular context and in Judaism.

Comparison of Torah and Secular Principles

In a system that is firmly based on evolutionary theory there is no intrinsic holiness, or indeed meaning, to a human life. In such a system, decisions affecting human life can be made with very broad latitude; the only constraints will be those decided and legislated by the current social ethos. Policies based on notions of quality of life and indeed the very definitions of that quality will shift with the spirit of the times.

Where evolution frames the reality, man is essentially dispensable because he is only a biological reality, protoplasm really, no different in principle than a monkey or an ameba. In such a worldview man's life is not painted on a canvas larger than any animal's. Accountability for human life cannot extend beyond the individual and the collective conscience.

In the Torah view however, the value of human life is immeasurably great, and accountability is measured on an absolute scale. These worldviews could hardly be further apart.

Ironically, Torah sees animals as having value and meaning, even sanctity – killing an animal is a deplorable act.[1] Man was originally not allowed to kill animals for food. Cruelty to animals is a stringent halachic prohibition, and there is a universal human prohibition of eating a limb or part torn from a live animal. Judaism sees foxhunting, bullfighting and other forms of torturing animals for sport as beneath contempt; a Jewish society would never tolerate such brutality. But despite all that, the distinction between humans and animals is crucial; human sanctity transcends the animal beyond measure.

THE FOUR PRINCIPLES

Modern medical ethics are generally predicated on the four basic principles of autonomy, justice, beneficence and non-maleficence.[2] From a Torah perspective, all of these are valid and important, but difficulty arises when their details are considered: in practice, the remit of each of

---

[1] "For he has spilled blood..." (Leviticus 17:4) referring to the inappropriate killing of an animal.

[2] Beauchamp TL and Childress JF, Principles of Biomedical Ethics, 5th ed., (Oxford, 2001).

these depends on its definitions and limitations, and these are often very different in the secular world than in Torah.

Other principles governing modern practice such as veracity, privacy and confidentiality may also have different limits in halacha.[3]

AUTONOMY

This is usually presented as the primary criterion in the hierarchy of secular medical ethical principles (although in practice there are scenarios in which it may need to be limited by one or more of the others). Indeed, beneficence and non-maleficence are effectively null in many cases where patient autonomy conflicts with these – the patient's wishes will determine what is beneficent for that patient. If a terminal patient chooses to die by refusing lifesaving therapy, allowing that death may be regarded as beneficent *because* that is what the patient wants, and withdrawing life support in such a case will not constitute a maleficent act for the same reason. Even where an action or omission may not be regarded as beneficent in this way, as for example in the case of refusal to accept a blood transfusion for religious reasons, that decision will be allowed and protected by law on the basis of the patient's right to choose autonomously. In such a case, autonomy is clearly being set above beneficence and indeed all other competing factors.

In the liberal Western tradition, autonomous self-determination is a core value, perhaps even the root value. This is not surprising – in a godless system, who but the individual should decide? Where the individual's choices do not seriously conflict with the interests of others, there is no reason to impose any constraints on those choices. In halacha, however, although there is wide scope for autonomous expression and indeed in many cases patients are required to make choices, that scope is far more limited. In halacha the individual finds himself in a world of values formed in the image of an Absolute; in such a world there certainly are constraints that should inform the individual's choices. Certain choices will accord with the Absolute standard, others will not.

In the secular world there is a range of opinion concerning how far autonomy should extend. Some theorists insist that autonomy is incompatible with *any* authority external to the individual – no state or religious authority can be allowed to determine action for an individual

---

[3] See below, page 232.

without compromising the individual's autonomy; not even a state or religious authority that the individual willingly accepts.[4] Others take a softer line and hold that autonomy is not compromised when an individual acts in accordance with external authority as long as the individual has accepted that authority autonomously.[5] Both positions require that individuals determine their own actions, however; the disagreement is only with regard to how extreme the individual's independence of choice ought to be.

There is also a debate in the current secular literature concerning whether autonomy implies a *duty* to choose,[6] or only a right.[7] All agree that there is at least a right to autonomous choice; the debate is only with regard to how insistently the patient should be required to choose even in circumstances where the patient may not wish to exercise such autonomy.

Where are the practical limits set in the secular system? There is presently only one generally agreed limit: where the expression of an individual's autonomous choice may harm others, that choice would not be acceptable.[8] [9] In some specific circumstances too, autonomy may be set aside – for example, when an autonomous choice can be made only when a patient is given sufficient information to make that choice but where provision of that information is likely to cause harm (such as severe depression or anguish). In such cases the obligations of beneficence and non-maleficence may be seen as justifying non-disclosure. In general, however, respect for autonomy is a fiercely defended value.[10]

---

[4] See Beauchamp and Childress, p. 104, note 4 for references.

[5] This is the position of Beauchamp and Childress; see p. 60 there.

[6] See Beauchamp and Childress, p. 105, note 9.

[7] Beauchamp and Childress argue strongly for this position; see p. 61 there.

[8] Beauchamp and Childress, p. 65.

[9] Secular courts have consistently held that parents who refuse lifesaving therapy for their children (such as refusing blood transfusion for a child due to religious beliefs) should be overruled. In a recent case an Atlanta judge allowed physicians to transfuse a pregnant woman against her wishes (due to religious conviction) in order to save her fetus during cesarian section.

[10] In a California case an emergency room physician intubated a severely ill AIDS patient in respiratory failure despite the patient's reported previous wishes not to be intubated. The physician did so because the patient's wishes were not

Where are the limits set in halacha? There are three categories of patient choice in medical halacha:[11]

1. Permitted choices; indeed there are situations in which the patient must choose (for example, between various halachically acceptable therapeutic options where each option has a different set of risks and benefits; or where risky therapy may reverse a terminal condition);[12]

2. Choices that are mandated by halachic obligation but cannot be forced on an unwilling patient; such a patient will be acting improperly in halachic terms but may not be coerced (for example, where therapy with a relatively low but significant risk may reverse a terminal condition);

3. Choices that are mandated by halacha and may be imposed against the individual's wishes (for example, where a safe and painless lifesaving therapy is available).

The halacha is often in sharp contrast with the current secular position in this area. Whereas the secular approach looks first to autonomous patient choice, in halacha that priority applies only in the first category above. In the second category an objective halachic obligation is defined and then secondarily posed for subjective choice; in the third category patient choice is not practically relevant.

Autonomy is not a primary or independent value in halacha, not only for the more obvious reason that in Torah a person is not a free agent to determine ultimate values, but for another reason too: in halacha one's body and life are not one's possessions.[13]

The Radbaz[14] brings this out by noting an apparent anomaly in the laws of testimony. In halacha it is a basic principle that one may not testify in matters affecting oneself (or a relative in general, due to a presumed

---

documented and due to the emergency nature of the situation there was no time to verify the details. The patient subsequently sued the physician in a California court for assault and "wrongful life."

[11] See above, Coercion and Consent, p. 155 for details and clinical applications

[12] For examples, see risking temporary life for the chance of long term life, p. 118, and Clinical Case 5, p. 98.

[13] See above, p. 153 and note 3 there.

[14] Radbaz on M. Torah, Sanhedrin 18:6.

vested interest). However, this prohibition is limited to cases involving capital or corporal punishment – one is entirely free to testify thus in financial cases. Why the discrepancy? If there is a suspicion of lack of objectivity in capital and corporal cases, the same concern should apply in financial cases. Or put another way, why is a litigant free to testify concerning himself where money is at stake, but not where the outcome will be lashes or a death sentence? The Radbaz answers that one is free to testify in monetary matters because one's money is in one's legal jurisdiction: your money is yours to deal with as you wish. *But your body and your life are not yours:* who are you to incur lashes or death when those will be imposed on a body or a life that are not yours?

In an extended analysis,[15] Rabbi Shlomo Yosef Zevin demonstrates that Shylock's contract with Antonio is intrinsically invalid halachically – not because of any prohibition of assault or injury that may protect Antonio from the loss of a pound of his flesh, but for the more basic reason that his body is not his to pledge in the first place.

Competence

A vexed issue in the area of respect for autonomy is the issue of assessing competence to decide. At exactly which point is the ability to choose compromised by mental or emotional factors or indeed by illness itself? Here too there is a significant difference between current secular norms and halacha. In the secular system, much emphasis is placed on assessing the patient's capacity to choose; *what* he chooses is of less concern. For example, in the case of a depressed patient who requests assistance in dying, a primary concern in secular law and practice will be to determine whether the depression has an undue bearing on the request to die. A real danger here is that in the effort to respect autonomy, patients may be allowed to make inappropriate decisions with catastrophic consequences. Evidence suggests that this may not be uncommon: between 1998 and 2006, only 12.6% of patients who received prescriptions for lethal drugs in Oregon were referred for psychiatric evaluation; in 2007, none of those receiving such drugs were referred.[16] A study conducted between 2004 and 2006 suggested that patients in Oregon who requested physician-

---

[15] R. SY. Zevin, L'Ohr HaHalacha 2nd ed. (Tel Aviv, 5717) pp. 318-335.

[16] Physician-Assisted Death – From Oregon to Washington State. N Engl J Med Dec 11, 2008.

assisted suicide were not all screened adequately for depression and that "some potentially ineligible patients" may have received prescriptions for lethal drugs.[17] At present, depression *per se* is not seen as invalidating compliance with a request to die; the only question is whether the depression may be compromising the patient's competence to decide.[18]

In halacha, a request to die in the setting of clinical depression should be seen as an indication for counselling or psychotherapy rather than as an indication for providing a prescription for lethal drugs. In fact, helping a patient to commit suicide instead of attempting to provide appropriate therapy for pain, anguish and depression constitutes a dereliction of *medical* duty, quite apart from the issue of ethical failure. It has been shown that when symptoms are treated aggressively, in many cases the desire to actively hasten death may disappear. An instructive example is that of a famous suicidal patient of the 1980s, Elizabeth Bouvia.[19] Quadriplegic and in pain, she abandoned her legal quest to commit suicide with medical assistance after she was given control over the administration of her own morphine and has continued to live ever since.[20] Judaism would see this as an example of a patient who was misdiagnosed by a wrong worldview; even the patient did not know what she needed until she was fortuitously given the correct treatment.

In the secular system, competence to decide is the primary issue, not the value of life. In halacha, treating the patient and saving life where possible are the primary issues.[21]

---

[17] Ganzini L, Goy ER, Dobscha SK. Prevalence of depression and anxiety in patients requesting physicians' aid in dying: cross sectional survey. BMJ 2008;337:973-5.

[18] See below, p. 237.

[19] Bouvia v. Superior Court, 179 Cal. App. 3d 1127, 225 Cal. Rptr. 297 (1986).

[20] Drugs can not only relieve depression and pain, they can also give patients a sense of control that permits them to live, as this case illustrates. It has been pointed out that in jurisdictions where physician-assisted suicide is legal, physicians are paradoxically more free to prescribe lethal drugs with the intent that patients use them to kill themselves than some less dangerous drugs that might prevent suicide by enhancing the quality of their lives. See Annas G.J, Death by Prescription. N Engl J Med 1994;331:1240-1243.

[21] See Appendix I, How a Rabbi Decides an Issue in Medical Halacha.

There are further Jewish concerns about the principle of autonomy as practised today. It has been noted that respect for autonomy is not applied evenly in the current ethos. For example, when a patient chooses to terminate life that decision will be respected even when the attending doctors believe that continued treatment would be reasonable; however, where a patient chooses to continue living where doctors believe that choice is unreasonable, there may be serious resistance and even flat refusal on the part of medical staff to continue treatment. But if patient autonomy is such a strong principle that it must be respected to end life even when life could be prolonged, then surely it must be accepted to prolong life when that is the patient's choice too. This is clearly not the case today.[22]

Put more starkly, an unreasonable choice to die must be respected; an unreasonable choice to live must not. This anomaly exists in modern practice perhaps because a fully autonomous decision to die is never really seen as unreasonable – as long as it is the patient's choice, it must be seen as reasonable. Choosing a life of "low quality" (as defined by the current ethos) is seen as intrinsically unreasonable. It seems that the defining value is not autonomy at all, but the broader question of the value of life and its quality.[23]

NON-MALEFICENCE

The principle of refraining from doing harm is usually traced to the axiom of *"primum non nocere"* or "first do no harm," commonly assumed to be Hippocratic. The phrase is not found in the Hippocratic Oath though it is often given as the Latin paraphrase, by Galen, of a Hippocratic Aphorism. A close approximation is: "to help, or at least to do no harm," from Hippocrates' *Epidemics*, Bk. I, Sect. V.

It is basic to all Jewish morality that one must not cause harm; there is no reason to take issue with this principle as such. Real problems arise, however, when definitions and details must be specified. What constitutes harm? In the modern context, quality of life judgments are made first;

---

[22] See Not a Doctor's Decision, p. 279.

[23] See below, Euthanasia, Suicide, Assisted Suicide and Withholding Therapy in Current Thought and Practice, p. 237.

only then are issues of non-maleficence seen to be relevant.[24] When a patient's quality of life is judged to be sufficiently inadequate, it follows that terminating the patient's life will not be a maleficent act[25] (on the contrary, it will be beneficent). For this reason, in practice there is often a major gap between halacha and modern secular norms. The basic position in Judaism is that there is no quality of life so poor that it justifies active termination of that life.

Many analyses of non-maleficence and beneficence in secular sources conclude that in general neither should be given primacy; there are circumstances where one or the other takes precedence. One correlate of this conclusion is that killing and letting die (extreme transgressions of non-maleficence and beneficence respectively) should ordinarily not be distinguished; one is not worse than the other.[26] This is not correct from a halachic perspective; both killing and letting die (inappropriately) are wrong, but killing is certainly worse, and in halacha there is a practical distinction too: killing will be actionable in some circumstances where letting die may not (although such letting die may be morally derelict). The most important difference between halacha and current secular practice in this area, however, is that in the secular world where it is seen as appropriate to withhold therapy (letting die) it is increasingly seen as appropriate to hasten death actively – this is the practical outcome of a policy that does not distinguish between killing and letting die. In halacha this is very definitely not the case: even in circumstances where therapy may be withheld (indeed even where it *must* be withheld) with the consequence that the patient will die, hastening death actively will certainly not be allowed.[27]

---

[24] "Central to this framework is an interpretation of the principle of non-maleficence that sanctions rather than suppresses quality-of-life judgments." Beauchamp and Childress, p. 113-114.

[25] Sometimes it may be "legitimate to invoke the 'do no harm' maxim as a justification for termination of life." Jonsen AR. Do no harm: axiom of medical ethics. In: Spicker SF, Engelhard HT, eds. Philosophical Medical Ethics: its Nature and Significance. Dordrecht:Reidel, 1977:27-41.

[26] See for example Beauchamp and Childress, chapter 4; Gillon R, Philosophical Medical Ethics (John Wiley, 1986), chapter 20; Hauser M, Moral Minds (Little, Brown 2006), p. xvi.

[27] See above, Withholding Treatment p. 103.

In reality there is some ambivalence in the secular world on the question of equating beneficence and non-maleficence as obligations. Although it is often stressed that in the context of terminal care there should be no distinction between passively withholding therapy and actively terminating life (for example by withdrawing life support), and the converse point is often made that failure to save life is just as culpable as taking life,[28] there are many situations in which it seems obvious that harming is worse than not helping, and that whereas non-maleficence can be enforced, beneficence cannot.[29]

With regard to non-treatment, four distinctions have been important in secular medical ethics[30] (and in various religious traditions):

1. Withholding vs. withdrawing treatment (and related distinctions between acts vs. omissions, and killing vs. letting die);

2. Ordinary vs. extraordinary treatment;

3. Feeding (and artificial feeding) vs. life-sustaining technologies;

---

[28] "[The] distinction between killing and letting die... has no moral importance." Rachels, J. Active and passive euthanasia. N Engl J Med 1975;292:78-80. This author and others state explicitly that not exerting oneself to save a drowning victim is as morally reprehensible as murder (see Hauser M, Moral Minds, in the prologue, and Gillon R, Philosophical Medical Ethics, p. 127) although it would seem that only an extreme utilitarian could hold this position. Indeed, the strong common intuition that suggests a very real difference between these two forms of moral failure has been advanced as a major element in critiques of utilitarianism (see for example, Bernard Williams, Morality, Cambridge Press).

[29] This seems to be the normative position in American law at present. In *McFall v. Shimp* (no. 78-1771 in Equity, C.P. Allegheny County, Pa., July 26, 1978) a man with aplastic anemia required a bone marrow transplant in order to survive; his cousin agreed to donate marrow and began the compatibility testing process but later changed his mind and refused. The court was asked to compel him to continue the testing and to donate if he proved compatible. The legal (and public) debate focused on whether the cousin had a duty of beneficence; the patient's lawyer argued that even if a legal duty of beneficence did not exist, there was an obligation of non-maleficence: according to this argument, agreeing to undergo testing and then backing out had caused a critical delay that violated the obligation of non-maleficence. The court ruled that the cousin had not violated any legal obligation but held that his actions were "morally indefensible." See Case 17, p. 168 for a substantially similar case in halacha.

[30] See Beauchamp and Childress pp. 119-132.

4. Intended effects vs. foreseen but unintended effects.

A number of authorities argue that all four of these distinctions are irrelevant or dangerous.[31] What is their place in halacha?

1. Withholding vs. withdrawing treatment: This distinction is certainly relevant in halacha; for a detailed discussion, see above (page 103).

2. Ordinary vs. extraordinary treatment: This distinction has a long history in some religious traditions and has been influential in Western medical ethical thinking. However, apart from the difficulty of defining the limits of "ordinary" and "extraordinary,"[32] it has little halachic relevance. Where these categories are broadly construed as "beneficial" and "burdensome" respectively they may have halachic relevance; however the terms "ordinary" and "extraordinary" are misleading and should be avoided.

3. Feeding (and artificial feeding) vs. life-sustaining technologies: In practice, the usual question here is whether artificial (medically administered) feeding should be distinguished from other forms of life-sustaining technologies such as ventilators. This question is the subject of disagreement. Some medical authorities and moral philosophers insist that although technologies like ventilators may be withdrawn or withheld, patients may never be starved to death; others see no distinction and allow the withdrawal of feeding tubes and intravenous hydration lines. There can be little doubt that the latter opinion has shaped much of modern law and practice over the past three decades; withholding nutrition and hydration from terminal patients is no longer uncommon.[33]

---

[31] See Beauchamp and Childress pp. 119-132; Gillon, chapters 20-22.

[32] These categories are radically differently construed by various authorities; see for example Beauchamp and Childress p.123 and Gillon, ch. 22.

[33] In the course of defending this practice, Beauchamp and Childress state (p.127): "Evidence also indicates that patients who are allowed to die without artificial hydration sometimes die more comfortably than patients who receive hydration. It is misleading to project the common experience of hunger and thirst on a dying patient who is malnourished and dehydrated. Malnutrition is not identical with hunger; dehydration is not identical with thirst; and starvation is very different from acute dehydration in a medical setting. Caregivers can also

In halacha, necessary food and liquid may never be withheld, although the operative principle in halacha is not the distinction between feeding and other "technologies."[34] Of course, where food or liquid are unnecessary or harmful, they should be withheld – for example, in a terminal patient who is in the acute process of dying; in such a situation food may be at best medically irrelevant. However it is crucial to distinguish this situation from that of a terminally ill patient *who needs food and liquids to survive for the present* – a patient who is expected to die within an hour may need neither food nor liquid, but a patient who is expected to die within a day or two needs liquid, and a patient who is expected to die within a few days or weeks needs both food and liquid; if nutrition or hydration are withheld such patients will certainly die of starvation or dehydration, and that is never allowed.

4. Intended effects vs. foreseen but unintended effects: The "principle of double effect" has a venerable history in ethics. It posits that an act that will produce both benefit and harm (or risk of harm) may be allowed under certain specific conditions. In its usual formulation, four conditions are posited as necessary to permit such an act:

(i) The act itself must be good.

(ii) The agent must intend only the good effect (although the bad effect can be foreseen).

(iii) The bad effect must not be a means to the good effect.

(iv) The good effect must outweigh the bad; or, the good effect must provide sufficient reason to permit the bad effect, that is, it must be sufficiently proportional.

Authorities question the cogency of these conditions; some reduce them to two (intention and proportionality), and some to just one

---

alleviate feelings of hunger, thirst and dryness of the mouth, and related problems by other means, such as ice on the lips...." Jewishly, this is misguided. The concern expressed here is entirely for the patient's comfort in the process of dying, but the real issue is not the patient's symptoms of hunger and thirst – the issue is whether the patient needs food and liquid to survive. The fact that he may "die more comfortably" without hydration does not justify allowing him to dehydrate to death. In halacha the obligation is clear: to provide the necessary hydration and to keep the patient comfortable too.

[34] See above, p. 114.

(proportionality). Many hold that the principle adds nothing useful in resolving ethical dilemmas.[35]

In halacha, actions that will benefit but also harm are certainly allowed and even mandated: abortion to save the mother's life, or amputation of a limb to save a life, for example. Are the classical secular conditions relevant in halacha? Only the fourth, proportionality, finds specific expression in halacha (when examined carefully, the other three will be seen to be inconsistent with halacha or to collapse into the broad requirement that the intended overall outcome must be good).[36] There is in fact much halachic discussion about what proportion of benefit to risk constitutes good enough reason to permit (or indeed mandate) incurring the relevant risk.[37]

Futility

Another vexed issue in this general domain is the question of futile treatment. There is no debate about the inappropriate nature of treatment that is clearly futile – no-one holds that it would be appropriate to continue mechanical ventilation on a patient who has died. The problems arise in distinguishing those situations in which treatment is futile from those in which it is not (what point defines death?) and in defining which types of treatment are futile and which are not.

---

[35] Beauchamp and Childress, p. 128-132. See also Gillon, ch. 21.

[36] The first is not meaningful halachically: an action that will lead to a good outcome and is halachically mandated must be performed; there is no need for deliberation about whether that action would be deemed "good" *a priori* in other circumstances. The second is halachically void: an inevitable effect of an action, despite being undesirable, cannot be deemed to be unintended in halacha. The third is not a necessary condition in halacha: where halachically sanctioned, an undesirable action may be performed in pursuing a necessary end – where a pregnancy must be aborted to save the mother's life, that is permitted despite the fact that the undesirable effect constitutes the means (this does *not* mean that forbidden means are generally justified by good ends – quite the opposite is true in halacha). The fourth is valid: temporary life may be risked in the attempt to achieve long-term cure, but only where the risk is small enough in proportion to the chance of cure (see Risk, p. 45, and Risky Treatment p. 118, for the specific values of this ratio).

[37] See Risk, p. 45 and Risky Treatment, p. 118.

In defining which situations ought to render treatment futile and what sorts of treatment ought to be regarded as futile, there is presently a wide range of opinion. Is treatment futile when it has little chance of success or only when it has no chance?[38] Here it is impossible to avoid value judgments.[39] Technical medical expertise can define statistical limits, but at what statistical limit a chance of cure becomes meaningful is not a technical matter. Similarly, what quality of life renders life itself futile is the subject of extreme disagreement between the secular and the Torah worlds.

This is typically where conflicts arise between the secular approach and halacha, and these conflicts are becoming sharper as modern practice and law increasingly enlarge the boundaries of what is considered futile.[40] Modern ethics and law hold that a doctor is not morally obliged to provide therapy that he considers futile, even against patients' or surrogates' wishes, and the doctor may not even be required to discuss the treatment. A common battleground of this conflict today is the area of treatment and life-support for terminally ill patients.[41]

One version of this conflict arises when treatment is extremely unlikely to have any beneficial physiological effect in a terminally ill patient: in the secular world such therapy will usually be regarded as futile; in Judaism,

---

[38] Some maintain that a treatment is futile only if it has no chance of success, some maintain that anything less than a 13% chance of success represents futility, others that the borderline should drawn when "in the last 100 cases, a medical treatment has been useless." See Truog R, Brett AS, Frader J. The Problem with Futility. N Engl J Med 1992;326:1561; Schneiderman LJ, Jecker NS, Jonsen AR. Medical Futility: Its Meaning and Ethical Implications. Annals Internal Med 1990;112:951; and Schneiderman, Jecker and Jonsen, Medical Futility: Response to Critiques. Annals Internal Med 1996;125:669-74.

[39] Beauchamp and Childress put it thus: "Indeed, 'futility' typically is used to express a combined value judgment and scientific judgment" (p. 134). "Claims of medical futility are often presented as objective and value-free, when in fact they are subjective and value-laden" (p. 192).

[40] "Increasingly, hospitals are adopting policies aimed at denying therapies that physicians judge to be futile..." (Beauchamp and Childress p. 134). Medicine is increasingly arrogating futility decisions to itself – physicians commonly make these decisions on the basis of technical considerations without regard to patients' religious or personal value systems; see p. 279.

[41] For an extreme example, see Not a Doctor's Decision, p. 279.

if continuation of therapy will serve to maintain the patient's sense of hope, it is far from futile and indeed may be obligatory (see page 289).

In the final analysis, futility decisions often collapse into value judgments and quality of life decisions. Thoughtful secular authorities concur on this point,[42] but that serves only to shift the disagreement from the subject of futility to that of the quality of life and its value.

BENEFICENCE

Here again the central problem is one of definition – what is beneficent? Not long ago in Western medicine beneficence meant saving the patient's life at virtually all costs; at least that was the default position. Life was seen as a paramount value. Today, facilitating suicide and even performing euthanasia are increasingly regarded as beneficent. What was actionable then as homicide is laudable now. This shift in values is to be expected in a democratic system: where society decides on its values, those values will change as the ethos of society changes over time. That is not the case in the world of Torah – although halacha is a dynamic process that engages the issues and challenges of each era as new technologies create new moral dilemmas, its underlying values do not change.

In the secular world there is a debate about whether beneficence is an obligation or a virtue (the distinction has practical importance: at least some obligations are enforceable; virtues are not).[43] There is general agreement that some beneficent acts are obligatory (where the risk, cost and effort of the benefactor are small and the need of the recipient is great) and some are simply virtuous but not legally obligatory (where risk, cost or effort of the benefactor is significant and the need of the recipient relatively small). Overall, three categories can be discerned: acts that are morally and legally obligatory, acts that are morally obligatory but not legally enforceable, and those that are virtuous but not obligatory.

---

[42] Beauchamp and Childress, p. 133.

[43] In McFall v. Shimp no. 78-1771 in Equity, C.P. Allegheny County, Pa., July 26, 1978 (see note 29 above), in which a man refused to donate bone marrow to his cousin who was dying of aplastic anemia due to his fear of possible complications, the court held that there was a moral obligation but not an enforceable legal one.

In the halachic view it is correct that risk to the benefactor must be weighed against need, and there is a nuanced spectrum ranging from obligation to virtue (in halacha, all virtues are in fact obligatory in some sense; however this is not the place for a detailed exposition). The differences between secular and halachic standards are in defining where the limits are to be set in weighing these proportions – how much of one's income should be given to charity is clearly defined in halacha (both a lower limit that is obligatory and an upper limit that is virtuous); in the secular world opinions vary widely. There is ongoing debate in modern ethics about levels of risk and expense that should be undertaken for patients or in rescue efforts;[44] halachic precedent provides guidelines for these situations.[45]

JUSTICE

There are many theories of justice in the secular world and it is clear that no consensus has emerged on setting up a fundamental hierarchy of values; this is a problem that continues to tax philosophers and social theorists. In medicine, the main challenges in this category arise in apportioning healthcare resources for individuals and for society at large. There are points of conflict between halacha and current secular standards in triage decision-making as well as points of agreement.[46]

Other Principles and Values

Besides these four foundational principles, a number of others govern modern medical ethical practice:

Veracity

Telling patients the truth is generally agreed to be a non-absolute value: there are situations in which withholding information and even distorting it may be justified, such as when open disclosure is likely to cause harm. However, defining the nature and limits of this obligation is problematic. It is often necessary to weigh the benefits of disclosure against its

---

[44] See "The rule of rescue" in Hope, T. Medical Ethics, a Very Short Introduction (Oxford University Press), pp. 32 - 41.

[45] See Risk, above, p. 45 and Costs, pp. 65-67.

[46] See Triage, p. 171 for a discussion of triage criteria in halacha and some points of divergence from secular approaches.

possible harm, and what is considered an appropriate balance has shifted significantly over the recent past. Physicians tend to far more open disclosure today than in a previous age when a more paternalistic style of medical practice was the norm; this shift has been dramatic. In studies performed in 1961 it was found that 88% of doctors sought to avoid disclosing a diagnosis of cancer, whereas in 1979 virtually all doctors surveyed (98%) followed a policy of disclosure. Many reasons for this shift in practice have been identified,[47] some of which may be reasonable from a halachic perspective such as the need to disclose a serious diagnosis where modern therapeutic options exist for which the patient's consent will be needed.

However, in halacha the patient's well-being is paramount: disclosure that may harm is generally prohibited, and it is a common experience nowadays that the secular approach errs on the side of excessive disclosure and also tends to insensitive and alarming disclosure (modern commentators have termed this "truth dumping" and "terminal candor").[48] This is not acceptable in halacha; even when bad news must be delivered there are halachic norms that govern the extremely sensitive manner in which this must be done.[49]

Privacy

Individuals have a right to privacy in modern law and ethics (there is debate about the foundations of this right: some suggest that it is simply an aspect of the principle of respect for autonomy, others see it as more primary). This is unremarkable from a halachic perspective.

Confidentiality

Confidentiality is an aspect of respect for privacy that is widely acknowledged as an obligation in medical ethics (although it is often unnecessarily compromised in modern practice).[50] In principle there need

---

[47] See Beauchamp and Childress, p. 285 and references there.

[48] Beauchamp and Childress, p. 286.

[49] See above, p. 101, note 2 and p. 113, note 45. See also Afterword, p. 289.

[50] Studies show that contrary to patients' expectations, their details are often inappropriately divulged – in up to 70% of cases. See for example Weiss B.D. Confidentiality Expectations of Patients, Physicians, and Medical Students. JAMA 1982;247:2695-97.

be no argument with this obligation from a halachic point of view. In halacha this obligation to a patient becomes null when danger to others (or to the patient) must be averted – in such cases information that would ordinarily be privileged must be divulged. This seems to be the consensus position in secular medical ethics and law at present too.[51]

MORAL DILEMMAS

A broader area of conflict between Torah and secular norms is the field of moral dilemmas – situations in which there may be agreement on the relevant principles, but not on their order of precedence.

It is noteworthy that there is broad agreement on moral principles at the widest level: all agree that there are ethical issues and standards, and almost regardless of the rationale underlying the framework that defines the standards, ethicists agree on the basic ethical issues. The broadest moral principles *in isolation* are not problematic: all agree that stealing, killing for no purpose, hurting people for no reason, breaking a promise for no reason and not recognizing a debt of gratitude are wrong. The problems begin *when basic principles clash.* May one kill for a higher purpose – for example, to save many lives? May one cause suffering for a greater good? Steal to save life or health? Break a promise when the cost of keeping it becomes too high? And what is "too high" in a particular case? Here, reasonable people can (and certainly do) disagree. And critically, there is no uniform or agreed way to resolve reasonable people's opinions on these matters – in a system that admits no outside standard, no clear resolution is possible. There is no agreed universal framework that defines a single clear hierarchy of priorities in the secular

---

[51] Although not without argument: in Tarasoff v. Regents of the University of California, 17 Cal.3d 425 (1976), a psychologist disclosed his client's intention to murder a young woman to the police but not to the intended victim; the threatened murder was in fact committed. The majority opinion held that full disclosure of the danger was improperly withheld; there is no obligation of confidentiality in such situations. The minority opinion held that even in such cases patient confidentiality should not be breached: the reasoning offered was that if such information is not treated in confidence, clients will not feel able to confide in their counsellors; this will hinder therapy and may in fact lead to violence that could have been averted by appropriate therapy. In halacha this debate has a clear resolution: an immediate and specific danger overrides a more distant putative long term interest.

model. There is therefore no resolution to many classical moral dilemmas; many moral theorists doubt that there ever will be.[52]

Medical ethical texts commonly present the classical bioethical dilemmas and delineate how they might be resolved in various competing moral systems; very seldom is an overall and definitive solution offered – there very seldom is one because there is as yet no overall system of priorities that is agreed.

In Torah, the ordering of principles is as fundamental an aspect of halacha as the principles themselves. It may require halachic expertise to identify the relevant principles and order them correctly in any given situation; but it is axiomatic in the process of the Oral Law that its dynamic is built on a definite framework that defines the principles and their interrelationship in a way that speaks to any human situation.[53] To be sure, the process of halacha can be complex; senior expertise may be required and there certainly is place for opinion – not all halachic experts will necessarily come to the same conclusion in any particular case. But underlying the application of that expertise and those opinions is a universal set of axioms and a universal hierarchy that orders them.

TORAH AND SECULAR LAW

There is a halachic principle that states "the law of the land is the law;" that is, the law of a legitimate secular jurisdiction is binding on Jews. It is beyond the present scope to delineate fully how far this principle extends, but it is clear that the law of a secular country does not oblige Jews to an extent that contradicts Torah law in matters such as medical decisions involving danger to life. A Jew is forbidden to actively hasten a patient's

---

[52] The English moral philosopher W. D. Ross, for example, pointed out that all mature, thinking people know that there are basic principles of conduct that oblige us, and that each of those principles must be followed unless it conflicts with another. These moral principles are as real as any law of physics: "[The] moral order expressed in these propositions is just as much part of the fundamental nature of the universe... as is the spatial or numerical structure expressed in the axioms of geometry or arithmetic." (Ross W. D. The Right and the Good. Oxford, 1930.) But he could not identify any meta-principle that informs us how to arrange those moral principles in a universal hierarchy.

[53] See Appendix I: How a Rabbi Decides an Issue in Medical Halacha.

death even where such action is entirely legal and even obligatory in a non-Jewish country (and in Israel too, for that matter, where secular Israeli law may contradict Torah law on such matters).

Fortunately, in modern practice in the West, respect is usually afforded (at least nominally) to individual religious convictions, and Jewish doctors seldom find themselves in situations where the law of the land demands of them to break a Torah law in a way where no resolution is possible. Almost always the individual doctor will be allowed at least to withdraw from caring for a particular patient on the grounds of religious belief rather than be forced to perform a halachically proscribed procedure. At present, despite many points of divergence from Torah, Western law and ethics have not reached the point of foisting actions and practices on unwilling minorities who see those actions as morally odious. At least for the present, a Jewish doctor can step back and declare himself unable to perform (or assist at) a particular abortion or sterilization or the shutting off of a ventilator on a living patient.

This is not to say that conflicts do not arise; they certainly do, and they can be extremely trying particularly for medical students and junior doctors in training. A large component of the solution to these dilemmas is in being well-prepared: a junior doctor who is clear about the halachic parameters governing the relevant areas of practice and who can present these in cogent and coherent fashion to the hierarchy of authority in advance of the need for their acute application will find that it is possible to minimize the zone of conflict.

Indeed, it is not uncommon for deeply committed and knowledgeable observant Jewish doctors to find their principles accorded a certain respect by non-Jewish colleagues who perceive the coherent and comprehensive structure of a system whose modern branches grow from ancient and sublime roots and whose values are clear and unchanging in a world of secular ethics whose moral questions are clear but whose answers shift with the times.

Euthanasia, Suicide, Assisted Suicide and Withholding Therapy in Current Thought and Practice

It is hard to imagine anything more opposed to the Jewish view than the current acceptance of euthanasia and assisted suicide. To be sure, there may be situations in which death would appear preferable to life, and in such extreme situations Judaism does not deny the reality or the sincerity of that perception. Nevertheless, actively hastening death or assisting suicide even in such situations is not part of normative halacha. This is famously expressed by Rabbi Yaakov Tzvi Mecklenburg:[1] commenting on the verse in Genesis[2] (from which a number of aspects of the prohibitions of murder and suicide are derived): "The blood of your lives will I require... and from the hand of man, from the hand of his brother, will I require the life of man," Rabbi Mecklenburg asks what the phrase "from the hand of his brother" adds. Why should one think that murder by a brother needs a special admonishment – surely it is included in the general prohibition of murder? He answers that even where murder is committed in a "brotherly" way, that is out of genuine compassion for the suffering of the victim, the verse indicates that such killing is forbidden (and actionable) no less than any other act of murder. Killing a victim "as a brother" may seem justified as an act of compassion, but the Torah outlaws it.

Assisting patients to die is now an accepted part of modern society and modern medicine. A recent report states: "Dutch doctors make suicide advice available to the public." The information given to the public

---

[1] HaK'tav V'ha'Kabbala 20.

[2] Genesis 9:5.

includes "advice on refusing food and fluids and taking a combination of drugs to induce coma and death."[3] Medicine has passed suicide as an acceptable option into the public domain.

Euthanasia now includes active killing of patients by doctors, sometimes by direct injection of neuromuscular blocking agents, and often *without the patient's request.*[4][5]

In current clinical practice it is not uncommon to allow patients to die by starvation and dehydration; often no attempt is made to dissuade a patient who chooses this option – all that good practice requires is an assurance that the patient is competent to decide. Even depression as a reason for such a decision is not seen as invalidating that decision; as long as the patient is of sound mind the decision is acceptable.[6]

In a typical case reported in the literature,[7] a psychiatric opinion confirms that the patient's "decision-making capacity was intact and not compromised by depression..." before the patient is allowed to die of starvation. Note that the psychiatric concern is only that the patient's

---

[3] Reported in the British Medical Journal 2008;336:1394-5.

[4] van der Heide A et al. End-of-Life Practices in the Netherlands under the Euthanasia Act. N Engl J Med 2007;356:1957.

[5] Meier DE, Emmons C, Wallenstein S, Quill T, Morrison RS, Cassel CK. A National Survey of Physician-Assisted Suicide and Euthanasia in the United States. N Engl J Med 1998;338:1193-1201. In this survey of American physicians, it is reported that: "Sixteen percent of the physicians receiving such requests... or 3.3 percent of the entire sample, reported that they had written at least one prescription to be used to hasten death, and 4.7 percent... said that they had administered at least one lethal injection."

[6] Appelbaum PS. Assessment of Patients' Competence to Consent to Treatment. N Engl J Med 2007;357:1834.

[7] A 58-Year-Old Woman with Headaches, Weakness, and Strokelike Episodes. N Engl J Med 2007;357:164. This diabetic patient, suffering from numerous problems including depression, requested (as did her family) that she be allowed to die. "After all her symptoms were controlled, and after a psychiatric consultant felt that her decision-making capacity was intact and not compromised by depression, she still wished to die. She specifically requested that nutrition and hydration, as well as insulin, be discontinued, despite our suggestion that insulin be continued to prevent discomfort from ketoacidosis. Insulin therapy was discontinued, and she died with her family at the bedside two days later. The family expressed appreciation that her wishes were honored."

depression is not compromising her decision-making ability, not that it may be the cause of the patient's wish to die. In Jewish terms, this should be regarded as psychiatrically incompetent quite apart from the question of moral incompetence.

A particularly disturbing current trend is represented by growing numbers of patients who are *refused* treatment against their will – patients (or their families) who request treatment and are refused on the grounds that the short-term prolongation of their lives is "futile" or that their degree of incapacity or suffering ought to preclude treatment despite their autonomous desire to live and receive treatment. As noted, this previously unthinkable situation represents a surprisingly inconsistent application of the value of autonomy: extreme respect for patient autonomy when it is expressed as the desire to die or refuse treatment, but none at all for autonomy when it is expressed as the desire to live or receive treatment in certain desperate situations. It seems that the premier value of autonomy is trumped by a new view of futility, and that the modern distaste for medical paternalism dissolves entirely when that paternalism manifests as the refusal to treat or prolong life.

Why are autonomy and the usual staunch rejection of paternalism being set aside to facilitate these unwilling deaths? Suggested explanations range from the ideological (such as the value that modern society assigns to quality of life rather than to life itself) to the pragmatic (allowing patients to die when they want to and insisting on it when they do not saves money).[8]

This gross humanitarian and ethical failure goes against Jewish values in the most extreme way. The means too, are antithetical to the Jewish approach: in Britain, food and hydration have been defined as treatment rather than staple and ordinary needs – this allows them to be denied to patients as "inappropriate treatment;"[9] [10] in halacha, on the contrary,

---

[8] Dr Colleen Clements, Canadian professor of psychiatry and ethicist, put it like this: "Patient choices are given supreme value when they are choices not to receive medical care, but are overridden when they are choices to receive medical care. Official opinion cries 'Medical futility' in going against patient wishes for medical care, thus saving money. It cries 'Patient autonomy' in supporting patient wishes to terminate care, which also saves money."

[9] The director of medical services at the Royal Hospital for Neurodisability, Dr Keith Andrews, stated: "It is ironic that the only reason that tube feeding has been identified as 'treatment' is so that it can be withdrawn…" Correspondence in BMJ, 25 November 1995.

medications are defined as staple and ordinary[11] with the consequence that they ought not to be denied any more than food and water.[12]

The selections that follow explore these and related issues and their development over the past few decades.

---

[10] The British Medical Association's Ethics Committee ruled in 1999 that doctors could withdraw food and fluids in the "best interests" of patients who could not speak for themselves. The BMA announced that "The doctor must first judge against a set of criteria whether the patient is benefiting from being kept alive..." Under the UK Mental Capacity Act of 2005, a doctor is legally obliged to comply with an Advance Directive refusing food and fluid, but is not bound by one requesting it.

[11] The Sages (Midrash Shmuel 52a:4) teach that the administration of appropriate medication should be seen no differently than any other necessary human engaging of the natural world. Maimonides (Mishna Pesachim 4:9) states that both foods and medicines were created to be used when needed; refusing to take a necessary medication would be as foolish as refusing to take food.

[12] The European Court of Human Rights concurs with the British approach: in 2006, 46 year old Leslie Burke (who suffers from Friedreich's ataxia) sought the right to receive artificial nourishment and water when he becomes too ill to speak for himself. The British Department of Health opposed Mr Burke's claim, saying that artificial nutrition and hydration count as medical treatment and that the Health Service cannot guarantee to provide the treatment a patient wants, only the treatment doctors believe is best. The Strasbourg court ruled that a patient does not have the right to stop doctors withdrawing food and water when his illness becomes advanced. The court said that although British law remains generally in favour of prolonging life, it would be "burdensome" if doctors had to apply to a High Court judge every time they wished to end a life by withdrawing food and water.

Euthanasia and Assisted Suicide
Changing Attitudes and Practices in Recent Times

The following anonymous feature article appeared in the January 8th, 1988 edition of the Journal of the American Medical Association:[1]

It's Over, Debbie

The call came in the middle of the night. As a gynecology resident rotating through a large, private hospital, I had come to detest telephone calls, because invariably I would be up for several hours and would not feel good the next day. However, duty called, so I answered the phone. A nurse informed me that a patient was having difficulty getting rest, could I please see her. She was on 3 North. That was the gynecologic-oncology unit, not my usual duty station. As I trudged along, bumping sleepily against walls and corners and not believing I was up again, I tried to imagine what I might find at the end of my walk. Maybe an elderly woman with an anxiety reaction, or perhaps something particularly horrible.

---

[1] JAMA 1988;259:272

I grabbed the chart from the nurses' station on my way to the patient's room, and the nurse gave me some hurried details: a 20-year-old girl named Debbie was dying of ovarian cancer. She was having unrelenting vomiting apparently as the result of an alcohol drip administered for sedation. Hmmm, I thought. Very sad. As I approached the room I could hear loud, labored breathing. I entered and saw an emaciated, dark-haired woman who appeared much older than 20. She was receiving nasal oxygen, had an IV, and was sitting in bed suffering from what was obviously severe air hunger. The chart noted her weight at 80 pounds. A second woman, also dark-haired but of middle age, stood at her right, holding her hand. Both looked up as I entered. The room seemed filled with the patient's desperate effort to survive. Her eyes were hollow, and she had suprasternal and intercostal retractions with her rapid inspirations. She had not eaten or slept in two days. She had not responded to chemotherapy and was being given supportive care only. It was a gallows scene, a cruel mockery of her youth and unfulfilled potential. Her only words to me were, "Let's get this over with."

I retreated with my thoughts to the nurses station. The patient was tired and needed rest. I could not give her health, but I could give her rest. I asked the nurse to draw 20 mg of morphine sulfate into a syringe. Enough, I thought, to do the job. I took the syringe into the room and told the two women I was going to give Debbie something that would let her rest and to say good-bye. Debbie looked at the syringe, then laid her head on the pillow with her eyes open, watching what was left of the world. I injected the morphine intravenously and watched to see if my calculations on its effects would be correct. Within seconds her breathing slowed to a normal rate, her eyes closed, and her features softened as she seemed restful at last. The older woman stroked the hair of the now-sleeping patient. I waited for the inevitable next effect of depressing the respiratory drive. With clocklike certainty, within four minutes the breathing rate slowed even more, then became irregular, then ceased. The dark-haired woman stood erect and seemed relieved.

It's over, Debbie.

(Name withheld by request)

This now-famous piece aroused strong responses. The following are drawn from among those that appeared in the press at the time:

New York Times

EUTHANASIA ESSAY PROMPTS PROTEST

February 1, 1988

An essay in The Journal of the American Medical Association describing a young physician's decision to inject a lethal dose of morphine into a terminally ill patient has drawn a flood of letters from doctors calling the action unethical and illegal...

As of Saturday, the editors said, they had received inquiries about the matter from law-enforcement officials. The Chicago Tribune reported today that Mayor Koch of New York had read the article and had notified Attorney General Edwin Meese, seeking possible legal action...

Letters Are '80 to 20 Against'

The publication, based in Chicago, has been inundated with letters protesting the essay, said Dr. George Lundberg, the editor. "I would say the mail is running 80 to 20 against publishing the piece at all, and the vast majority is running against the physician's action," Dr. Lundberg said.

Some experts say the actions described in the article were both unethical and illegal, but Dr. Lundberg said a growing acceptance of euthanasia by physicians prompted him to publish the essay over objections by members of his staff...

'Active, Direct Killing'

Dr. Mark Siegler, a professor of medicine and the director of the Center for Clinical Medical Ethics at the University of Chicago, called the action described in the essay a case of "active, direct killing."

"As far as I know such an action is a crime, perhaps even premeditated murder, in every American jurisdiction as well as being a violation of every canon of responsible medical practice and medical ethics," Dr. Siegler said today. "Debbie's remaining time was snuffed out by an unthinking on-call resident who was conditioned for this action by an intellectual climate of vague notions of 'death with dignity,'" he said....

The following appeared three weeks later:

ESSAY ON MERCY KILLING REFLECTS CONFLICT ON ETHICS FOR PHYSICIANS AND JOURNALISTS

By ISABEL WILKERSON, SPECIAL TO THE NEW YORK TIMES

February 23, 1988

An anonymous essay in The Journal of the American Medical Association, describing the killing of a cancer patient by a resident physician, has astonished doctors and touched off a struggle between local prosecutors and the American Medical Association, which has vowed to protect the author's identity... Medical ethicists are questioning whether, as physicians, the editors should have reported the incident to the authorities...

'Let's Get This Over With'

According to the essay, the resident had never seen the patient before, but administered a fatal dose of morphine after hearing the patient's only words, "Let's get this over with."

A Disservice to the Profession

Dr. Mark Siegler, a professor of medicine and director of the Center for Clinical Medical Ethics at the University of Chicago, said... "This could change medicine profoundly and irreversibly"... "It undermines the profession if the public believes that doctors have the power to kill people, and occasionally do..."

Revival of an Old Debate

As expected, the incident has revived a longstanding debate in the medical community about euthanasia, even as signatures are being gathered in California to put an initiative on the ballot that would make "mercy killing" legal under certain circumstances.

While many doctors have condoned for some time the practice of withdrawing life support systems at the request of terminally ill patients, legalizing the direct killing of those patients is deplored by most physicians.

A poll conducted last June by Louis Harris and Associates and made public last month showed that physicians are far more adamant on the issue than the general public.

The poll... showed that 66 percent of the doctors considered it wrong for a physician to comply with a patient's wishes to end his life, as against 38 percent of the general public.

Some Fears and Arguments

Opponents of mercy killing say the essay only underscores their fears and arguments.

"This is a perfect example of why this kind of conduct should not be legalized," said Giles Scofield, legal counsel for Concern for Dying, a patient's rights group based in New York. "Some would say there is a fine line between the withdrawal of treatment and active euthanasia. This doctor clearly crossed that line."

Advocates of euthanasia also found the essay troubling.

"We're shocked by the speed and spontaneity with which it happened," said Derek Humphry, founder and director of the Hemlock Society, a Los Angeles-based group that promotes voluntary euthanasia. "People say, 'Let's get this over with,' when the doctor comes in to draw blood. That's not a request for death."

Some physicians say the essay points up a problem in the training of residents. "The cold, bitter anger in the essay makes you wonder, 'What are we doing in the socialization of our doctors?'" said Dr. Arthur Caplan, director of the Center for Biomedical Ethics at the University of Minnesota.

"There was a quick inference, an irresponsible leap and no consultation with anyone else," Dr. Caplan said. "It was horrific, but it ought not cast a pall over a discussion of mercy killing."

Change in Attitude Feared

"If you go to the bedside of a patient and the option of killing the patient exists, as it did in the mind of this resident, doctors will be less inclined to think of alternative medical possibilities," Dr. Siegler said. "It will change the mind and attitude of even the most conscientious doctors. And patients will be afraid that their doctor may be a great believer in death with dignity when all they need is their asthma medicine."

The Rev. John Paris, a professor of medical ethics at Holy Cross College in Worcester, Mass., said such fears were not wholly unwarranted now, adding, "I think it happens more often than the public would like to believe."

The article and the response it generated raise several issues.

Apart from the obvious issue of active euthanasia and the break with tradition that this specific act, its admission and publication represent in the history of Western medicine, the article reveals an unexpected carelessness and callousness. In fact, much of the criticism generated was directed against the manner in which the act was performed as much as against the act itself.

This young and relatively inexperienced doctor, still in training, sets the stage by describing the mindset that underlies this clinical encounter: he is exhausted and frustrated at finding himself up again at night, concerned that he is likely to be "up for several hours" and upset that he will "not feel good" the next day. It is already obvious that he needs rest as much as any patient he is going to encounter tonight. In fact, that turns out to be exactly his clinical challenge: "...a patient was having difficulty getting rest, could I please see her;" and when he muses that "I could not give her health, but I could give her rest" the sinister specter is raised of a disgruntled, sleep-deprived doctor choosing between what threatens to become another dreaded "several hours" of draining work trying to relieve a terminal patient's pain and desperation, and some quicker solution that will give *him* the rest that he needs and craves.

Any experienced doctor knows the stark difference between decisions made in a mood of well-rested thoughtfulness with extensive exploration of the available options together with supportive colleagues in the bright light of day, and the murky and strangely depersonalized process that the darkness of an exhausted night tempts.

That is the setting. Then, with no discussion with the patient beyond her brief and highly ambiguous comment, no discussion with her family although her mother (the probable identity of the older woman) is right there beside her, no consultation with her own physicians (this is a "large, private hospital"), no more personal knowledge of the patient and her clinical situation than some "hurried details" from a night nurse and the chart, he decides....

The stark horror of a young, exhausted physician arriving in the dead of night on a service not his own to encounter a patient whom he has never seen who desperately needs symptomatic relief, without so much as examining her and with no discussion or consultation and no attempt to relieve her symptoms summarily ending her life is beyond comprehension. Even for those who consider some form of euthanasia to be a legitimate option, what has happened to the basic requirement of ascertaining the patient's wishes without doubt? What of the simple professional courtesy of consulting with the patient's private physician before intervening? What of the careful attempt to eliminate possible error – in prognosis, in clinical judgment – that haunts clinical medicine at every turn? What of an attempt to titrate the analgesic against the pain, surely the most basic approach to this clinical situation? And what of the law?

It is noteworthy that even the pro-death camp was surprised: *"'We're shocked by the speed and spontaneity with which it happened,' said Derek Humphry, founder and director of the Hemlock Society."*

The moral incompetence represented by this incident is clear (as indeed, is its medical incompetence: "....a violation of every canon of *responsible medical practice* and medical ethics"). It is instructive to note, however, that not all the responses were critical, and that many, both within the profession and without, approved of such action, and very many approve of euthanasia in general. In the poll cited, fully a third of doctors felt that it is acceptable for a physician "to comply with a patient's wishes to end his life," and *almost two thirds* of the general public found such conduct acceptable.

Since then, the pendulum has swung steadily towards greater acceptance of various forms of euthanasia, including active euthanasia, suicide by starvation and physician-assisted suicide. Society and the medical profession have come to accept these in varying degrees and further movement in the same direction is taking place, including the suggestion of practices that would previously have been considered beyond the pale of legitimate discussion, such as the active destruction of very ill or severely handicapped newborns.[2]

Diane

Not as stark as "Debbie" perhaps, but also a landmark in this slide of values and also clearly opposed to halacha, was the open admission and description of a doctor who prescribed barbiturates for the purpose of suicide that appeared in the New England Journal of Medicine in March, 1991.[3] The following is excerpted:

---

[2] These have become more than mere suggestions: see the following sections.

[3] N Engl J Med 1991;324:691-694.

Death and Dignity
A Case of Individualized Decision Making

Timothy E. Quill, M.D.

Diane was feeling tired and had a rash. A common scenario, though there was something subliminally worrisome that prompted me to check her blood count. Her hematocrit was 22, and the white-cell count was 4.3 with some metamyelocytes and unusual white cells....

The bone marrow confirmed the worst: acute myelomonocytic leukemia.... This is an area of medicine in which technological intervention has been successful, with cures 25 percent of the time.... As I probed the costs of these cures, I heard about induction chemotherapy (three weeks in the hospital, prolonged neutropenia, probable infectious complications, and hair loss; 75 percent of patients respond, 25 percent do not). For the survivors, this is followed by consolidation chemotherapy (with similar side effects; another 25 percent die, for a net survival of 50 percent). Those still alive, to have a reasonable chance of long-term survival, then need bone marrow transplantation (hospitalization for two months and whole-body irradiation, with complete killing of the bone marrow, infectious complications, and the possibility for graft-versus-host disease – with a survival of approximately 50 percent, or 25 percent of the original group). Though hematologists may argue over the exact percentages, they don't argue about the outcome of no treatment – certain death in days, weeks, or at most a few months.

[O]ur oncologist broke the news to Diane and began making plans to... begin induction chemotherapy that afternoon. [But she] decided that she wanted none.... she was convinced she would die during the period of treatment and would suffer unspeakably in the process... She articulated very clearly that odds of 25 percent were not good enough for her to undergo so toxic a course of therapy...

I have been a longtime advocate of active, informed patient choice of treatment or nontreatment, and of a patient's right to die with as much control and dignity as possible. Yet there was something about her giving up a 25 percent chance of long-term survival in favor of almost certain death that disturbed me. I had seen Diane fight and use her considerable inner resources to overcome alcoholism and depression... I gradually understood the decision from her perspective and became convinced that it was the right decision for her...

A week later she phoned me with a request for barbiturates for sleep. Since I knew that this was an essential ingredient in a Hemlock Society suicide, I asked her to come to the office to talk things over. She was more than willing to protect me by participating in a superficial conversation about her insomnia, but it was important to me to know how she planned to use the drugs and to be sure that she was not in despair or overwhelmed in a way that might color her judgment. [It] was... evident that the security of having enough barbiturates available to commit suicide when and if the time came would leave her secure enough to live fully and concentrate on the present... I made sure that she knew how to use the barbiturates for sleep, and also that she knew the amount needed to commit suicide. We agreed to meet regularly, and she promised to meet with me before taking her life, to ensure that all other avenues had been exhausted. I wrote the prescription with an uneasy feeling about the boundaries I was exploring - spiritual, legal, professional, and personal. Yet I also felt strongly that I was setting her free to get the most out of the time she had left, and to maintain dignity and control on her own terms until her death.

The next several months were very intense and important for Diane. Her son stayed home from college, and they were able to be with one another and say much that had not been said earlier. Her husband did his work at home... She spent time with her closest friends...

Bone pain, weakness, fatigue, and fevers began to dominate her life... it was clear that the end was approaching... She called up her closest friends and asked them to come over to say goodbye, telling them that she would be leaving soon. As we had agreed, she let me know as well. When we met, it was clear that she knew what she was doing, that she was sad and frightened to be leaving, but that she would be even more terrified to stay and suffer...

Two days later her husband called to say that Diane had died. She had said her final goodbyes to her husband and son that morning, and asked them to leave her alone for an hour. After an hour, which must have seemed an eternity, they found her on the couch, lying very still and covered by her favorite shawl. There was no sign of struggle. She seemed to be at peace. They called me for advice about how to proceed. When I arrived at their house, Diane indeed seemed peaceful...

I called the medical examiner to inform him that a hospice patient had died. When asked about the cause of death, I said, "acute leukemia." He said that was fine and that we should call a funeral director. Although acute leukemia was the truth, it was not the whole story. Yet any mention of suicide would have given rise to a police investigation and probably brought the arrival of an ambulance crew for resuscitation. Diane would have become a "coroner's case," and the decision to perform an autopsy would have been made at the discretion of the medical examiner. The family or I could have been subject to criminal prosecution, and I to professional review, for our roles in support of Diane's choices. Although I truly believe that the family and I gave her the best care possible, allowing her to define her limits and directions as much as possible, I am not sure the law, society, or the medical profession would agree. So I said "acute leukemia" to protect all of us, to protect Diane from an invasion into her past and her body, and to continue to shield society from the knowledge of the degree of suffering that people often undergo in the process of dying...

The following is the comment of a consultant psychiatrist, head of a department of psychiatry at one of Britain's major university hospitals, on "Debbie" and "Diane":

> " 'It's Over, Debbie' is genuinely shocking, but perhaps the most striking thing is that the shock is attenuated now as we become more used to such an approach. It somehow started to alter the climate in thinking, perhaps the most pernicious aspect of the case.

> 'Diane' is more understandable on a superficial approach. The author appears to be genuinely caring, involved, and reflective about his practice. Yet, eventually, he allows himself to collude with the patient. Despite his reservations that a patient with husband and son should spurn a 25% chance of long-term remission, for reasons that remain unclear he 'became convinced it was the right decision for her.' The patient's past history of alcoholism and depression together with her counter-intuitive decision concerning her treatment does not concern him sufficiently to get a second opinion. One wonders whether his being a 'longtime advocate of... a patient's right to die with as much control... as possible' prevents him from seeking an opinion that may scupper the assisted suicide. In the end, and with some resonance of the first case ('Debbie') the doctor practices assisted suicide (albeit not euthanasia) without any of the checks and balances necessary to ensure a correct decision has been made. So even by the standards of those supporting assisted suicide, his decision, taken unilaterally, appears extreme. I would also add that

many patients asking for help to die are often, on closer questioning, asking for help to live – only with the necessary psychological, physical and social support. I think doctors need to be more aware of the subtexts of their patients' questions and requests."

This consultant expresses his reservations with regard to assisted suicide and euthanasia decisions in general:

"I find the issue of assisted suicide problematic from a clinical point of view as well.

While undoubtedly there will be a small group of people who have undertaken the calm and rational decision to terminate their lives, there is a clear concern that there will be a larger group of people who have been coerced into doing so. These coercive influences can be extremely subtle and difficult to pick up.

People who are dying are aware of the burden that this may place on others. This includes both the imposition of the caring role on others, and equally importantly the financial constraints which their illness may impose, including the costs of additional help domestically and often the costs of nursing homes and other such expenses. They may be concerned that relatives see their need for expensive care as using up their inheritance. Those with terminal illnesses are obviously in an extremely vulnerable psychological state and may be unduly sensitive to the suggestion or implication that they are placing a financial, emotional or physical burden on their family. These subtle, and in some cases overt, forms of coercion will be keenly felt. There is no way, nor could there be any way, of being able to pick up these kinds of issues, particularly where capacity is presumed, and particularly where the person concerned internalises those thoughts as their own.

Coupled with this is the (often erroneous) notion that it is 'understandable' that a person with a terminal illness would wish to end their life.

There is also the issue of psychiatric assessment. Capacity decisions in which there is a component of mental illness are amongst the most complex that psychiatrists must make.[4] Although many decisions are

---

[4] Physicians commonly fail to detect patients' impaired ability to decide: See Appelbaum PS. Assessment of Patients' Competence to Consent to Treatment. N Engl J Med 2007;357:1834.

quite clear cut, there is a range of decisions in which an element of judgment is called for. The same problems apply here as to the assessment of capacity, including the 'understandability' of feeling low and depressed, without this being taken to have influenced the decision to die.

The term 'unbearable suffering' is used. Modern medicine has many limitations, but palliative care should not be one of them. In current clinical practice, no patient should ever 'suffer unbearably.' This, however, is given as the central justification for someone wishing to terminate his or her own life. In many cases it is clear that what is meant by 'unbearable suffering' is that the family are suffering unbearably watching their loved one die. I think the term is loose and is potentially open to interpretation and hence abuse.

While there may be attempts to provide safeguards in the process of assessing the nature of a patient's wish to die, on closer scrutiny these do not stand up. 'Unbearable suffering' and 'mental competence' are open to interpretation. Any practising psychiatrist in this field knows that such decisions in the real world are very complex.

This process invites doctors to become moral arbiters, because inevitably some clinicians will take a view based on little more than their own opinions. Unfortunately history teaches us that doctors are no more or less able to make moral decisions than anyone else."

Many previously controversial practices have passed beyond the stage of public debate and are commonplace; clinicians are now more often involved in decisions about individual patients' competence to decide when to stop treatment (or feeding) than in the morality of such practices in themselves. The next case, in which a hospital psychiatrist is asked for her opinion and a decision in such an instance, presents this issue and frames the state of modern practice in this area.

Mind Reading[1]

E... E...., M.D.

I was called in to see a man I did not know. No one knew him. His usual doctor was on vacation, and the social worker who paged me was covering for another social worker.

"Can't it wait a week?" I asked. The patient had been in the hospital for three years without a psychiatric evaluation.

"I don't think so," the social worker said. "He hasn't taken food or fluids for two days. But," she added, trying to encourage me, "he does take every pill."

The consultation question was the patient's competence. Did he mean to kill himself? The chart gave no help, with its notes full of vital signs and bowel functions. Three times a day, he received a cupful of medications: pills for seizures and diabetes, hypertension and constipation, depression and anxiety. The social worker who didn't know him was correct; he took them all, then turned his head from the pudding that followed.

The nurses had a somewhat fuller picture. Before his admission, he had manned a carnival booth with his wife, crossing the country from one school parking lot to the next. They had no children, and their lifestyle was raucous. He smoked and drank in carnival quantities until, in his late 50s, a stroke left him half paralyzed and speechless.

His wife had signed the medical directives form on admission. She had checked off "care and comfort measures only." Now she no longer visited and was not returning phone calls. An off-duty nurse had spotted her in the local market with a different hair color and a new man. The nurse shook her head to remember it. "I didn't tell him anything," she said, "but he knows. She doesn't come anymore. I try to feed him, and he pushes my hand away with his cheek. I say to him, 'You know if you do that you're going to die,' and he shakes his head yes. But if he wants to die, then why does he take all his pills?"

I went to the patient. His wheelchair was locked in front of the TV, his right leg dangling off the footrest, his right arm contracted at the elbow and wrist. There was a documentary on about the first lunar landing. His eyes were open, following the dusty steps of Buzz Aldrin, while a nurse tried to coax a spoonful of pudding into him...

---

[1] N Engl J Med 2004; 351:420-422.

I had to refer to the consult form for his name. When I introduced myself, his eyes moved from the form to me. Then they closed, firmly but without offense. I thought it was a sensible response to a stranger who has been called in to make critical decisions without intimate knowledge. I hoped I would have done the same myself.

I apologized for interrupting and left. Looking back through the doorway, I saw his eyes open and fix on the television. He seemed perfectly alert and historically involved. The nurse sat on the edge of his bed and said something. He nodded, and they watched together. Giant steps for mankind were being made.

The covering medical doctor waited at the nursing station. "Sad, sad," he said busily. "What do you want to do?"

Competence is a legal state. The decision, especially when intervention is involved, must be rendered by a judge. But judges rely heavily on psychiatrists' opinions in issuing their own. Competence is also a function-specific state, and it comes in shades; someone might be competent to handle his finances but not competent to refuse his medications. He could be full of insight and judgment in one setting but not in another. It easily becomes confusing...

Medical competence has a number of components. Ethicists diagram them for clarity. The patient must have cognitive capacity. He must concentrate and attend, register information and retain it. He must comprehend his diagnosis, undistracted by a treatable set of circumstances including psychosis, suicidal depression, and delirium (any of which can impede insight and judgment). He must be able to weigh the risks and benefits of accepting treatment — food and drink, in this case — and must understand the consequences of refusing them — here, it meant death.

On a blackboard with colored chalk, the variables of cognition, understanding, and judgment create a complex but manageable set of intersecting circles. This case did not feel manageable. I tried to break it into its components. Cognition: difficult to assess in the absence of speech and given the patient's refusal to comply with any exam; however, he seemed able to maintain attention to television, to follow simple commands, and to respond to the nurses, who had not reported deterioration in these capacities.

Impediments to judgment: psychiatrically, someone had diagnosed depression at some point (I could find no note about it) and started an antidepressant; maybe he was inadequately treated. Electroconvulsive therapy (ECT) will rapidly alleviate life-threatening depressive symptoms, including the refusal to eat or drink. But it cannot remedy personal devastations. It can't, for instance, return missing love. Here, I leaned lower over the consult form and hoped that no one could read my thoughts. The man had sensible reasons to wish for death — no future health to anticipate, no one to anticipate it with.

Other reversible impediments: Was he delirious? hyponatremic? hypercalcemic? hypoxic? febrile? septic? having a second stroke? Blood tests and imaging would rule these conditions in or out. Was there a physical reason he couldn't swallow, such as pain? But why, why did he take his pills?

Nobody at the nursing station wanted to petition for an emergency guardianship to force feedings or ECT on a man with seizures, diabetes, hypertension, hemiparalysis, speechlessness, and lovelessness. Tacitly, I knew, I was being asked to document the reasoning behind the majority opinion. If he had come to a decision in sound mind, we wanted to support it on paper. The paper part was critical. Families of ghosts can be litigious.

The nurse who had been trying to feed him came up to the station. "God bless him," she said. "I wouldn't wish that life on a dog." Heads nodded. Even those of us who did not know him could agree on this. I was scribbling away, behind schedule, trying to imagine those clean intersecting circles on the board. But ultimately, we who didn't know him were not making judgments according to those clean criteria. We were making them on the basis of our own impressions of his life and our own standards of living.

I passed the consult form to the covering doctor. We agreed that it was easy enough to check for reversible signs of mental-status change. If nothing leapt out of the laboratory tests or vital signs, treatment would not be forced. It was the best we could do but incomplete; our answers did not rise to the complexity of the questions he had raised. I went back to my own floor, and the doctor went to his.

A world full of less imperative tasks intervened after that. It might have been a month or so later that the social worker and I met in parallel cafeteria lines. We had almost passed one another before I recognized her and remembered. What had become of the consult patient? Had anyone ever understood why he took his pills but refused his food — extended one arm for help and used the other to fight it off?

"He died a couple of days after you saw him," she said, sounding as if she, too, had just remembered. Even regular members of his health care team had been unable to reconcile his contradictions. They could not feel certain that his actions were intentional. But, given the absence of an acute reversible condition, they could not justify interrupting him, either.

The social worker and I stood together uncomfortably. When our separate lines began to move at different paces, the space between us widened. Neither of us mentioned the patient by name. I thought afterwards that we might both have forgotten it.

– From Harvard Medical School, Boston.

Despite being entirely legal and fully sanctioned by the medical system, this is a case of flagrant abandonment of a patient. The current medical, social and legal ethos demands only an assessment of mental competence before allowing such an act; in Judaism such conduct represents failure to save and sustain a human life.

But this case report demonstrates something else as well: how far society's values have pervaded medicine – not long ago a case handled like this would undoubtedly have been judged medically incompetent in its open admission of failure to offer what medicine is all about: treating the patient.

It appears that psychiatry, of all medical specialties the one that might be expected to see patients in a more sensitive light than the merely biological, and even in the most prestigious of American medical institutions, has no more to offer than to condone a depressed patient's decision to starve to death. And in this particular case that decision was taken despite the patient's curiously ambivalent "mixed messages" – refusing food but taking his medications. Is this so clearly a hopeless case from a psychiatric point of view? Is it so clear that there is no possibility that underlying this patient's reactive depression a desire to live can be coaxed out, gently and sensitively over time? And if not, is depression due to serious illness and deep loneliness enough to sign a patient's death warrant? Is that the appropriate medical response?

This case makes it clear that all that is required from psychiatry in such circumstances is an assessment of the patient's competence to decide; *what* the patient decides is not the issue, even if that decision is to die of starvation. The value of autonomy has become so paramount that it supersedes even the notion of attempting treatment for a patient who so desperately needs it. It seems that doctors have profoundly forgotten their most basic function – the attempt to make the patient whole in body and mind.

Many elements of this candid report from one of the Western world's pre-eminent medical institutions bear study:

I was called in to see a man I did not know. No one knew him. His usual doctor was on vacation, and the social worker who paged me was covering for another social worker...

Shades of "Debbie" here. Surely if this momentous and irrevocable decision is going to be made, the treating physician should at least know the patient well. Is this a decision to make after one brief visit to an uncommunicative patient who is signalling conflicting messages? By a doctor who is unable to interview the patient? What psychiatrist can be so confident in these circumstances that no attempt to help such a patient could possibly be productive? The primary approach here should be to keep him going at all costs until his own doctor gets back. And if that does not prove feasible, why not contact the doctor on his vacation? A man's life is at stake.... Perhaps his usual doctor has seen him thus previously and has found a way to pull him through...

"He hasn't taken food or fluids for two days. But... he does take every pill..."

This is interesting psychiatrically... what does it mean? Is the patient to be written off before this challenging question is resolved?

The consultation question was the patient's competence. Did he mean to kill himself?...

This consultant has been asked only that, and that is all that will be assessed. But where is the consultation for general assessment and treatment? Surely there is a duty to refer this patient for emergency psychiatric and social work assessment... *"The patient had been in the hospital for three years without a psychiatric evaluation...."* Do we no longer care if our patients kill themselves as long as we know they are mentally competent to do so? In Judaism there is an obligation to prevent a suicide just as there is an obligation to prevent a murder or to prevent death by disease.

This non-terminally ill patient who is receiving "pills.... for depression and anxiety" is going to be allowed to die without a general psychiatric evaluation. Is the proper order of things to evaluate a patient who is being treated for depression and anxiety only when a life-and-death crisis looms, and then only to ensure that he is competent to decide to die?

Depression as a reason for deciding to die is not seen as sufficient to invalidate that decision; the only question is whether the depression renders the patient incompetent. Of course depression may rob a patient of the will to live – that is a feature of depression. The first approach should be an attempt to improve the patient's state of mind; that ought to be the therapeutic goal, not simply acquiescence. What could represent a greater medical failure than the failure even to attempt a cure? The patient's lack of will to live *is the clinical problem* here, not an indication to abandon treatment. If a patient were holding a gun to his head about to commit suicide, would an attending psychiatrist be acting professionally if he stopped the patient only long enough to ensure that he is competent to make such a decision before allowing him to proceed? The patient's life has become irrelevant; it is only the competence to decide to destroy it that matters.

Three times a day, he received a cupful of medications: pills for seizures and diabetes, hypertension and constipation, depression and anxiety. The social worker who didn't know him was correct; he took them all, then turned his head from the pudding that followed.

Is this man trying to kill himself... or is he perhaps indicating that he has no appetite; indeed cannot enjoy anything. He is mourning; food has no taste in his sadness. And a mourner needs consolation, not collusion in hopelessness.

His wife had signed the medical directives form on admission. She had checked off "care and comfort measures only."

This tells us a lot about her, not about him. It is highly dubious if such a statement should be allowed to appear in a chart; only when there is no trace of doubt concerning a family member's motivations should such directives be allowed to stand, and then of course only when the patient is incompetent to represent himself may they become relevant. In the case we are considering, this wife's directives are entirely irrelevant, and potentially dangerous.

Now she no longer visited and was not returning phone calls. An off-duty nurse had spotted her in the local market with a different hair color and a new man.

We now have more than sufficient cause for the patient's depression. He needs help in discovering a reason to live, as many in his type of situation have managed to discover against all odds. He needs a young person, any person, to take an interest in him, read to him, perhaps, talk to him, take him out, find a way to communicate with him... those simple things are no less to be called treatment than the medications that he mysteriously continues to take.

But if he wants to die, then why does he take all his pills?...

Indeed, why?

.... his eyes... closed, firmly but without offense. I thought it was a sensible response to a stranger who has been called in to make critical decisions without intimate knowledge.

Perhaps, but one should not be making critical decisions without intimate knowledge. This decision must be delayed until that priceless psychiatric commodity is available.

This life-and-death case involves a number of elements of doubt, and in cases of doubt we must surely err on the side of life; the ethical default position must surely be full and aggressive attempts at therapy where the clinical picture is not clear. If there is ever a place for abandoning therapy, it must certainly be where all else has failed and no possible therapeutic option can be found, not where clinical uncertainties abound. Only a system that has clearly lost sight of the value of life and medicine's basic commitment to that value could approach a case such as this and declare its default position to be the condoning of death.

And even a slavish respect for autonomy cannot be invoked as the reason for allowing this death – there is enough cause to doubt what this patient's real autonomous wishes are.

I apologized for interrupting and left.

Why not stay awhile? Does a consultant psychiatrist not have any tricks of the trade up her sleeve that can be used to engage a depressed patient? No doubt time is a problem for a busy psychiatrist: *"I was scribbling away, behind schedule..."* But is a patient's life to be scribbled away because we do not have enough time for him? A life-and-death decision is being made here by a visiting consultant who sees the patient once, spends almost no time with him, fails to engage him in any significant way and does not begin to resolve the contradictions that he presents.

The nurse sat on the edge of his bed and said something. He nodded, and they watched together.

It seems that someone, at least, can engage him. There is hope yet, for that.

Competence is a legal state... and it comes in shades... It easily becomes confusing...

Again, competence is not the whole story here. Of course it is a necessary element in clarifying the clinical psychiatric problem, and if competence is lacking the problem is solved. We know what to do. But where there *is* competence and yet no will to live, that is where the real problem begins, not ends.

He must [be] undistracted by... suicidal depression...

But our patient very likely has at least an element of suicidal depression. What is a more likely interpretation of a depressed patient's refusal to eat? And if that is the case, then an argument can be made that even by the secular and legal standard he should not be regarded as competent.

... someone had diagnosed depression at some point (I could find no note about it) and started an antidepressant; maybe he was inadequately treated.

Indeed he is inadequately treated, and unfortunately he is not about to receive adequate treatment now. But it is not more drugs that this man needs.

Electroconvulsive therapy... cannot remedy personal devastations. It can't, for instance, return missing love.

Of course not. But must the solution become condoning his death?

The man had sensible reasons to wish for death...

This is religious and philosophical territory, not medical. But before we consign him to fulfilment of his "sensible" death wish, we ought at least to try to help him wish for something better and give him whatever meager means we can think of to achieve it, difficult though it will no doubt be. Where is this hospital's chaplain? Does he or she have time to talk to patients, to get to know them, to try to "resolve their contradictions"?

If he had come to a decision... we wanted to support it on paper. The paper part was critical. Families of ghosts can be litigious.

The law is clearly important, and so of course it should be. The tragedy here is that it is just another thing that is more important than his life.

If nothing leapt out of the laboratory tests or vital signs, treatment would not be forced...

To save this man's life something will have to *leap out* of the lab tests or vital signs. If there is some clue buried in the chart or in the subtle physical signs that a careful examination may evoke (that every patient, surely, deserves) that may save him, we are not going to find it. If it does not leap out at us, we are going to let him die. Surely, in the name of all that is best in the practice of clinical medicine, something should have to leap out at us absolutely unavoidably to force us to allow him to die, not to live. What is the default – life or death?

But, given the absence of an acute reversible condition...

One that leaps out of the chart, that is.

It might have been a month or so later that the social worker and I met in parallel cafeteria lines... What had become of the consult patient?

In the old world of medical values, the consultant would surely have known. Simple clinical curiosity would have led the doctor back to observe the development of an unresolved clinical question. The minimum awareness of continuity of care, too, would have a psychiatric service follow up on a patient who has been allowed to starve, surely, not forget about him until chance brings a reminder.

Had anyone ever understood why he took his pills but refused his food — extended one arm for help and used the other to fight it off?... Even regular members of his health care team... could not feel certain that his actions were intentional...

Doubt that his actions were intentional, yet allowed to die on the assumption that they were. The default could not be clearer: clarity is needed to save a life, doubt is enough to discard it.

This candid report from one of the world's premier medical institutions indicates clearly where modern medicine stands in terms of the values that inform its approach to such dilemmas.

The following are the comments of an experienced consultant psychiatrist on reading this report:

"The patient is either unable or unwilling to communicate, and therefore his intentions must be inferred from his behaviour. From his behaviour, it is assumed that the patient is making an attempt to end his life. This is despite behaviour that one would call, at the very least, ambivalent. There then follows further cognitive bias to support the notion that the patient must be suicidal. This is to say that arguments that support the notion of suicidality are maximised, while those against it are overlooked. For example his wife's supposed infidelity, based on a hearsay report of a sighting of a woman with different hair colour seen with another man (which suggests misidentification for a different person as much as it proves infidelity) is over-emphasised, and the subsequent 'lovelessness' or 'missing love' mentioned twice more in support of his decision to end his life. There is by contrast a minimisation of considerations that would not support the notion of suicidality. For example, it is plausible that the patient is protesting against the hospital food. Or the patient may have dental problems (an abscess, for example) that make chewing food painful, but taking tablets bearable. The point is that the mute patient becomes a blank canvas onto which the beliefs of the staff are projected, representing their own beliefs about the value of life under such circumstances. I think this is a crucial aspect of the case.

But let's assume he is actually trying to die. Does he have capacity with regard to this decision? We really do not know. His understanding is unclear, his ability to weigh in the balance such decisions unknown, and his ability to communicate the decision non-existent. As a clinician, this would give me significant cause to doubt the patient's decision-making capacity.

If he does not have capacity, then what is the reason for this? And will he regain his capacity at some point in the future? It appears that psychiatric problems have been considered and discarded, although I would be concerned that little time has been spent exploring this, and the author was rather too easily put off at clinical interview. Nevertheless, if capacity is lacking, one must act in the best interests of the patient. One would be hard put to make a case that someone's death is in their best interests.

I think the author is insightful about the shortcomings of the decision-making process, and perhaps understandably the decision she made does not sit comfortably with her."

The Medicalization of Death

An area that should be of particular concern to doctors is the escalating involvement of medical personnel in euthanasia, apart from the more general issue of societal attitudes. Aspects of doctors' direct involvement in this field that have received attention in recent years have been active and passive euthanasia, assisted suicide, and medical participation in legal executions.

It is instructive to review the modern history of suicide assisted by doctors. The following is excerpted from The New England Journal of Medicine, May 27, 1993:[1]

Kevorkian and the Suicide Machine

by George J. Annas

Jack Kevorkian decided to test his suicide machine in Michigan because he was convinced that Michigan had no laws against assisted suicide. This belief was based on his own reading of two Michigan cases, People v. Roberts and People v. Campbell. The first is a 1920 case in which Frank Roberts pleaded guilty to the charge of murder for killing his wife, Katie. Katie Roberts was terminally ill, practically helpless, and suffering from multiple sclerosis. At his wife's request, Frank Roberts mixed a quantity of Paris green (which contains arsenic) in a drink and placed it within his wife's reach. Katie Roberts drank the potion with the intention of taking her own life and died a few hours later. After being sentenced to life imprisonment on the basis of his guilty plea, a sentence required under Michigan law for murder "perpetrated by means of poison," Roberts appealed. His primary argument was that since suicide was not a

---

[1] N Engl J Med 1993;328:1573-1576.

crime in Michigan, there could be no crime of being an accessory before the fact to suicide – that is, since Katie Roberts committed no crime in killing herself, Frank Roberts could have committed no crime in helping her. The Michigan Supreme Court agreed that if there is no crime of suicide there can be no crime of being an accessory to suicide, but Roberts was not charged with being an accessory to suicide, but with murder, to which he pleaded guilty. The court concluded that the facts supported a finding of guilty of murder by poison.

In 1983, the Michigan Court of Appeals dismissed the indictment of Steven Paul Campbell on the charge of murder in connection with the suicide of Kevin Basnaw. On the night of his suicide, Basnaw had been drinking heavily with Campbell. Just two weeks earlier, Campbell had [discovered Basnaw in an intimate relationship with] Campbell's wife. Basnaw talked about suicide but said he didn't have a gun. Campbell offered to sell him one and ridiculed him. Finally, the men drove to the home of Campbell's parents to get a gun and bullets, after which Campbell left Basnaw at home. The next morning Basnaw was found dead with a self-inflicted wound to the temple. The prosecutor relied on Roberts to justify a charge of first-degree murder against Campbell. The appeals court agreed that the case could not be distinguished from Roberts but ruled that Roberts was no longer good law. The court found that "the term suicide excludes by definition a homicide. Simply put, the defendant here did not kill another person." The court invited the legislature to pass a statute against this type of conduct, which it said laws in other states had characterized as crimes ranging from negligent homicide to voluntary manslaughter, but not murder. The court concluded that Campbell's conduct, although "morally reprehensible," was not "criminal under the present state of the law."

As of May 1, 1993, Kevorkian had been involved in the deaths of 15 people (11 women and 4 men), 2 of whom used his "suicide machine" and 13 of whom used carbon monoxide. The suicide machine consists of three hanging bottles connected to an intravenous line. When the line is in place, it delivers a saline solution. The subject can then push a button that switches to the second bottle, containing the sedative thiopental. A third bottle, containing potassium chloride, is later activated automatically by a timer, and death follows within minutes.

After this method was first used by Janet Adkins in June 1990, I observed that the "suicide machine stands as a hybrid between medical and nonmedical technology" and that if Kevorkian had used a noose or helped Adkins "point a gun at her head and indicated when to pull the *trigger, there seems little doubt that he would have been charged with and convicted of manslaughter (the reckless endangerment of another's life), if not murder." Kevorkian was in fact charged with murder in the death of Adkins, but the medical trappings of the machine seemed to help persuade the trial judge that Kevorkian's acts were medical in nature – and thus presumptively benign. Relying on Campbell, Judge Gerald McNally dismissed all charges, ruling that Adkins had caused her own death and that Michigan had no specific law against assisting a suicide...*

Kevorkian, a pathologist, had trouble starting the intravenous line in Janet Adkins, making five attempts to enter a vein. With his second subject, Sherry Miller, he tried unsuccessfully four times to start the infusion and eventually returned home to get a cylinder of carbon monoxide. Later that same day he was successful in starting an intravenous line in Marjorie Wantz, but thereafter he abandoned the suicide machine and has since relied exclusively on the use of carbon monoxide. On December 15, 1992, the day Kevorkian supplied carbon monoxide to his seventh and eighth subjects (who, like the earlier subjects, were women), Governor John Engler signed Michigan's anti-assisted suicide bill, which was to become effective on March 30, 1993. Kevorkian stepped up his activities, however, and after his list of cases grew quickly to 15, Michigan's legislature made the statute effective immediately (on February 25, 1993) and also clarified the exceptions to the new crime of assistance to suicide...

On the surface, the statute might seem to criminalize actions like those described by Timothy Quill in an earlier issue of the Journal. Quill prescribed barbiturates to a terminally ill patient ["Diane"] with cancer who said she might use them to kill herself at some indeterminate future time. However, assuming a Michigan physician writes a prescription for drugs that have a legitimate medical use (but also could be used to commit suicide) with the intent "to relieve pain and discomfort and not to cause death," the physician's action should qualify as an exception...

The Slippery Slope

The most powerful argument against the legislative expansion of the power of physicians to assist patients in suicide is the danger that this greater latitude will result in abuses that disproportionately affect especially vulnerable populations – the poor, the elderly, women, and minorities... already marginalized members of society could be deprived of their human rights by making them appear somehow less than fully human. This is especially true in the context of cost containment and economic constraints.

Kevorkian is fond of describing his detractors as Nazis, but his own actions (and our response to them) require that we examine the Nazi experience carefully. Kevorkian's primary method of inducing death, for example, is carbon monoxide poisoning. This was the method personally chosen by Adolf Hitler at the outset of the Nazi euthanasia program on the advice of his medical advisor, Werner Heyde. Heyde conducted an experiment in 1940 on various ways to kill people and concluded that carbon monoxide gassing was the most humane. Even though it was difficult to see gas poisoning as a medical act, the Nazi physicians nonetheless persisted in stressing that "only doctors should carry out the gassing." It is remarkable how much commentary has been devoted to Kevorkian's suicide machine and how little to his much more frequent use of carbon monoxide gas. There is nothing medical about the latter method, which has no legitimate medical use; nonetheless, some of us seem to accept the idea, as did the Germans, that if a physician performs the act, it must be "medical," and if it is medical, it must be acceptable.

For similar reasons, state-ordered executions in the United States are moving from the gas chamber to lethal injection. Medical organizations throughout the world have quite properly declared that the participation of physicians in executions is unethical. The primary reason is that physicians should not permit their caring profession to be subverted for the nonbeneficent goals of the state. The medicalization of executions makes them appear more humane and thus much more acceptable to society.

The same may be said about assisted suicide. If suicide is assisted by a physician instead of a relative or friend (even using poison gas), society is much more likely to see this assistance as acceptable, even expected. Although proponents currently insist on contemporaneous, competent, voluntary, and informed consent, the terms "physician-assisted suicide" and "euthanasia" are already being used almost interchangeably. This linkage indicates that it will be as difficult to retain personal consent at the time of death as a prerequisite to physician-assisted death in the United States as it has proved to be in the Netherlands, where almost half of all lethal injections given to incompetent patients are given in cases in which the patient has never expressed a wish for euthanasia. When we decide to rely on substituted judgment, our own definition of another person's best interests, or proxy consent, we quickly move from assisted suicide to direct killing by physicians...

In some countries, these activities by doctors have entered the mainstream of acceptability and practice. In 1991 the Dutch government released the results of a study on medical decisions to end life. In this study,[2] (performed in the Netherlands more than ten years before such activities became legal there) 54% of physicians said they had practiced euthanasia at least once; 34% had not but would be willing to do so under appropriate circumstances.

Two years later, a new report[3] provided more information on one subgroup of those decisions: life-terminating acts performed without the patient's explicit request. In this study, the researchers interviewed 405 physicians in detail, reviewed questionnaires completed after more than 5,000 deaths, and prospectively followed 322 physicians for 6 months. Results indicated that 0.8% to 1.6% of all deaths in the Netherlands were caused by drugs given to hasten death without the patient's explicit request. In 59% of these cases, the physician had information about the patient's wishes short of an explicit request; no discussion with the patient was possible in the remaining cases. In 98% of all cases, the physician had discussed the decision to hasten death with the patient, the patient's relatives, or colleagues. Most patients were thought to be suffering unbearably with no hope of palliation, and 86% were expected to die within a week.

Follow-up studies[4] published in 1996 prompted the following responses:

Euthanasia and Physician-Assisted Suicide in the Netherlands [5]

To the Editor: In their articles on physician-assisted death in the Netherlands (Nov. 28 issue), van der Maas et al. and van der Wal et al. omit some information that has been of particular concern to international observers and is contained in their fuller Dutch report.

---

[2] van der Maas PJ et al. Euthanasia and other medical decisions concerning the end of life. Lancet 1991;338:669-674.

[3] Pijnenborg L et al. Life-terminating acts without explicit request of patient. Lancet 1993;341:1196-1199.

[4] van der Maas PJ, van der Wal G, Haverkate I, et al. Euthanasia, physician-assisted suicide, and other medical practices involving the end of life in the Netherlands, *1990-1995*. N Engl J Med 1996;335:1699-1705.

[5] Correspondence. N Engl J Med 1997;336:1385-1387.

The 1990 study documented that 50 percent of Dutch physicians suggest euthanasia to patients. Neither the physicians nor the study investigators seem to recognize how much the voluntariness of the process is compromised by such a suggestion. A frightened and suffering patient is inclined to listen to a suggestion made by the doctor, even when the doctor is telling the patient that his or her life is not worth living...

The investigators minimize the number of patients put to death who have not requested it by omitting from this category cases in which patients were given pain medication without discussion of the doctors' explicit intention to use the medication to end their lives; these cases are instead treated as deaths secondary to pain medication. These deaths have increased by 40 percent — from 1350 deaths (1 percent of all deaths in the Netherlands) in 1990 to more than 1900 (1.4 percent) in 1995 — a comparison the investigators choose not to make. In over 80 percent of these cases, the patient made no explicit request for death...

Herbert Hendin, M.D. *American Foundation for Suicide Prevention New York, NY 10005*

To the Editor: The report by van der Maas et al. presents the data in a misleading manner, which makes the situation appear more favorable than it is.

Some of the data are presented as the percentage of change, which emphasizes the magnitude of change, whereas other data are presented as absolute numbers, giving an impression of minimal change. Thus, we are told of a 37 percent increase in the number of requests for euthanasia from 1990 to 1995. But the change in the incidence of euthanasia is given in absolute percentages (2.4 percent in 1995 vs. 1.7 percent in 1990), which of course seems to be a trivial increase, whereas the actual increase is 41 percent, or more than an additional 1000 patients whose lives were terminated. The influence of such framing of data on their interpretation has been well documented.

The authors also report data on life expectancy as if these estimates were straightforward facts. The inability of physicians to predict life expectancy for critically ill patients is well known. Categorical statements, such as the statement that patients whose lives were deliberately terminated had "only a few hours or days to live," are not reassuring.

Shimon M. Glick, M.D. *Ben Gurion University of the Negev, Beer Sheva, Israel 84105*

To the Editor: Dutch physicians still do not report the majority of cases of euthanasia and assisted suicide, as required by law. The required safeguard of consultation with another physician occurred in 94 percent of reported cases but in only 11 percent of unreported cases. Without independent consultation by physicians knowledgeable about palliative care, there can be no assurance that physician-assisted death occurs only as a voluntary measure of last resort. In the absence of such consultation, I find it difficult to concur with Dr. Angell's conclusion in her accompanying editorial, "As far as we can tell, Dutch physicians continue to practice physician-assisted dying... under compelling circumstances."

Franklin G. Miller, Ph.D. *University of Virginia, Charlottesville, VA 22908*

In addition, euthanasia in the Netherlands appears to be practised not only on terminally ill adults, and not only by medical practitioners:

To the Editor: In 1991, a Dutch psychiatrist gave a lethal dose of barbiturates to a severely depressed 50-year-old woman at her request. Although physically healthy, the woman had recently gone through a bitter divorce, and her two children had died. The Dutch Supreme Court found the doctor guilty but exempted him from any penalty, ruling that in matters of assisted death, there is no distinction between mental and physical suffering.

In March 1993, a Dutch gynecologist gave a lethal injection to a three-day-old girl born with multiple handicaps, including spina bifida, hydrocephalus, and leg deformities. This physician was cleared of murder charges because he had obtained the consent of the parents and followed official guidelines for euthanasia in adults. It has also been reported that a growing number of older Dutch children with cancers and degenerative diseases are having their lives ended through euthanasia.

In July 1994, a Dutch nurse gave a lethal injection to a friend with AIDS at the friend's request. Under Dutch law, only a physician can perform euthanasia. The nurse was found guilty of this violation, but she was given only a two-month suspended sentence.

These events indicate that in addition to... involuntary euthanasia... there are other disturbing trends in the Dutch practice of physician-assisted death...

Kenneth J. Simcic, M.D. *William Beaumont Army Medical Center, El Paso, TX 79920-5001*

Anatomy of a Disaster
Hurricane Katrina – a Medical Ethical Nightmare

The idea that there may be, at least in some circumstances, a medical *duty* to "euthanize" suffering patients who cannot be saved, and perhaps even without their knowledge or consent, has entered the consciousness of medicine in this generation. Philosopher Peter Singer of Princeton University advocates killing suffering or handicapped babies and others whom he does not regard as "persons," and in the Netherlands today at least some acts in this category are perpetrated and accepted. What "Debbie" began as an outrageous anomaly has passed into mainstream thinking, and more than occasionally into the world of practice.

Hurricane Katrina, which struck New Orleans in August 2005, tested a number of medical ethical issues, including triage and euthanasia, in the harshest way.

Katrina resulted in massive floods in New Orleans, stranding doctors and patients in the city's hospitals for days in extremely trying and sometimes desperate circumstances. A doctor who was present described the situation as follows, and raises the issues of triage and euthanasia:[1]

---

[1] N Engl J Med 2006;355:2067-2069.

Murder or Mercy? Hurricane Katrina and the Need for Disaster Training

Tyler J. Curiel, M.D., M.P.H.

Katrina's floodwaters crippled emergency power generators, transforming hospitals into dark, fetid, dangerous shells. Extremely high indoor temperatures killed some people. We were under tremendous strain: in addition to the dire medical circumstances of many of our patients, we confronted uncertainty about our own evacuation, exacerbated by the tensions of threatened violence by snipers and frazzled soldiers and guards. I saw some competent professionals reduced to utter incoherence and uselessness as the crisis unfolded. I saw others perform heroic deeds that surprised me. Clearly, a better personnel selection process was needed.

[Dr]DeBlieux [ICU head at Charity Hospital] did rate patients according to their potential for survival. "Red meant critical care. Black meant moribund — comfort care only. We had rated a number of patients red, and treated them accordingly. We finally got them evacuated to the airport. I found out later that the airport personnel re-rated them black, and gave comfort care only. We were devastated." The same patients, he explained, received different levels of care depending on the availability of resources at specific locations. "The airport was just too swamped, and they didn't have anything to spare," he noted. Acknowledging that conditions at Memorial, where the heat was extreme, were worse than those at Charity, DeBlieux added, "Now you have to imagine what decisions might have been made at Memorial [Hospital], with its specific conditions."

What might lead a health care professional to consider euthanasia in such a situation? If a terrorist bombs a building and we identify trapped people who are doomed to die before they can be rescued, should we offer to kill them or oblige them if they ask us to do so? If professionals who do undertake euthanasia in such circumstances have had no training in coping with disaster, does that change their accountability? When is such killing murder, and when, if ever, is it medically justified, humane, or legal?

At Tulane, we faced our share of these difficulties after Katrina. I cared for a woman with severe graft-versus-host disease caused by a bone marrow transplant. Given her dismal prognosis, I omitted her from the priority evacuation list — predicting a much greater chance of survival for other patients, including a man with a life-threatening low platelet count due to idiopathic thrombocytopenic purpura. Blood was oozing from his gums, bowels, and skin, and I couldn't treat him because all our blood products had been destroyed by the heat. Although he was at great risk for bleeding into his brain, which could precipitate paralysis or death, I never considered ending his life. Would someone else in the same position have done so?

"Would someone else in the same position have done so?" The answer to that question is disturbing. The following is excerpted from a report in the New England Journal of Medicine:[2]

Dr. P... and the Hurricane — Implications for Patient Care during Disasters

Susan Okie, M.D.

During the flood after Hurricane Katrina in August 2005, health care providers in marooned New Orleans hospitals worked in almost unimaginably difficult conditions while awaiting rescue. Nowhere was the situation more desperate than at Memorial Medical Center, where for 4 days a small staff struggled to care for critically ill patients in a dark building with no electric power, no fresh water, a flooded first floor, a nonfunctional sanitation system, and an interior temperature above 100°F.

Dr. A.M. P..., a cancer surgeon on the faculty of Louisiana State University School of Medicine, was supervising residents at Memorial when Katrina hit on Monday, August 29, and she remained at the hospital after the storm....

At least 34 patients died at Memorial during and after the storm, and shortly thereafter, media reports began to suggest that some had been euthanized. In July 2006, Louisiana's attorney general, Charles Foti, shocked the country by arresting [Dr]P... and two nurses, accusing them of administering morphine and midazolam to kill four elderly patients on September 1, 2005, the day patient evacuation was completed. In a television interview aired in September 2006, [Dr]P... denied the

---

[2] N Engl J Med 2008; 358:1-5.

accusation, stating, "I did not murder those patients. . . . I do not believe in euthanasia. I don't think it's anyone's decision to make when a patient dies. However, what I do believe in is comfort care, and that means that we ensure that they do not suffer pain."

A grand jury considered possible murder charges in the deaths of these four patients plus five others on the same floor, and the attorney general agreed not to pursue charges against the nurses in exchange for their testimony against [Dr]P... This past August, the grand jury refused to indict [Dr]P... she still faces three civil suits that have been brought by relatives of patients who died. After the grand jury's decision, she acknowledged in an interview that she had administered morphine and midazolam to the nine patients knowing that their deaths might be hastened, but she said that she did not intend to kill them...

....By the morning of Thursday, September 1, about 25 of the sickest patients in the complex had been evacuated by helicopter, and staff members were moving other patients, ... to staging areas to await evacuation by helicopter or boat. The staff apparently decided that these nine could not be rescued, but it is unclear who made that decision and whether it was based on the patients' medical conditions, their resuscitation status (five of the nine reportedly had do-not-resuscitate [DNR] orders), or other considerations. According to written responses that [Dr]P... provided for this article, "The standard of rescue [had] changed from Tuesday to Thursday; initially the sickest patients were evacuated first. When we realized that help was not imminent, ... the standard of rescue changed to that of reverse triage. It was recognized that some patients might not survive, and priority was given to those who had the best chance of survival. On Thursday morning, only category 3 patients [the most gravely ill] remained on the... unit."

The story so far is incomplete... The version we have comes from an affidavit that was issued at the time of [Dr]P...'s arrest by the Louisiana Department of Justice and from a summary of evidence that was released by that department last July... According to the documents, Susan Mulderick, the Memorial "incident commander" who oversaw patient care and evacuation during and after Katrina, allegedly told employees at a meeting on the morning of September 1 that she did not expect [the] nine critically ill patients to be evacuated. Later, she allegedly told three... employees that the plan was not to leave any living patients behind. Therese Mendez, a nurse executive for LifeCare, stated that Dr. P... told her on the morning of September 1 that a decision had been made to administer lethal doses of medication to the remaining patients *on the seventh floor. Steven Harris, [the] pharmacy director, stated that [Dr]P... also informed him of the decision and showed him about 27 vials of morphine; he later told the attorney general that he gave her midazolam and additional morphine.*

Diane Robichaux,... assistant administrator, stated that during a discussion of the patients' mental status, she informed [Dr]P... that at least one patient, Emmett Everett, 61, was alert, oriented, and interactive, although he weighed 380 lb and was paralyzed. Kristy Johnson, ... director of physical medicine, said she watched [Dr]P... and two nurses draw liquid from vials into syringes and that she guided them to patients' rooms on the seventh floor. She said that outside Everett's room, [Dr]P... appeared nervous and said she planned to tell him she was giving him something for dizziness. Johnson also said she heard [Dr]P... say, regarding another patient, "I had to give her three doses, she's fighting." She said [Dr]P... asked her for a list of remaining... patients and their room numbers, and then instructed the... staff to leave, saying the patients were "in our care now."

Dr. John Skinner, Memorial's director of pathology, stated that because of plans to finish the evacuation and lock down the hospital by 5 p.m., he made rounds throughout the hospital during the afternoon of September 1 to document all deaths and to make sure no one had been left behind. He said he encountered Dr. P... on the seventh floor with a patient who appeared to be alive and offered to help her evacuate the patient, but she said she wanted to talk with an anesthesiologist first. Skinner said he returned to the seventh floor around 3:30 p.m. and found that all the patients there were dead.

Establishing the causes of the deaths of the nine patients was problematic. The bodies lay in the sweltering hospital for 10 days before they were recovered, and autopsies were not performed for another week or more. This past February, after considering the opinions of multiple experts, Orleans Parish coroner Frank Minyard announced that he could not determine whether the patients had died from natural causes or homicide. On the autopsy reports, the classification of the deaths has been left blank. Toxicology studies of liver and purge fluid documented the presence of significant levels of morphine in all nine patients and of midazolam in seven; levels of one or both drugs in brain tissue were also measured in eight patients. However, because of the extent of decomposition, these results may not accurately reflect what the levels were when the patients died.

The patients, four men and five women, ranged in age from 61 to 90 and had varied medical problems. Richard Deichmann, Memorial's chief of medicine, said in an interview that some... patients were dependent on ventilators and others had chronic, nonhealing wounds or required tube feeding or hyperalimentation. Before Katrina, they were "just long-term patients who weren't well enough to really go home," he said. However, as hospital conditions deteriorated, many patients got sicker or became dehydrated — for example, Ireatha Watson, one of the nine patients, was coded and resuscitated after developing a temperature of 105°F and probable aspiration.

About 2000 people... had taken shelter at Memorial... In Code Blue, his harrowing Katrina memoir, Deichmann describes "dozens of people sprawled on the floors and corridors of the hospital, lifting their voices to ask for water and assistance." Routines for tasks such as drug ordering and charting broke down; the approximately 25 physicians in the hospital, assigned to nurses' stations, were to sort patients into triage categories so that sicker patients could be evacuated first. To evacuate nonambulatory patients, employees had to carry them on stretchers down multiple flights of stairs to the second floor, pass them through a narrow opening in a wall into the parking garage, and then either transport them to the helipad on the garage roof or load them onto boats. "Our intention was that we were going to evacuate all the patients, [but] we decided early on that the patients that were 'no codes'. . . were going to be lower on the priority list," Deichmann said. "Lots of no-code patients were evacuated. Some of them died awaiting evacuation."

Wednesday night or early Thursday morning, hospital administrators received word that no government rescue was forthcoming. Staff morale plummeted... In his book, Deichmann writes that Susan Mulderick, the incident commander, asked him on Wednesday whether euthanasia should be considered for some patients with DNR orders but that he immediately dismissed the idea... On Thursday, staff members and rescuers managed to round up a fleet of private fishing boats that evacuated scores of patients, and helicopter flights resumed.

As a doctor responsible for patients who, it had apparently been determined, were not going to be rescued, [Dr]P... was faced with a dire choice, noted R. Alta Charo, a professor of law and bioethics at the University of Wisconsin. "From her perspective, these people are now terminal — because of their biological status, their medical condition, and the environmental context... and they're terminal under particularly terrifying conditions: extreme discomfort, [probably] panic, and the *prospect of being abandoned while helpless," said Charo. If [Dr]P... could not save them, then her next obligation "would seem to be palliation... to give them enough medicine that they're not in any pain and they're not in any panic and it may or may not hasten their deaths." If her intent was to relieve suffering, Charo added, "then I don't think anybody in the ethics community would bat an eye. If it [was] specifically to hasten death... then it becomes a little more questionable." Furthermore, [Dr]P... had a duty to inform any conscious, competent patients of the circumstances and offer them a choice about accepting the medications — "not a choice," noted Charo, that "we are willing to take away from people capable of making it."*

... [Dr]P... argues that "the conditions faced were similar to battlefield conditions" and that civilian medical training does not prepare physicians for such circumstances: "There's nothing that teaches reverse triage, military evacuation strategies, or how to prepare oneself for the feelings of helplessness and sorrow that come when there is little to do for a patient based on lack of resources."

These disturbing reports raise important points. One is the assumption that it is better to kill patients rather than allow them to suffer helplessly, and that this may in fact be a doctor's duty. This is radically contrary to Jewish law.

Another is the observation that despite the paramount position of patient autonomy in the present hierarchy of medical ethical values, these patients do not appear to have been given a choice. Apparently medical paternalism, even to the extent of deciding to kill patients without their choice, has a place in such scenarios. The reasons for this, however, are not clear.

The comment of the ethicist consulted on these events is revealing. After opining that it would be proper to relieve suffering even if shortening life may turn out to be a by-product of that effort, the professor goes on to say: *If her intent was to relieve suffering... "then I don't think anybody in the ethics community would bat an eye. If it [was] specifically to hasten death... then it becomes a little more questionable."* A little more questionable? In Jewish law it is hard to imagine anything that could be more questionable.

What are the principles of triage to be applied in these circumstances? It seems that the priorities used as described in the reports would generally accord with halacha:[3] it is correct to save the sickest patients first if that is the way to save the most lives. Assuming that those who are not as ill will survive until evacuation becomes possible, those who need immediate lifesaving evacuation should be given priority. When the situation changes, however, and it becomes apparent that if the sickest are saved first, those remaining are likely to die before evacuation, it may be appropriate to apply the "reverse triage" described. The general principle to be applied is to proceed in such a manner as to save the maximum number of lives.

What may be done to relieve suffering in such extreme circumstances? It is certainly appropriate to treat pain and distress, even where such treatment carries risk (as outlined above,[4] provided that all the conditions mentioned there are fulfilled).

At what point may the doctors in such a situation take steps to save themselves? The relevant principle here is that one's own life generally takes precedence over others'; therefore when it becomes clear that no more can be done to rescue or treat patients except at grave danger to the medical personnel, they no longer have an obligation to treat and may desist. Of course, nothing may be done to harm patients or in any way compromise them medically, and all efforts to rescue every patient must continue from a distance.

In practice, doctors have a duty to do everything possible for every patient in such a situation, both medically and emotionally. When nothing more can be done, the doctor must stay with the patient until the stark choice arrives – remain when that means that both doctor and patient will die, or leave. At that point, but not before, the doctor is free to leave.

And even then, the patient must not be given a feeling of abandonment and hopelessness – in halacha, causing such anguish is regarded as materially harming a patient whose situation is fragile and is clearly forbidden.[5]

---

[3] See Triage, p. 171.

[4] See Analgesia in Dangerously or Terminally Ill Patients, p. 112.

[5] See above, p. 101, note 2 and p. 113, note 45. See also Afterword, p. 289.

Materialism and Medical Ethics

The following is excerpted from an article in the Jerusalem Post, December 27, 2007:

Not a Doctor's Decision

by Jonathan Rosenblum

A Winnipeg case currently winding its way to its grim conclusion pits the children of Samuel Golubchuk against doctors at the Salvation Army Grace General Hospital. According to the pleadings, Golubchuk's doctors informed his children that their 84-year-old father is "in the process of dying" and that they intended to hasten the process by removing his ventilation, and if that proved insufficient to kill him quickly, to also remove his feeding tube. In the event that the patient showed discomfort during these procedures, the chief of the hospital's ICU unit stated in his affidavit that he would administer morphine.

Golubchuk is an Orthodox Jew, as are his children. The latter have adamantly opposed his removal from the ventilator and feeding tube, on the grounds that Jewish law expressly forbids any action designed to shorten life, and that if their father could express his wishes, he would oppose the doctors acting to deliberately terminate his life.

In response, the director of the ICU informed Golubchuk's children that neither their father's wishes nor their own are relevant, and he would do whatever he decided was appropriate. Bill Olson, counsel for the ICU director, told the Canadian Broadcasting Company that physicians have the sole right to make decisions about treatment - even if it goes against a patient's religious beliefs - and that "there is no right to a continuation of treatment." That position was supported by Dr. Jeff Blackner, executive director of the office of ethics of the Canadian Medical Association. He told Reuters: "[W]e want to make sure that clinical decisions are left to physicians and not judges." Doctors' decisions are made only with the "best interest of the individual patient at heart," he said, though he did not explain how that could be squared with the undisputed claim that this patient would oppose the doctors' decision. Meanwhile, an Angus Reid poll of Canadians showed that 68% supported leaving the final decision with the family. The claim of absolute physician discretion to withdraw life-support advanced by the Canadian doctors would spell the end of any patient autonomy over end-of-life decisions. So-called living wills, which are recognized in many American states, and which allow a person to specify in advance who should make such decisions in the event of their incapacity, would be rendered nugatory....

And in a follow-up article (July 2008), after the patient's death:

After the entry of a temporary injunction, the hospital pursued an aggressive legal and public relations campaign. At one recent hearing, the hospital was represented by a team of... seven... attorneys...

Three doctors resigned from the hospital's intensive care unit claiming they were being forced to violate their ethical beliefs by continuing to treat Mr. Golubchuk rather than simply hastening his death...

[Mr. Golubchuk was described as "awake, alert, sitting up in a chair at times, more interactive and shaking hands purposively..."]

One editorial in the journal of the Canadian Medical Association went so far as to accuse the Golubchuk children of using their religious beliefs to gain special treatment for their father. And numerous letters appeared in the Canadian press decrying or ridiculing the Golubchuk's religious fanaticism.

In Mr. Golubchuk's case there could be no dispute about what his wishes were. This was no replay of the... Terry Schiavo case. Yet the hospital and his doctors viewed those wishes as irrelevant. The Statement of the

College of Physicians and Surgeons of Manitoba on Withholding and Withdrawing Life-Sustaining Treatment, published after the issuance of the first injunction, explicitly provides that "physicians have the authority to make medical decisions to withhold or withdraw life-sustaining treatment from a patient without the consent of the patient or the patient's family."

This case is disturbing not only because it represents a step further from an ethical worldview that is already at odds with halacha, but also because it is a radical departure from conventional secular ethical criteria. The approach of this Canadian hospital and indeed that of the Canadian Medical Association and the College of Physicians and Surgeons of Manitoba demonstrated here diverges sharply from one based on the widely accepted basic values of modern medical ethics. Autonomy, the value usually given precedence, is here discarded entirely: no argument was made that Mr Golubchuk had chosen or would have chosen to have his therapy withdrawn. It is manifestly clear that he and his family staunchly adhered to a halachic standard that requires the continuation of life-sustaining treatment in situations such as his. But a new value appears to be given greater priority than the patient's wishes in this case: the concept of low quality of life, or its probable short duration, or perhaps the two combined – these suggest to the Canadian doctors involved that continuing treatment is "futile." Their idea of the futility of treatment overrides the basic principle of patient autonomy, and indeed even the basic Western respect for freedom of religious expression. The patient's personal wishes and his religious convictions are seen as entirely irrelevant, and not because justice, beneficence or non-maleficence are perceived to have been compromised here, but simply because there is a conviction that the value of this patient's life is purely a clinical matter – *"[W]e want to make sure that clinical decisions are left to physicians..."* – and then that the correct clinical decision is that this patient's continued life is futile.

(It is more than likely that the doctors in this case would assert that they have not abandoned the value of patient autonomy altogether – in cases where they consider treatment to be reasonable but the patient chooses to reject it they would respect that choice. In other words, they fully subscribe to the primacy of patient autonomy *where that autonomy is expressed as the choice to die*; it is only where the choice is to live that they deny it. But that is unthinkable: can they be so morally derelict as to claim loyalty to a value that they will trample when it does not yield their personal preference?

If the current system of values claims to place the patient's autonomous choice as paramount and then allows only the choices that it has already decided are acceptable, it has made a mockery of its most basic value. You cannot have it both ways: if you are serious about autonomy you must grant it freely and honor it impartially.)

This approach goes further than any old-style medical paternalism – *"Doctors' decisions are made only with the 'best interest of the individual patient at heart...'"* even when that decision is to terminate a patient's life against his and his family's wishes. This is a sweeping arrogation of the right to define the value of life itself that brushes aside the broadly accepted modern canon. It is hard to imagine a more extreme deviation from the consensus on the core values forming the framework of modern Western medical ethics. If these senior spokesmen of Canadian medicine accurately reflect the attitude of their profession in their country, one is forced to conclude that (in that country at least) we are entering a new era in which deference is no longer given to patient autonomy or the notion of freedom of religion, and not even in matters of life and death.

Indeed, the very idea of individual rights is threatened here: the hospital's legal representative announced publicly that *"there is no right to a continuation of treatment."* This is dangerously close to denying the right to life itself, and there is hardly a more basic right than that.

This deprivation of a patient's most fundamental right is fully endorsed by the College of Physicians and Surgeons: *"... physicians have the authority to make medical decisions to withhold or withdraw life-sustaining treatment from a patient without the consent of the patient or the patient's family."* What major new principle is the basis for this sinister "authority" that trumps the least contentious of all rights?

"[W]e want to make sure that clinical decisions are left to physicians and not judges"...

But of course this is not a clinical decision. Clinical medicine concerns itself with questions of how to care for ill patients, not with the deeply philosophical question of the meaning and value of life – that is a spiritual and religious issue. How to prolong a patient's life by means of clinical skill, therapeutics and technologies is a medical question; *whether* to prolong that life or not is a profoundly existential question. In situations that require such ultimately existential decisions, medicine can be no more than a loyal handmaiden. Clinical medicine is not predicated on a specific value system or religion any more than any other science. It is true that the science and art of medicine reach deeply into the human experience; to be sure, medicine seeks insight into the nature of the human being both biologically and psychologically, but it makes no pretensions of being the final arbiter of the deepest philosophical issues of the meaning of life and its ultimate value.

This should be obvious. But the really perplexing question is this: what underlies these doctors' total discounting of any element beyond the technical? This is *entirely* a spiritual or existential issue. Medical futility simply means that the patient cannot be kept alive beyond a certain point – that judgment is certainly "clinical"; whether the patient *should* be kept alive until that point is a moral and religious question, not a clinical one. What gives a doctor the confidence to assert categorically that there is no moral issue here, only a medical one? A patient wishes to remain alive, that is clearly his personal conviction and an expression of his religious values, and his doctors see only a "clinical" issue – how is this possible? What sort of fundamental blindness is this?

The answer must be that society has so pervasively entered a mode of reductionist materialism that in the popular mind no other view is possible. The rejection of a religious view is based on the conviction that religion has nothing meaningful to say, that it *could not* have anything relevant to add. Those Canadian doctors and judges have decided that religion can be no more than a personal whim, mere superstition, and if the decisions to be made in this case are not clinical, they are nothing – there is no other system of knowledge to consider. What is not scientific is less than irrelevant; it does not exist in reality.

When a doctor assumes that a religious question is medical he demonstrates that in his worldview one needs no religious qualification to adjudicate religious matters; he does not even realize that such qualification could exist. He accepts that medical opinions need knowledge and credentials – you would look foolish holding forth on a technical medical issue if you had no medical knowledge. But he does not begin to realize that Torah knowledge is at least as rigorously necessary in its own domain; that if there is one area that needs an immense effort of study and due qualification it is Torah. In the world of Torah, nothing could be further from mere superstition and personal whim than genuine knowledge and objective halachic expertise.

This is a peculiar blindness. It is not merely a matter of a too-superficial understanding of religion; the doctor who opines that there are no issues here other than clinical ones is not merely inadequately educated religiously – his ignorance is much more profound. He cannot identify a religious issue when he sees one because it has never occurred to him that the world of the spirit may have anything objective about it. This is a symptom of an ethos that allows anyone to say anything about religion with no fear of contradiction; religion is no more than personal feeling, and everyone's feelings must be equally valid.

This has been recognized by observers of modern society. Dorothy Sayers complained about the "the present climate of opinion [in which] biologists [air their opinions] about metaphysics; inorganic chemists, about theology..." When it comes to religion, one needs no credentials or qualifications; scientists offer opinions on spiritual matters without even a passing thought that real knowledge may be required. This can be seen everywhere – a popular modern exercise is the debate between science and religion, but it is striking that very often the protagonists are duly (even superbly) qualified scientifically but have no formal religious training. When a widely read weekly magazine published a debate on this subject[1] the two protagonists chosen were a famously atheistic Oxford biologist and a famous geneticist who is a religious Christian – but who has no professional religious credentials and claims no deeper religious education. Who would dream of convening a serious debate in any other area of human enquiry where neither party to the debate has more than the most amateur of acquaintances with the subject?

This same biologist presumes to write a book on the subject of religion; but what gives a man the idea that he can deal seriously with a subject that he has never studied deeply? Anyone with more than a passing knowledge of religion who reads his material is struck by its extreme incompetence, not only in its lack of authentic sources and arguments but its patent unawareness even that there is such material. Here is one comment on this phenomenon:

> *"Imagine someone holding forth on biology whose only knowledge of the subject is the Book of British Birds, and you have a rough idea of what it feels like to read Richard Dawkins on theology. Card-carrying rationalists like Dawkins, who is the nearest thing to a professional atheist we have had since Bertrand Russell, are in one sense the least well-equipped to understand what they castigate, since they don't believe there is anything there to be understood, or at least anything*

---

[1] Time, November 5, 2006.

worth understanding. This is why they invariably come up with vulgar caricatures of religious faith that would make a first-year theology student wince. The more they detest religion, the more ill-informed their criticisms of it tend to be. If they were asked to pass judgment on phenomenology or the geopolitics of South Asia, they would no doubt bone up on the question as assiduously as they could. When it comes to theology, however, any shoddy old travesty will pass muster... critics of the richest, most enduring form of popular culture in human history have a moral obligation to confront that case at its most persuasive, rather than grabbing themselves a victory on the cheap by savaging it as so much garbage and gobbledygook." [2]

Thomas Nagel's critique of Dawkins is equally devastating, as are all the critiques offered by professional philosophers and qualified thinkers. The point is clear: in the popular notion, religion is not something that has objective reality; it is *by definition* subjective. In the popular mind, everyone's ideas about religion are equally valid, and Nobel prize-winning scientists pontificate about the validity of the Bible though they cannot even read it in the original.

A sharp (and sadly amusing) reminder of this blindness to the requirement for rigorous religious qualification and its out-of-hand dismissal by the modern scientific establishment was provided in a debate that took place some years ago between eminent scientists and religious thinkers. On that occasion the religious side included some genuinely knowledgeable authorities, including one rabbi with a particularly incisive wit. The first speaker was a famous atheistic astrophysicist; as usual, a person with no religious training or credentials at all. He began the debate thus: "Ladies and gentlemen, I don't know much about religion, but I think it can be summed up as: 'Do unto others as you would have them do unto you...'" And from there he proceeded to build his argument. The rabbi was next to speak, and he began thus: "Ladies and gentlemen, I don't know much about astrophysics, but I think it can be summed up as: 'Twinkle, twinkle, little star...'"

This is an unusual debate: usually, each side understands the other but disagrees with it. To debate a subject, you must understand what the opposition is saying; how can you debate meaningfully otherwise? But here the chasm is so wide that one of the sides does not even

---

[2] Terry Eagleton; in the London Review of Books, 19 Oct, 2006.

acknowledge that there is another side at all. The secular side has no idea that there is cogent evidence on the other side; on the contrary, it is convinced that the very idea of religion *means* that area of human interest that has no evidence. (The same biologist quoted above writes off religion with this: "Faith is belief without evidence." He does not begin to realize that *that* sort of faith has nothing to do with Judaism – evidence is as critical in Judaism as it is in science; the last thing Judaism would endorse is completely arbitrary, blind faith.)

There can be little doubt that the basis for this phenomenon is the evolutionary underpinning of Western thought (or perhaps both are symptoms of an even more fundamental secularism). If it is clear that we are nothing but accidental biological organisms whose minds are no more than accidents in a material medium, then of course any talk of transcendence and the Absolute is nonsense, or at best irrelevant. In a secular and material worldview, we are animals.

And yet there is a reluctance to give up the human. Many of these same materialists who insist that we are no more than biological matter also wax eloquent about our humanity and wonder at the beauty and elegance of the world and our place in it in a way that is very far from the brute awareness of the merely animal.

But again, you cannot have it both ways. Either there is no more than the brute matter of the physical, and imputing meaning to such a world is sheer delusion, or our consciousness is a window to something higher that is real and one must acquire the tools to access that higher dimension – and ignoring it would be to live in delusion.

And you cannot have it both ways when it comes to the question of the difference between humans and animals. If you are convinced that there is nothing beyond biology, you must either elevate animals to the human, or demote us to the animal. In the final analysis the difference will be no more than semantic – if we are on the same level as animals it makes little difference where we stand and how we act; in essence it makes no real difference whether we eat at elegant tables with prim etiquette or drool over our oats at the same trough.

In fact, both approaches are found today. Some elevate the animal: in some modern jurisdictions primates have been given civil rights. Language has been enlisted to smooth this change in consciousness – National Geographic magazine published its July, 2008 issue with a cover story entitled: "Who Murdered the Mountain Gorillas?" Letters to the editor included one praising this egalitarian use of language (as well as one castigating this blurring of the human-animal boundary).

And some demote the human: as noted, a well-known Princeton philosophy professor suggests killing handicapped infants (at parents' discretion, for the first 28 days of life, or on a "case by case basis"). He claims that some people with life-long cognitive disabilities never become "persons," and it is not wrong to kill beings who are not "persons." This philosopher, who favors animal rights, writes that bestiality does not constitute a transgression of our status as humans because humans are animals ("we are great apes"). But if all humans are animals, what does he mean by a "person"? Are degrees of cognition enough to make some animals "persons" and others not?

This effacing of the human-animal boundary is dangerous: if we are all in the same boat, it makes no difference whom you throw overboard. Of course, the materialist will say that is fine; it truly makes no difference.

But does he really mean that? In his inalienably human heart he knows that his humanity is real and that it should oblige. Incidents such as the following point to this hidden ambivalence:

When the lady seated next to the rabbi received her vegetarian airline meal, he asked if she were eating vegetarian because of a concern for kosher food, perhaps? "No," she replied pointedly, "I don't eat other animals." We are simply another species. The rabbi made no comment, but the correct response to that statement is: "Why not, lady? Other animals do..."

If you are no more than animal, from where do you derive the morality that makes eating animals unfair? That is not the rule of the animal; indeed, if she had assimilated the idea of her animal identity deeply enough, instead of making moral points to the rabbi she ought to be taking a bite out of his neck.

There is deep conflict here. At the intellectual level, modern atheists insist that there is no higher meaning or purpose to existence; we are accidents of physics and biology. Yet at another level they enthuse about the beauty and grandeur, and even the *meaning* of human existence. But if nothing transcends the material, our lives can have no meaning; in fact the very concept of meaning becomes incoherent. Meaning is a transcendent thing, a meta-concept. You cannot manufacture meaning; at least not that sort. The illusory grasp of an imaginary value can be no more than a pathetically empty thing, an essentially accidental confluence of electrochemical brain events no more meaningful and reaching no further than any physiological process in an earthworm. Man's sense of self, his morality, his sense of love and honor, his sense of guilt and shame – nothing *really* matters, and of course euthanasia makes sense; why not? As a famous atheistic surgeon put it, we put dogs out of their misery when they are suffering; we ought to do the same for people.

In fact, there is more than conflict; there is confusion. A medical journal editor writes:[3]

> *"The pity of it all is that opponents of the theory of evolution have missed the main point. The central idea of the theory is not the Victorian image of a hairy ape with a human face. On the contrary, the theory unveils the beautiful thought that all living creatures are related – in a sense, we are all one. This concept, if properly understood, can inspire more faith...."*

Of course we are all one, and in a sense more profound than this writer begins to admit – we are all part of a cosmic Oneness that pervades far more than our biological relatedness. Certainly the bodies of all living creatures are made of the same stuff and manifest the same patterns (it is not in the material body or its basic responses that the difference between human and animal is to be found). Indeed that unifying theme weaving through its myriad variations should inspire thoughts of beauty and faith.

But if the relatedness of all living creatures means that nothing transcends the animal, and if the animal amounts to no more than accidental arrangements of material substance, then how is it that *"[T]his concept, if properly understood, can inspire more faith..."*?

More faith? In what? What possible definition of faith can he mean? What place can there be for any sort of faith in a world that is no more than a menagerie? In what animal heart or brain can faith assume a meaning? Only a human could be so confused as to evoke beautiful thoughts and a sense of faith from the commonality of brutes.

---

[3] Editorial; N Engl J Med 2005;353:1439.

Afterword

"Abandon hope, all ye who enter here..."

Serious illnesses with little hope of cure have become death sentences in modern practice. Previous generations of doctors fought for the smallest hope; now hope is abandoned without a fight when things look bleak. Modern doctors are too ready to capitulate to serious illness and "poor quality of life," and old age has become a death sentence in itself.

Abandoning hope is not allowed in Judaism. But abandoning hope is not only bad religion, it is very bad medicine. Hope is therapeutic; the abandoning of hope may become self-fulfilling. The doctor must always focus on hope and transmit it to the patient no matter how small the chance of cure, not only because that is humane, but because it is good medicine.[1]

In halacha, even when it is necessary to convey a catastrophic diagnosis to a patient, the discussion must begin with a positive statement.[2] No

---

[1] "[H]opelessness is a strong predictor of adverse health outcomes, independent of depression and traditional risk factors." Everson SA et al. Hopelessness and Risk of Mortality and Incidence of Myocardial Infarction and Cancer. Psychosomatic Medicine 1996;58:113-121.

See also: Murray Parkes C et al. Broken Heart: A Statistical Study of Increased Mortality among Widowers. BMJ 1969;1:740–743; Phillips DP et al. Psychology and Survival. Lancet 1993;342:1142-5; and Whitney SN et al. Beyond Breaking Bad News: the Roles of Hope and Hopefulness. Cancer 2008;113:442-5.

[2] Concerning the confession to be said before dying, Y.D. 338:1 states that the gravely ill person should be told: "Many have recited the confession and did not die..."

situation should be presented as utterly hopeless, no matter how dismal it may be.[3] Some form of treatment beyond mere palliation must always be given to a conscious patient,[4] even if only to avoid the dangerous realization that definitive care has ceased because all is lost. It is essential to realize that this is not futile therapy, and not merely because it may have a psychological effect – indeed, even if active therapy served no purpose beyond maintaining an atmosphere of hope it would be justified; but the fact is that hope and a positive attitude are essential elements affecting the physiological too.[5]

Today's hospice and terminal care programs whose policy is explicitly or tacitly to abandon hope of cure and focus instead on facilitating a dignified death are contrary to the letter and spirit of Jewish law. Programs that define the expected outcome as death with palliation and exclude all possibility of therapeutic care as a policy are condemning their patients to a hopelessness whose torment may be worse than that of their illnesses.

Medical Treason: Healers and Executioners

We have moved with surprising rapidity from an era in which life was an end in itself, sacrosanct, above and beyond other values, to a time in which patients are abandoned or assisted in dying, and the door is ajar on an era in which doctors are to become executioners.

But even if an argument could ever be made for hastening death, no doctor should be the agent of that function. The doctor should always be fighting for life wherever that is possible and must always be perceived in that role; no conflict of interest can be allowed to enter the doctor-patient relationship. The doctor is the patient's advocate for life and cure; the

---

[3] See Moed Katan 26b; Sh. Aruch Y. D. 337 and Shach there (subs. 1). See also Nishm. Avraham Y.D. 337:2 and 338:1. See p.101 above.

[4] Igr. Moshe Ch. M. 2:75. Such treatment need not necessarily include medications; dietary or other directions may suffice. The point is to avoid transmitting the message that all therapy is hopeless.

[5] See Segerstrom SC, Miller GE. Psychological Stress and the Human Immune System: A Meta-Analytic Study of 30 Years of Inquiry. Psychological Bulletin 2004; 130, No.4; and Kiecolt-Glaser JK, Glaser R. Depression and immune function: Central pathways to morbidity and mortality. Journal of Psychosomatic Research 2002;53:873-876.

patient's trust in that advocacy must never be tainted with the knowledge that at some point it may transform into an advocacy for death. Trust is basic to the doctor-patient relationship;[6] when a patient knows that his doctor may become his executioner at some time and that in at least some circumstances the patient may have no say in judging when that time has arrived, that trust will surely dissolve. At the root of the doctor-patient relationship must be the secure knowledge that the doctor will pursue only life, cure and relief, and never betray that agenda. The nature of medicine requires that patients place their lives in their doctors' hands; the steadier those hands in their dedication to patients' life and safety, the greater will be that trust. The surest way to destroy the therapeutic nature of the doctor-patient relationship is to place vulnerable patients' lives and health in ambivalent hands.

Where palliative expertise is necessary, that too is part of the doctor's function, but any suggestion of a doctor playing the role of executioner is odious in the extreme. If that role were ever to be filled, why should it fall to a physician? Surely the very last candidate for that job should be the one whose entire professional essence is nurturing and guarding life and health. When a healer crosses the line from promoting life and hope to extinguishing those, he has betrayed his essence.

The natural sensitivity that leads a healer to shrink from becoming an agent of death is widely shared among medical professionals in the context of legal execution.[7] The consensus is that even doctors who support the death penalty should not be involved in its execution; the act of taking life is simply incompatible with the nature of a healer. In the context of clinical medicine, however, that sensitivity is far from universal.

---

[6] Halacha regards the doctor-patient relationship itself as therapeutic; a personal relationship with a particular physician may constitute an essential component of the therapy. For practical expressions of this see Y.D. 336:1 and Nishm. Avr. Vol. I, p. 225.

[7] "Physicians and other health care providers should not be involved in capital punishment, even in an advisory capacity. A profession dedicated to healing the sick has no place in the process of execution." Physicians and Execution. Editorial. N Engl J Med 2008;358:403-404.

"Even physicians who support the death penalty should stay out of its execution..." Annas, GJ. Toxic Tinkering — Lethal-Injection Execution and the Constitution. N Engl J Med 2008;359:1512-1518.

A New Ideal

Facilitating death has moved beyond acceptance in today's medicine; it is now part of its essence. The following is excerpted from a roundtable discussion on the future of primary care in the United States that was convened to address, among other things, the need for more primary care physicians. One of the goals of the discussion was to show young physicians why primary care can be a rewarding field worth considering when choosing a career path. The excerpt describes an encounter in the professional life of one of the panelists, a senior primary care practitioner, and conveys the satisfaction she experiences in fulfilling her role as physician:

When I met Mrs. C, she told me, "I am 82 years old. I have lived a good life. I am ready to die. Please do not do anything to prolong my life..." By the time she was 94, she had become quite frail... [O]ne day... [s]he wouldn't get out of bed. She wasn't eating... Soon, she developed a fever... [H]er family wanted to bring her in [to the hospital]. She refused. Her temperature rose higher. She was no longer responsive. I heard the anxiety in her daughter's voice as she reported this latest development. I offered to come see her that night.

When I arrived, 22 family members were waiting. The anxiety was palpable. Mrs. C was unconscious in a bed in the front parlor. I greeted the relatives, some of whom were also my patients, and went to examine Mrs. C. She was dehydrated, unresponsive, burning with fever. She would clearly die unless I did something drastic. In my mind, I could hear my patient's clear and consistent instruction. I laid my hand on her hot, dry forehead and silently said good-bye.

Then I sat down with her family. "Shouldn't we take her to the hospital?" "What about giving her oral antibiotics?" "We can't just let her die here." The questions poured over me.... I reminded them that she would not want to go to the hospital. I talked about how hard it is to do nothing but said I believed that by being here with her and allowing her to die as she had asked, they were doing something very important: respecting and loving her... I suggested they be with her, talk to her, say their good-byes. I gave them a prescription for morphine in case she became uncomfortable and said they could page me at any time.

Then I left. The room was calm. People were hugging each other. I had walked into a room of fear and anxiety and left a room of peace – not because of me... but because of my role as physician.

Two hours later, the family paged me. Mrs. C had died peacefully. After I left, her family had gathered around her bed, telling stories, laughing, and crying. They had sung her favorite hymns as she slowly stopped breathing. Later, one of the letters I received from her family said, "Without your presence, this moment would have been very difficult for all of us... The firm guiding hand of the doctor was felt"...

For me, this is the essence of primary care: comprehensive, longitudinal, and relational...[8]

Here, an experienced doctor and teacher shares her experience of primary care in a manner that may be hoped to inspire graduates to go into this field. Of all the cases she has handled in years of practice she chooses to demonstrate the appeal of primary care with a case of allowing her patient to die; indeed, of convincing a family against its instinct to allow their mother to die. Of course, she is honoring her patient's wishes; that is exactly what respect for autonomy requires – the patient wishes to die because she has *"lived a good life"* and is *"ready to die"* and that is enough. The fact that she has an undiagnosed condition that may be eminently treatable is irrelevant, and her family's opinion is irrelevant; the doctor has become the patient's advocate for death and has applied a *"firm guiding hand"* to fulfil that role.

That this is against everything Judaism teaches goes without saying, and all this is entirely unremarkable in the modern context where autonomy is paramount. What is remarkable, however, is that this case should be chosen to show the greatness and goodness of primary care medicine. This is the case that will best express *"my role as physician,"* that will inspire young doctors to choose that role. With years, perhaps decades, of experience in the practice of medicine this doctor could no doubt have told of night hours at a bedside waiting for a crisis to pass, saving a fragile newborn life, witnessing the miracle of an apparently hopeless

---

[8] Treadway, K: "Sustaining Relationships," from The Future of Primary Care, N Engl J Med 2008;359:2086-8. The author is an assistant professor on the faculty of Harvard Medical School and in the Department of Medicine at Massachusetts General Hospital.

case recover against all odds, helping a devastated patient discover a reason to live, coaxing a bereaved mother back into the mainstream of life, helping parents with borderline coping skills manage without compromising their dignity, converting tragedy into cure with an astute and timely diagnosis, examining the newborn child of parents she cared for when they themselves were born, attending the wedding of a young person she helped through the dark days of a childhood malignancy that she helped beat, attending a woman in labor whose infertility she shared and defeated, sharing a family's pain when she was unable to prevent tragedy...

Surely the glory of primary care lies in those moments. Every experienced doctor cherishes the memory of the spark of clinical intuition that led to an excellent diagnosis, or perhaps even more, the knowledge that consistent, methodical and thorough practice has prevented disease and averted much suffering. From a multitude of medical memories, is this the case to recall for the purpose of showing the reward and satisfaction of primary care, indeed for showing the very essence of primary care? *"For me, this is the essence of primary care..."* Even if this case raised no ethical issues at all, the fact that it is chosen as the vehicle for demonstrating the desirability of a particular field of medicine shows clearly that facilitating death has become an integral part of medicine, and perhaps even an ideal.

Moments of Eternity

In July of 1944, in Slabodka, when Rabbi Abraham Grodzenski was bedridden in a hospital that the Germans were about to burn with the patients inside, he asked to be moved to a place where it seemed that he might be able to survive a little longer.[9] Quoting his teacher, the Alter of Slabodka, Rabbi Grodzenski commented on the words of Jonah the prophet: when Jonah is unavoidably about to be cast into a raging sea to avert tragedy from his fellow seafarers, he says "Lift me and cast me..." The Alter pointed out that the words "Lift me" are unnecessary, they appear to add nothing to the narrative; had Jonah simply said "Cast me..." the scene would have been equally clear. Those extra words, said the

---

[9] R. Yitzchak Grodzenski. See also the introduction to Torat Avraham. In the event his injuries were too severe, he could not be moved and was burned to death; 13th July, 1944.

Alter, teach a critical lesson: even when death is inevitable and rapidly approaching, if an extra few seconds of life can be gained, they are to be seized, not spurned. "Lift me..." – that will be one action, it will take a second or two; and then "Cast me..." if you must. But I will have gained a second or two of life.

The supreme value of even the briefest moments of life was clear in a previous age; now it has little meaning. Grasping a few seconds of life – in the modern secular context that is an empty and desperate gesture, a mere spasm of self-deception; in Judaism it is a profoundly ethical act.

APPENDICES

Appendix I

How A Rabbi Decides An Issue in Medical Halacha

(Based on a presentation by Rabbi Yitzchak A. Breitowitz, JD, PhD.)

I. Approach to the Process

Secular law is primarily concerned with *who* is authorized to make a decision in medical ethical issues. Courts and legislatures are thus occupied with advance directives, surrogate decision-making and ethics committees. This is so because the primary value the law seeks to uphold is the autonomy of the individual. The problems that concern this system include having to decide whether a particular patient is competent to exercise autonomy – what mental states compromize that ability, etc. Once the law identifies "who" should be making the decision in a specific medical ethical situation, it has essentially no primary interest in "what" that person decides – for himself if he is the patient, or on behalf of the patient if he is appropriately authorized to do so. By contrast, Jewish law is far more interested in the substance of the decision, and in principle the resolution should not depend on the identity or personal predilections of the decider (though there certainly are situations in halacha in which the individual is free to choose between halachically valid options).

So secular law asks *who* decides and leaves the appropriate decider to express his autonomy as he chooses; Jewish law asks *what is to be decided* and attempts to come to a definitive conclusion on the issue, even when that conclusion may not concur with the wishes of any particular individual.

II. Limited Role of Autonomy in Jewish Law

My body is not my own; it is the property of God who has entrusted it to me for care and preservation. Thus, the premise of the pro-choice movement (we have absolute control over our bodies) is fundamentally flawed (apart from the fact that abortion involves a fetus as well as a mother) from the halachic perspective. There is even discussion in halachic literature concerning the permissibility of elective cosmetic surgery both in terms of the surgical risks and in terms of the "mutilation" of God's property. (By and large, however, it has been allowed.)

Rabbi Shlomo Yosef Zevin wrote a classic article demonstrating that in the *Merchant of Venice*, Antonio's contract with Shylock to pay a pound of flesh in the event of a loan default is unenforceable under Jewish law – just as Antonio cannot pledge assets that he does not own, he cannot create such a pledge on his body; he does not own it.

III. Limited Role of Charisma/Inspiration

Halachic decision-making is not a matter of a Rabbi secluding himself and getting a direct answer from God which he then communicates with *ex cathedra* authority. Indeed, based on the verse "It [the Torah] is not in Heaven," the Talmud declares that prophecy *may not* be taken into account in the resolution of halachic questions (even if it were available). Halachic resolution depends on a solid empirical grounding in the facts coupled with a reasoned application from the primary texts that Jewish law considers to be definitive, namely the Talmud and halachic Codes. *Ad hoc* decision-making that is not rooted in these texts is generally illegitimate.

IV. Written Torah/Oral Torah

Although the Pentateuch is the highest source of law in Judaism, the meaning of that written Torah can be understood only by means of the oral interpretation that was handed down simultaneously with it. In its essence, the Oral Law is a core of principles and interpretations. The applications of that core, which originated in Divine revelation, grew more numerous as each generation applied the core principles to new situations. The particular applications sometimes generate disagreement. Although the core principles were part of a received tradition, the specific applications are the function of the Torah leadership (halachic authorities) of each generation to apply.

Jewish law forbade the writing down of the Oral Law, ensuring that the meaning of the tradition would be communicated through living human interaction. Only when (as a result of Roman persecution in the first and second centuries of the common era) the Oral Law was in grave danger of attrition and fragmentation was it reduced to the written form that is known as today's Mishna. Several hundreds of years of commentary on the Mishna eventually formed the work known as Gemara. (There is both a Babylonian and Palestinian Gemara though the Babylonian is regarded as the more authoritative.) Mishna and Gemara together form the work known as Talmud, second in importance only to the Pentateuch whose understanding and practical application depend on it.

V. Talmud: Source of Principles of Jewish Law

The Talmud is not a code of law; it rarely provides definitive halachic rulings. Rather, it is a transcript of hundreds of years of debates espousing a multiplicity of positions. It illuminates the process and conceptual structure of halacha through reasoned analysis, logic, analogy, and proof-text but very often does not indicate a final rule. All halachic decision-making, however, is ultimately grounded in Talmudic conceptualization. The classic and definitive codifications of Judaism – Rambam's Mishna Torah, Tur, and Shulchan Aruch are all based on conclusions derived from the Talmudic *sugyot* (treatments). The responsa literature – a vast body comprising thousands of volumes from every part of the Jewish world – applies Talmudic discussions and the rulings of the codes to contemporary situations, thereby ensuring that halacha remains a living, vital tradition.

VI. Halachic Reasoning: Induction and Deduction

Halachic reasoning involves a combination of inductive and deductive logic. First, relevant primary data – sources and rulings in particular cases extracted from Talmud and Codes – have to be identified and collected. Second, through inductive reasoning, a hypothesis is formulated that explains the specific collection of rulings by reference to a more general principle. Third, through deductive reasoning, this principle can be applied to new situations that are not explicitly covered by the earlier rulings but can now be subsumed under the principle that is believed to explain those earlier rulings. Uncertainty, ambiguity, and disagreement among halachic scholars can arise at any stage of this process.

Identification of primary data: this may be widely scattered with no real indexing. Especially in the case of Talmud, concepts that are highly relevant in one area may be discussed extensively in apparently unrelated areas. Moreover, various rulings or conclusions that appear to be stated as definitive in the course of a discussion may not survive the conclusion of a debate though the Talmudic text does not always make this point clear. Moreover, even a conclusion that appears to be "final" may be contradicted, superseded, or modified elsewhere in Talmud, or subjected to limitations or conditions not apparent from a particular discussion but derivable by implication from another Talmudic source.

Even after the primary data and rulings have been identified, there remains the problem of interpretation – What does rule X mean? There may be sharp disagreements among commentators and codes.

Generalization: As is true in physical science, data may often fit a variety of hypotheses and the plausibility of a given explanation may be subject to multiple views.

Application: Finally, application of the generalized principle to new cases may pose difficulties in determining whether or not the "new case" fits the parameters enunciated by the principle. This may require a re-examination or reformulation of what the generalization really encompasses as well as a careful understanding of the factual aspects of the "new case" to determine whether it is embraced by the paradigm.

In daily practice we often rely on the decisions of the great *poskim* (halachic authorities) of our day without deriving a conclusion ourselves from more primary sources. Nevertheless, even if in practice most Rabbis "follow the authorities," an original definitive decision can be reached only by one competent enough to go through all the steps of the process.

VII. The Crucial Importance of Knowing and Understanding the Facts on the Ground

Even if the Rabbi has full mastery of the halachic sources, his decisions may prove incorrect unless he fully understands the medical background of the case at hand.

VIII. The Art and Science of Proper Categorization

It is critically important to define the question correctly so that the appropriate analogies will be drawn. If a situation is perceived or described in a certain way, then one set of halachic categories and constructs will be brought to bear. If the situation is perceived differently, other halachic concepts may become relevant. The process of "shaping" or identifying critical and significant components is often the most crucial step in being able to resolve the halachic quandary properly. Thus: "The question of the wise is half the answer."

In addition, halachic and technical breadth are necessary in order to correctly identify all the issues that may be relevant to a given situation (analogous to "issue spotting" in secular law).

IX. The Modifying Role of Secondary Features Particular to the Case in *psak* (halachic ruling)

In theory, halacha ruling should not be subjective but should be predicated exclusively on the *posek's* (halachic authority's) objective understanding of the principles of Jewish law as derived from its authoritative sources. However, in cases of genuine unresolved disagreement (some authorities conclude one way, others conclude another way), the halachic system may allow the consideration of certain broader factors. These include, in part, concepts such as *"hefsed merubah"* (great financial loss), *"sha'at ha'dechak"* (a situation of urgency or special pressing need), *"shalom bayit"* (promotion of domestic tranquillity in a marriage), *"darchei noam"* (the ways of the Torah are ways of pleasantness). It must be emphasized that these factors alone are rarely taken into account in determining halacha on a primary level. In the event that the more primary objective halachic considerations are balanced, however, these factors may tip the scale.

(It should also be noted that some subjective conditions become objectively significant even on the primary level. For example, abortion is halachically permitted if the continuation of the pregnancy endangers the mother's life. This endangerment may very well include severe psychiatric trauma which carries a suicide risk. Whether or not a given event, for example rape or incest, creates such a risk depends entirely on the subjective mental state of the woman. Obviously, the Rabbi cannot answer such a question with his nose buried in the books, but must be sensitive to the individual characteristics of the questioner.)

X. Hearing the Question Not Asked

The burden of identifying the correct question and ferreting out the relevant information does not always rest on the questioner who after all may be ignorant of what Jewish law regards as significant. Moreover, it is not enough to simply answer the precise question asked – the Rabbi must have the sensitivity to address the "question behind the question," concerns that might be highly relevant but which were not explicitly articulated by the questioner. Thus, the Rabbi must be far more than the equivalent of a database.

> Example: A woman once asked the Beis Ha'Levi (the Rav of Brisk) whether one could fulfil the obligation of the Four Cups (of wine) at the Passover Seder with milk. The Beis HaLevi answered in the negative and immediately gave the woman funds to buy meals for all of Passover. His disciples asked him why he had not simply given her enough money for wine. His answer: the last two cups of the Seder are drunk after the meal. If the woman planned to use milk for the last two cups, it could only be because she had no meat to serve at the Seder meal. If there is no meat for the Seder – usually the most festive Pesach event – there is obviously none for the rest of the holiday. Accordingly, she needs funds for the entire holiday. The duty of the Rabbi is to address the entire problem, or more accurately, the entire person – not merely the segment of the problem that is explicitly raised.

XI. The Individualized Nature of *psak halacha* (halachic ruling) and the Competence of the *posek* (halachic authority)

R. Yitzchak Hutner, a renowned Rosh Yeshiva, once told a disciple: "Do not rely on anything that I ever said to someone else. Each *psak* (ruling) is unique."

See also the comments of Rabbi Moshe Feinstein in the introduction to his first volume of responsa *(Igrot Moshe Orach Chayim I)* where he writes that his responsa represent suggested approaches and general guidelines for each Rabbi to use his own judgment and discretion in applying the responsa to the facts of his particular case.

Moreover, Rabbi Feinstein argues that each Rabbi bears the responsibility of analyzing the primary sources on his own rather than blindly accepting his (Rabbi Feinstein's) reading of them. This means that the Rabbi must not only be able to apply the halacha to specific individual questioners and situations, but he must have mastery of the primary sources so that he can come to a personal understanding and ruling on his own. Real *p'sak* (ruling) is not simply the copying of a precedent; a *posek* must be competent to rule in his own right.

XII. The Importance of Empathy and Respect for the Feelings of the Questioner Even Where Consideration of Such Feelings Has No Direct Impact on Halachic Resolution

This consideration should apply to physicians no less than to rabbis.

XIII. *"Elu V'Elu..."*

Unlike mathematical truth where there may be only one "true" answer, halachic answers may be multiple. Thus, the Talmud states concerning the opposing and exclusive views of Bet Hillel and Bet Shammai: *"Elu v'elu divrei Elokim chayim"* – "These and those are words of the living God." There must be a commitment to the theological postulates of the system and to the accepted halachic methodology and use of authoritative texts; if those are present and correctly applied, the conclusion that the conscientious Rabbi arrives at will have the imprimatur of valid *psak*.

We are not suggesting unlimited flexibility – there are clearly standards and parameters that are absolute but as is obvious to any student of halacha, within the framework there is room for play at the joints.

XIV. Make for Yourself a Teacher

There is an obligation to develop a relationship with a Rabbi on a permanent rather than *ad hoc* basis: *"Aseh l'cha Rav"* – "Make for yourself a teacher." (*Pirkei Avot* – Ethics of the Fathers). Some of the relevant criteria in choosing a Rabbi are:

The Rabbi chosen should be knowledgeable in medical applications.

He should know you as a person to be able to take account of your individual circumstances.

It is improper to "shop around" – to look for the Rabbi who will give you the answer you want, that is, a different Rabbi for each type of question. However, with respect to categories of questions, it is legitimate to have various authorities to turn to – in halacha and personal counselling, for example. Decisions concerning whom to ask should be based on general considerations of competence, judgment, and experience.

A competent Rabbi (like a good doctor) knows when to refer to greater authority, or to non-rabbinic experts for technical expertise.

Appendix II

Modern Historical Overview of Euthanasia and Assisted Suicide in Western Countries

The following is an overview of some of the developments and milestones in the history of euthanasia and assisted suicide in the West over the past century.

- 1906 - First euthanasia bill drafted in Ohio. Unsuccessful.

- 1935 - World's first euthanasia society founded in England.

- 1938 - The Euthanasia Society of America is founded by the Rev. Charles Potter in New York.

- 1958 - Cambridge law professor Glanville Williams publishes "The Sanctity of Life and the Criminal Law," proposing that voluntary euthanasia be allowed for competent, terminally ill patients.

- 1958 - Lael Wertenbaker publishes "Death of a Man" describing how she helped her husband commit suicide.

- 1967 - The first living will is written by attorney Louis Kutner and his arguments for it appear in the Indiana Law Journal.

- 1968 - Harvard Medical School committee defines "irreversible coma," later to be accepted as definition of death – "brain stem death" in 1980.

- 1969 - Elisabeth Kubler-Ross publishes "On Death and Dying," opening broader discussion of the subject of death.

- 1970 - The Euthanasia Society (US) distributes 60,000 living wills.

- 1973 - American Hospital Association creates Patient Bill of Rights which includes informed consent and the right to refuse treatment.

- 1973 - Dr. Gertruida Postma, who gave her dying mother a lethal injection, receives light sentence in the Netherlands. Euthanasia movement (NVVE) launched in that country.

- 1974 The first American hospice opens in New Haven, CT.

- 1975 - Henry P. Van Dusen, 77, and his wife, Elizabeth, 80, leaders of the Christian ecumenical movement, commit suicide rather than suffer from disabling conditions.

- 1975 - Dutch Voluntary Euthanasia Society (NVVE) launches its Members' Aid Service to give advice to the dying. Receives 25 requests for aid in the first year.

- 1976 - New Jersey Supreme Court allows Karen Ann Quinlan's parents to disconnect the respirator that keeps her alive, saying it is affirming the choice Karen would have made. Despite removal of the respirator she lives for another eight years.

- 1976 - California Natural Death Act is passed. Gives legal standing to living wills and protects physicians from being sued for failing to treat incurable illnesses.

- 1976 - Ten more U.S. states pass natural death laws.

- 1978 - Doris Portwood publishes "Commonsense Suicide: The Final Right." It argues that old people in poor health might justifiably kill themselves.

- 1978 - "Whose Life Is It Anyway?" a play about a young artist who becomes quadriplegic, is staged in London and on Broadway, raising questions about the right to die. A film version appears in 1982.

- "Jean's Way" is published in England by Derek Humphry describing how he helped his terminally ill wife to die.

- 1979 - Artist Jo Roman, dying of cancer, commits suicide at a much-publicized gathering of friends that is later broadcast on public television.

- 1980 - President's commission recommends acceptance of brain death as standard definition of death in the US. Accepted throughout US and most Western countries over next few years.

- 1980 - Pope John Paul II issues Declaration in Euthanasia opposing mercy killing but permits the greater use of painkillers to ease pain and the right to refuse extraordinary means for sustaining life.

- 1980 - Hemlock Society founded in Santa Monica, California, by Derek Humphry. Distributes how to die information. Right to die societies formed in Germany and Canada.

- 1980 - World Federation of Right to Die Societies formed in Oxford, England, comprising 27 groups from 18 nations.

- 1981 - Hemlock publishes how-to suicide guide "Let Me Die Before I Wake."

- 1981 - British pediatrician Dr Leonard Arthur acquitted of the attempted murder of a newborn with Down's syndrome for whom he had prescribed analgesia and "nursing care only" after the baby had been rejected by his mother.

- 1983 - Author Arthur Koestler, terminally ill, commits suicide after publishing his reasons. His wife Cynthia, although healthy, chooses to commit suicide with him.

- 1983 - Elizabeth Bouvia, a quadriplegic suffering from cerebral palsy, sues a California hospital to let her die of self-starvation while receiving comfort care. She loses, and files an appeal.

- 1984 - Advance care directives become recognized in 22 states and the District of Columbia.

- 1984 - The Netherlands Supreme Court approves voluntary euthanasia under certain conditions.

- 1985 - Professor Peter Singer, Princeton, suggests that killing handicapped infants be allowed (at parents' discretion for first 28 days of life, or on a "case by case basis"). Singer claims that some people with life-long cognitive disabilities never become "persons," that some people who acquire cognitive disabilities cease to be "persons," and it is not wrong to kill beings who are not "persons." (Professor Singer, who favors animal rights, holds that bestiality does not constitute a transgression of our status as human beings because human beings are animals.)

- 1985 - Betty Rollin publishes "Last Wish," her account of helping her mother die after a long battle with breast cancer.

- 1986 - Roswell Gilbert, 76, sentenced in Florida to 25 years without parole for shooting his terminally ill wife. Granted clemency five years later.

- 1986 - Elizabeth Bouvia is granted the right to refuse feeding by an appeals court. Given control over her pain relief medications, she declines to take advantage of the permission and is still alive over 20 years later.

- 1986 - Americans Against Human Suffering is founded in California, launching a campaign for what will become the 1992 California Death with Dignity Act.

- 1988 - Journal of the American Medical Association prints "It's Over, Debbie" describing a resident doctor giving a lethal injection to a young woman dying of ovarian cancer.

- 1988 - Unitarian Universalist Association of Congregations passes a national resolution favoring aid in dying for the terminally ill.

- 1990 - Washington Initiative 119 is filed, the first state voter referendum on the issue of voluntary euthanasia and physician-assisted suicide.

- 1990 - American Medical Association adopts the position that with informed consent, a physician can withhold or withdraw treatment from a patient who is close to death, and may also discontinue life support of a patient in a permanent coma.

- 1990 - Dr. Jack Kevorkian assists in the death of Janet Adkins, a middle-aged woman with Alzheimer's disease. Kevorkian subsequently flouts the Michigan legislature's attempts to stop him from assisting in additional suicides.

- 1990 - Supreme Court decides the Cruzan case. The decision recognizes that competent adults have a constitutionally protected liberty that includes a right to refuse medical treatment.

- 1990 - Congress passes the Patient Self-Determination Act, requiring hospitals that receive federal funds to tell patients that they have a right to demand or refuse treatment.

- 1991 - Dr. Timothy Quill, writing in the New England Journal of Medicine, describes his provision of lethal drugs to "Diane," a leukemia patient who chose to die at home by her own hand rather than undergo therapy that offered a 25 percent chance of survival.

- 1991 - Nationwide Gallup poll finds that 75 percent of Americans approve of living wills.

- 1991 - Derek Humphry publishes "Final Exit," a how-to book on "self-deliverance." Sells 540,000 copies in 18 months. It is translated into twelve other languages.

- 1991 - Washington State voters reject Ballot Initiative 119, which would have legalized physician-aided suicide and aid in dying.

- 1992 - California voters defeat Proposition 161, which would have allowed physicians to hasten death by actively administering or prescribing medications for self-administration by suffering, terminally ill patients.

- 1993 - Advance directive laws passed in 48 states by this date.

- 1993 - Compassion in Dying is founded in Washington state to counsel the terminally ill and provide information about how to die without suffering and "with personal assistance, if necessary, to intentionally hasten death."

- 1993 - Oregon Right to Die, a political action committee, is founded to write the Oregon Death with Dignity Act.

- 1993 - In the UK, the Bland judgment legalises removal of the means of life from patients declared to be in a persistent vegetative state.

- 1994 - Death with Dignity Education Center is founded in California.

- 1994 - The California Bar approves physician-assisted suicide.

- 1994 - Washington State's anti-suicide law overturned. In Compassion v. Washington, the court finds that a law outlawing assisted suicide violates the 14th Amendment. "The court does not believe that a distinction can be drawn between refusing life-sustaining medical treatment and physician-assisted suicide by an uncoerced, mentally competent, terminally ill adult."

- 1994 - In New York State, Quill et al v. Koppell is filed to challenge the New York law prohibiting assisted suicide. Quill loses, and files an appeal.

- 1994 - Oregon voters approve Measure 16, a Death With Dignity Act initiative that would permit terminally ill patients, under proper safeguards, to obtain a physician's prescription to end life in a humane and dignified manner.

- 1994 - U.S. District Court issues a temporary restraining order against Oregon's Measure 16, following that with an injunction barring the state from putting the law into effect.

- 1995 - Oregon Death with Dignity Legal Defense and Education Center founded to defend Ballot Measure 16 legalizing physician-assisted suicide.

- 1995 - Washington State's Compassion ruling overturned by the Ninth Circuit Court of Appeals, reinstating the anti-suicide law.

- 1995 - U.S. District Court rules that Oregon Measure 16, the Death with Dignity Act, is unconstitutional on the grounds that it violates the Equal Protection clause of the Constitution.

- 1996 - The Northern Territory of Australia passes voluntary euthanasia law, the Rights of the Terminally Ill Act. Four patients died under the Act. Nine months later the Federal Parliament overturned it.

- 1996 - The Ninth Circuit Court of Appeals reverses the Compassion finding in Washington state, holding that "a liberty interest exists in the choice of how and when one dies, and that the provision of the Washington statute banning assisted suicide, as applied to competent, terminally ill adults who wish to hasten their deaths by obtaining medication prescribed by their doctors, violates the Due Process Clause."

- 1996 - A Michigan jury acquits Dr. Kevorkian of violating a state law banning assisted suicides.

- 1996 - The Second Circuit Court of Appeals reverses the Quill finding, ruling that "The New York statutes criminalizing assisted suicide violate the Equal Protection Clause because, to the extent that they prohibit a physician from prescribing medications to be self-administered by a mentally competent, terminally ill person in the final stages of his terminal illness, they are not rationally related to any legitimate state interest."

- Charles E. Hall, who has AIDS, asks court permission for a doctor to assist his suicide. The court refuses.

- 1997 - U.S. Supreme Court reverses the decisions of the Ninth and Second Circuit Court of Appeals in Washington v. Glucksberg and Quill v. Vacco, upholding state statutes which bar assisted suicide. The court also validates the concept of "double effect," acknowledging that death hastened by palliative measures does not constitute a prohibited act so long as the intent is the relief of suffering.

- 1997 - Dutch Voluntary Euthanasia Society (NVVE) reports its membership now more than 90,000, of whom 900 made requests for help in dying.

- 1997 - Britain's Parliament rejects by 234 votes to 89 the seventh attempt in 60 years to change the law on assisted suicide.

- 1997 - Oregon's Death with Dignity Act officially takes effect. The people of Oregon vote by a margin of 60-40 percent against Measure 51, which would have repealed the Act. This law allows physician-assisted suicide; not active euthanasia.

- 1998 - Dr. Kevorkian assists the suicide of his 92nd patient in eight years. His home state, Michigan, passes new law making such actions a crime. Kevorkian continues helping people to die - 120 by November.

- 1998 - Oregon Health Services Commission decides that payment for physician-assisted suicide can come from state funds.

- 1998 - 16 people die by making use of the Oregon Death With Dignity Act, receiving physician-assisted suicide in its first year of implementation.

- 1999 - Dr. Kevorkian sentenced to 10-25 years imprisonment for the 2nd degree murder of Thomas Youk after showing video of death by injection on national television.

- 1999 - 26 people die by physician-assisted suicide in the second year of the Oregon physician-assisted suicide law.

- 1999 - The British Medical Association's Ethics Committee rules that doctors can withdraw food and fluids in the "best interests" of patients who cannot speak for themselves, such as disabled newborns, Alzheimer's and seriously disabled stroke patients.

- 2001 - Kevorkian's appeal rejected.

- 2001 - Multiple sclerosis patient Diane Pretty asks UK court to allow her husband to help her commit suicide. The London High Court, the House of Lords, and the Court of Human Rights in Strasbourg all say no. She dies in hospice a few weeks later.

- 2002 - Dutch law, the Euthanasia Act, allowing euthanasia and physician-assisted suicide passed. The Act officially legalized an existing practice, since physicians had not been prosecuted for these actions as long as they were consistent with standards established in the early 1990s.

- 2002 - Belgium passes similar law to the Dutch, allowing both voluntary euthanasia and physician-assisted suicide.

- Final Exit Network formed to help dying people who request assistance.

- 2004 - Lesley Martin in New Zealand completes a seven-month prison sentence for the attempted murder by morphine overdose of her terminally ill mother.

- 2005 - Terry Schiavo, aged 41, who for over ten years was in a persistent vegetative state, allowed to die.

- 2005 - A hospital in Lausanne, Switzerland permits the right-to-die group, EXIT, to help a terminally ill adult who wants assisted suicide.

- 2005 - Doctor charged with second degree murder for allegedly "euthanizing" nine patients who she believed would not be evacuated in the aftermath of Hurricane Katrina in New Orleans.

- 2006 - The Suicide Materials Offences Act takes effect in Australia, making it a crime to discuss or advise on euthanasia or assisted suicide by telephone, email, internet or fax. Books, ground mail and personal meetings not affected.

- US Supreme Court upholds Oregon's assisted suicide law.

- 2007 - Surveys in the United States and the Netherlands show that active euthanasia including injection of neuromuscular blockers and potassium chloride is relatively common, and often performed without a direct request by the patient

- 2008 - Dutch doctors disseminate information to general public on how to commit suicide.

- 2008 - Washington state residents vote to allow physician-assisted suicide for patients with an illness expected to lead to death within 6 months, the Washington Death with Dignity Act (similar to Oregon law). Act takes effect in March 2009. (In 1991, Washington voters had rejected a proposal that would have allowed doctors to administer the lethal drugs. As of December 2008, no US state allows this.)

- By 2009, physician-assisted suicide legal in Belgium, the Netherlands, Luxembourg, Switzerland and in the US states of Oregon and Washington. Euthanasia legal in Belgium and the Netherlands since 2002.

Appendix III

The Dollar Value of Life

The following is excerpted from a Stanford Graduate Business School research initiative:

Putting Dollar Value on Extending Life Poses Ethical Dilemma According to Stanford Business School Research

STANFORD, Calif., May 15, 2008   [T]he single biggest factor contributing to the astronomically rising cost of healthcare is the emergence of expensive new technology...

New research from Stanford and Wharton shows that $50,000 – the average figure used internationally as a "threshold" for making medical allocation decisions – is low. A more realistic figure is probably a minimum of $129,000, which represents what it would cost to give a person an additional "quality-of-life adjusted" year of life. Moreover, the researchers argue, making decisions on whether insurance should cover medical interventions based on their cost-effectiveness leads to profound ethical dilemmas.

Outside the United States, countries such as the United Kingdom and Australia that offer national health care have developed explicit systems to determine the overall cost-effectiveness of a new medical intervention. This includes calculating the incremental cost of a treatment against the incremental improvements in the patient's health, and comparing that figure to a threshold number. "As long as the ratio is below that threshold number, a given treatment is accepted as part of the healthcare offerings; otherwise, it's rejected," explains Stefanos Zenios, the Charles A. Holloway Professor of Operations, Information, and Technology at the Stanford Graduate School of Business...

If Medicare were to begin accepting or rejecting coverage on treatments made available by new technologies based on cost, what might a realistic threshold look like? To make such a determination, [researchers] ran computer models using data from more than half a million patients who underwent kidney dialysis – an expensive procedure covered under Medicare that has typically been used as a benchmark for evaluating the cost-effectiveness of all new technologies internationally. "We found that starting dialysis earlier than the current practice allowed by Medicare would be more expensive, but would likely be associated with longer life and fewer medical complications," Zenios said.

In such a case, the average incremental cost was approximately $129,000 for a "quality-adjusted" year of life... Based on surveys of patients with kidney failure, one "quality of life" year is deemed the equivalent of about two years of life under dialysis...

"Say a new type of treatment for cancer comes along," explains Zenios. "If the incremental cost of that new technology was more than $129,000 for a quality-of-life adjusted year, then the recommendation would be that Medicare not cover that new technology."

But... Medicare would quickly be faced with a host of ethical concerns if it started applying the $129,000 threshold differentially to selective groups. For the sickest patients, the researchers determined that the average cost of an additional quality-of-life year was much higher: $488,000. "Applying the $129,000 threshold in a very sharp way for specific groups and individuals would mean that the sickest subgroups of patients would be denied access to expensive treatments such as dialysis."

For some policy makers, such a decision might be tempting, given that the sickest benefit the least from dialysis, and if the threshold were raised to even half that, or $240,000 per quality-of-life year, 90 percent of patients could be treated...

The issue of treating patients differently depending on their health poses ethical questions... [T]he authors maintain that the average figure – $129,000 – could be used as a global figure for the purposes of accepting or rejecting an entire technology for coverage, but not for accepting or rejecting specific subgroups once that technology has been approved.

How much money we should allocate to helping the sick, sicker, and sickest will only continue to be debated ever more vociferously as newer, costlier technologies continue to emerge...

Appendix IV

Risks Associated with Some Current Dangerous Occupations

The following article gives some idea of the risks of relatively dangerous modern occupations.

America's most dangerous jobs
A government report says fishermen continue to lead the nation in fatality rates.
By Les Christie, CNNMoney.com
August 9 2007

NEW YORK (CNNMoney.com) – Last year was a safer one for workers in the United States; 5,703 died on the job, down slightly from the 5,734 fatalities in 2005. The rate was 3.9 per 100,000 workers, slightly lower than the 4.0 per 100,000 in 2005.

But recent events - In January, the Coast Guard found a fishing boat submerged in 36 feet of icy water off Cape Cod after a winter storm; an early August medical plane crash in New Mexico left five dead; and the story of trapped mine workers in Utah, which continues to unfold - underscore the perilous natures of many vocations.

What are the best companies to work for?

These examples of death and danger on the job are just a few of the stories behind the statistics released every August by the Bureau of Labor Statistics in its report of fatalities in the work place.

Several industries dominate the BLS data. Year in and year out, the single deadliest U.S. job is commercial fisherman, and this year was no exception. At 141.7 deaths per 100,000 workers, fishermen had, by far, the highest fatality rate among all the listed U.S. occupations.

For fishermen, storms come up quicker than they can be outrun. Rogue waves wash them overboard. Heavy equipment bangs around the decks. Power winches and hoists yank ropes around that can snag a seaman's foot and drag him overboard.

Fishing is often pursued under harsh conditions. In the boat found in January, four crewmen were missing and presumed dead and the bodies of two, including the captain, Antonio Barroqueiro, were later recovered.

Barroqueiro had lost his younger brother to the sea 14 years ago. Fishing fatalities often run in families. The Fisherman's Memorial in Gloucester, Mass. has repeated many family names over the years.

The best jobs in America

People who fly for a living also face danger daily, earning them the number-two spot on the BLS list. The highest rates of fatalities for commercial pilots come not from the big airlines, who log thousands of daily flights mostly without incident, but among the more modest levels of the flying industry such as crop dusters and bush pilots.

Occupational aircraft -related fatalities jumped last year to 215, a 44 percent increase, after falling in 2005 to 149. The fatality rate was 87.8 per 100,000, second only to the fishing industry.

Top 10 dangerous jobs	
Occupations with the highest fatality rates in 2006.	
Occupation	**Deaths per 100,000 workers**
Fishermen	141.7
Pilots	87.8
Loggers	82.3
Structural iron and steel workers	61.0
Refuse collectors	41.8
Farmers and ranchers	37.1
Power linemen	34.9
Roofers	33.9
Drivers	27.1
Agricultural workers	21.7

Source: Bureau of Labor Statistics

[A]nother occupation that produces more than its fair share of fatalities is timber cutting, landing it at the number three spot on the BLS list. Loggers work with dangerous tools, often on steep slopes, threatened by the tremendous weight of the trees. Like workers in many other dangerous pursuits, they're often under pressure to work quickly, increasing risk.

In 2006, 82.1 per 100,000 loggers died on the job.

Coal mining deaths were not in the top 10 jobs with the highest fatality rates, but the rate nearly doubled last year, jumping 84 percent to 49.5 fatalities per 100,000 workers, largely due to the Sago mine disaster that killed 12. A total of 47 fatalities were recorded in 2006, up from 22 in 2005.

Numerically, the occupation that produced the most deaths in 2006 was the massive construction industry. 1,226 workers died in construction accidents, for a 3 percent increase. Structural iron and steel workers died at a rate of 61 per 100,000.

Crime against workers was a factor in many fields. When pizza delivery man, Boston Smithwick, was robbed and shot outside Pittsburgh last April, he was the second such employee of the Vocelli Pizza shop killed in the past two years. Taxi and limo drivers and convenience store clerks are also common victims of robbery and murder.

But this kind of fatality has fallen precipitously, down 50 percent since 1994. In 2006, they dropped 9 percent to 516 year over year.

Texas had the highest number of fatalities per state - 486. California recorded 448 and Florida 355.

Appendix V

Transport Modes – Risks

Relative risks

- Motorcycles have the highest fatality of all modes, on average 20 times higher than for car occupants.
- Cycling and walking have on average 7 to 9 times higher fatality than car travel per distance travelled.
- Rail and air travel are the safest modes per distance travelled, followed by bus.
- Bus travel has a 10 times lower fatality risk than car travel per trip.

(Data from European Transport Safety Council report; 2003)

Quantitative risks

Mode of transport	Deaths per 100 million miles
Commercial airliners	0.006
Bus	0.022
Rail	0.029
Car	0.849
Truck	0.898
Bicycle	21.235
Motorcycle	22.909
Pedestrian	84.030

(Data for US, published in New York Times, 1992)

Flying and Driving

Scheduled airline travel has a fatality rate of less than 1 per million departures. Scheduled airline travel is safer than driving per passenger mile; however, scheduled airline and car travel have approximately the same risk per hour of travel.

A quantitative study concludes that for average or high-risk drivers, it is always safer to fly than to drive. For low-risk drivers, nonstop flying is safer than driving on rural interstate highways (where driving risk is lowest) for a trip distance of more than 303 miles.[1]

---

[1] Data from: Sivak M, Weintraub DJ, Flannagan M. Nonstop Flying Is Safer Than Driving. Risk Analysis, 2006, Vol.11, pp. 145-148.

Appendix VI

Current Selection Criteria for Renal Dialysis and Transplantation

Currently, patients are selected for dialysis and transplantation where resources are limited on the basis of a set of more or less widely accepted criteria. In a large US survey,[1] criteria used included:

1. Medical Benefit: whether or not the prospective recipient will live longer because of the treatment.

2. Likelihood of Medical Benefit: how likely is it that the desired medical outcome will in fact occur.

3. Quantitative Prognosis: the length of expected survival with treatment.

4. Qualitative Prognosis: the quality of life the prospective recipient may expect if accepted for treatment.

5. Age.

6. Psychological Stability: the ability of the prospective recipient to cope emotionally and intellectually with the treatment regimen.

7. Environment: how supportive (financially, emotionally, etc.) the prospective recipient's family, friends, and community are likely to be.

8. Disproportionate Resources: whether or not the prospective recipient will likely require particularly long or expensive treatment.

9. Ability to Pay: whether or not the prospective recipient has enough money or insurance to pay for the required services.

10. Sex: whether the prospective recipient is male or female.

---

[1] Kilner, JF. Selecting Patients When Resources Are Limited: A Study of US Medical Directors of Kidney Dialysis and Transplantation Facilities. Am J Public Health 1988; 78:144-147.

11. Willingness: the expressed or implicit desire of the prospective recipient to undergo treatment.

12. Constituency: whether or not the prospective recipient is a member of a particular group, identified by geographical location, veteran status, etc.

13. Progress of Science: how much scientific knowledge may be gained from treating the prospective recipient.

14. Social Value: how much society, including people individually, will benefit if the prospective recipient is treated.

15. Unique Moral Duties: whether or not the physical life of at least one other person - or something equally important - depends upon whether or not the prospective recipient lives.

16. Random Selection: whether cases are ever such that they should be treated as fundamentally similar and, therefore, recipients selected by lottery or on a first-come first-served basis.

(These are not the only criteria used: intelligence as measured by IQ, mental illness, criminal records, employment status, alcoholism and drug addiction are among others that are also sometimes considered.)

The quoted study reports responses of 453 medical directors of renal dialysis and transplantation facilities to patient selection questionnaires concerning selection criteria being used today as well as those which would be employed were resources to become further limited relative to need. The following is the order of importance given to the various criteria:

* qualitative prognosis, psychological stability, likelihood of medical benefit, quantitative prognosis, medical benefit (virtually all);

* willingness, age (very large majority);

* unique moral duties, disproportionate resources, environment, progress of science, social value (majority);

* ability to pay, random selection, constituency (very large minority);

* sex (virtually none).

Qualitative prognosis, quantitative prognosis, medical benefit, ability to pay, and especially age are the criteria employed today whose influence would increase if resources are further limited.

In general, four major approaches to rationing scarce medical resources have been used or suggested;[2] each with serious disadvantages:

The Market Approach: this approach would provide resources to those who could pay for them with their own funds or private insurance.

The Committee Selection Process: this approach uses hospital ethics committees or publicly constituted bodies to make selections.

The Lottery Approach.

The Customary Approach: this approach uses various sets of selection criteria such as those mentioned above.

Kidney Allocation Criteria in the UK

In Britain, all kidneys from deceased heartbeating donors are allocated to recipients according to a national system (United Kingdom Kidney Allocation Scheme, 2009; first published April 2006) based on a number of factors including waiting time for a transplant and the degree of tissue type match with the donor.

Children are given high priority for well-matched kidneys as they may require more than one kidney transplant during their lifetime; a good match will facilitate finding a suitable donor in the future.

The national system is based on five tiers:

A. Difficult to match paediatric patients - highly sensitised or HLA-DR homozygous

B. Difficult to match paediatric patients - others

C. Difficult to match adult patients - highly sensitised or HLA-DR homozygous

D. Difficult to match adult patients – others & favourably matched paediatric patients

E. All other eligible patients

---

[2] Annas GJ: The prostitute, the playboy, and the poet: Rationing schemes for organ transplantation. Am J Public Health 1985; 75:187-189. See this review for a critique of each suggested approach.

Within Tiers A and B, children are prioritised according to their waiting time. In the remaining Tiers, patients are prioritised according to a points score based on a number of factors:

1. Waiting time (favouring patients who have waited longest)

2. HLA match & age combined (favouring well-matched transplants for younger patients)

3. Donor-recipient age difference (favouring closer age matches)

4. Location of patient relative to donor ((favouring patients who are closer in order to minimise the transportation time of the kidney)

5. HLA-DR homozygosity

6. HLA-B homozygosity

7. Blood group match

CLINICAL CASES

Clinical Cases

The clinical cases appearing throughout the book are given below without their descriptive titles or halachic resolutions; the page references indicate where those can be found.

Clinical Case 1: (p. 42)

A 35 year old man was diagnosed with an indolent lymphoma. One expert advised chemotherapy, another advised watchful waiting with no therapy. Their respective reasons were: immediate chemotherapy may avert or delay the change to an aggressive form of the disease; on the other hand chemotherapy is unlikely to eradicate the disease entirely, and if aggressive transformation takes place it may be less responsive to therapy because tolerance is likely to have developed due to the earlier therapy, so it would be better to hold chemotherapy in reserve for use when it is most likely to be effective.

In addition to these considerations, the patient had recently married and was concerned about the damage chemotherapy would almost certainly cause to his fertility. He sought rabbinic advice.

His rabbi suggested obtaining a third expert medical opinion. The third consultant agreed with the strategy of withholding chemotherapy, and the rabbi advised following the majority medical view.

It is now five years later. The disease is stable, although one superficial lymph node may have enlarged slightly; the bone marrow is clear. The same three experts all maintain their original recommendations. The patient now has children, but is still desirous of maintaining fertility. He again seeks halachic guidance. How should he be advised?

Clinical Case 2: (p. 60)

A civilian doctor is called to attend to a patient where the only access to the patient is by driving along a road that is exposed to occasional shooting from hostile villages. Is the doctor obliged to comply?

Clinical Case 3: (p. 69)

An employee is a "Hatzola" (community paramedical organization) volunteer. Responding to emergency calls during working hours means interrupting his work whenever he is called. His employer objects and wishes to dismiss him, claiming that he is not required to suffer the loss to his business caused by the employee's frequent absences. In addition to the question of dismissal itself, a likely consequence is that the volunteer may choose to give up his lifesaving work to avoid losing his income. Is the employer correct?

Clinical Case 4: (p. 95)

A woman presents in her eighth week of pregnancy with an intra-uterine contraceptive device (IUCD) seen in situ on ultrasound examination. The question of extraction of the device is raised, and the following risks are ascribed:

Risk of aborting the pregnancy during extraction of the device: 25%

Risk of spontaneous termination of the pregnancy due to the device if retained in utero: 35%

An obstetric consultant recommended extraction of the IUCD (after careful localization by ultrasound) on the grounds that the overall risk to the fetus would thereby be minimized (25% vs 35%).

A second expert opinion stated that the cumulative risk of abortion and premature birth due to retention of the IUCD would be approximately double the risk of accidentally terminating the pregnancy during extraction, and that in addition the following approximate quantitative factors should be considered:

Risk of amnionitis due to retained device: 10 - 15%

Risk of future fertility problems as consequence of infection: 5%

Risk of prematurity: 10%

The woman seeks halachic guidance. How should she be advised?

Clinical Case 5: (p. 98)

A 42 year old woman who has one child from a previous marriage has recently remarried. She is 12 weeks pregnant when a breast carcinoma is discovered; she undergoes immediate mastectomy while pregnant. She is advised to terminate the pregnancy and begin chemotherapy; however she wishes to continue with the pregnancy and delay chemotherapy until after delivery. Is her choice halachically acceptable?

Clinical Case 6: (p. 130)

A man with an implanted defibrillator has widely metastatic cancer. The device is designed to defibrillate only: it is not functioning continually as a pacemaker. He requests that the defibrillator be inactivated – due to his terminal situation, in the event of a lethal arrhythmia he does not want to be resuscitated by the device. Does his request accord with halacha?

Clinical Case 7: (p. 131)

A 65 year old woman had a left atrial mass, thought to be a myxoma, excised together with the mitral valve which was replaced with a prosthetic valve. The mass proved to be a pleomorphic sarcoma (a malignant condition which carries a risk of recurrence). Now, six weeks after surgery, the patient has developed heart failure; on ultrasound scanning a mass is seen just above the prosthetic valve. The differential diagnosis includes a vegetation due to infective endocarditis, thrombus, or recurrence of tumor. The patient is receiving appropriate medical treatment; her surgeons do not want to re-operate. The question of a biopsy arises; the risk of death or major complication due to the biopsy is estimated to be 20%. The chance of tumor recurrence at this stage is thought to be 3%. Should the biopsy be done?

Clinical Case 8: (p. 131)

A 50 year old man has hepatitis-C related chronic cirrhosis. He has declining liver function and is not expected to survive one year without liver transplantation. A live donor transplant is recommended; his chances of surviving the transplantation surgery are presently excellent but will decline significantly if it is delayed. The overall five-year survival rate for liver transplantation is currently over 75%; this particular patient's probability of five-year survival is thought to be closer to 85%. Should transplantation be performed, and if so, when?

Clinical Case 9: (p. 132)

Two brothers aged 12 and 17 have chronic granulomatous disease (CGD). Survival in CGD is currently between 20 and 30 years (with wide variability). Hematopoietic stem cell transplantation (HSCT) is proposed; if successful it will be curative. The procedure has a 75% success rate and a 25% mortality. The boys and their parents do not want the procedure. Does halacha accord with their choice?

Clinical Case 10: (p. 133)

A 30 year old woman has CML (chronic myelogenous leukemia). There is a risk of transformation to AML (acute myelogenous leukemia) of approximately 25% per year; she is unlikely to survive more than a few months after AML develops. She is offered marrow ablation and rescue transplantation, a procedure with a mortality of 60 - 70%. Should she choose the 30 - 40% chance of cure and accept the high risk of the procedure?

Clinical Case 11: (p. 133)

A newborn suffers from a degenerative neurological disease; the child is blind and has multiple abnormalities including exomphalos. Around 95% of children with this syndrome do not survive for 18 months; death is usually due to failure of muscle function including swallowing and respiratory muscles. Should this newborn be treated? If the child encounters respiratory difficulties, is ventilation required?

Clinical Case 12: (p. 134)

A 61 year old woman is admitted in acute-on-chronic renal failure. She had a primary breast carcinoma resected eight years previously; she now has secondaries in her spine which appear to be slowly progressive but no other evident spread of disease. She is independent and enjoys a relatively good quality of life; her bone pain is controlled on multiple analgesics (which may be related to her renal disease). She has recently refused chemotherapy after multiple cycles because her disease is no longer responding; she has not refused any other form of treatment, and she has not signed a DNR order. The hospital staff tell her family that treatment is futile and recommend palliative care only. How should she be treated?

Clinical Case 13: (p. 150)

Analyse the following case report (published in AHRQ WebM&M, an Agency for Healthcare Research and Quality online journal produced by an editorial team at the University of California, San Francisco):

The Wrongful Resuscitation

(Joan M. Teno, MD, MS. April 2008.)

The Case:

An 80-year-old man with diabetes, peripheral vascular disease, bilateral below-the-knee amputations, and poor quality of life had previously been resuscitated from sudden death. After his recovery, he completed a DNR (do not resuscitate) form signifying his desire to avoid such treatment in the future.

The patient presented to the emergency department in extreme pain and was found to have a ruptured abdominal aortic aneurysm. Although his DNR form was with him, neither the emergency department staff nor the consulting surgeon looked at it. The patient was rushed to the operating room, where his aneurysm was repaired.

Postoperatively, an internist came upon the DNR form in the patient's chart and discussed resuscitation preferences with the patient and the family. The patient reconfirmed his desire to avoid resuscitation and heroic procedures, expressing anger that he had been taken to the operating room for the aneurysm repair. The family agreed with the patient's choice. The internist wrote a DNR order in the chart, but the surgeon... was furious, changing the code status back to "full code." Ultimately, the internist consulted with the hospital ethicist, who convinced the surgeon to honor the patient's and family's wishes. The DNR order was reinstated, and the patient later died of a cardiac arrest during the hospitalization.

[From] The Commentary:

[T]he actions of the surgeon in this case raise important concerns... A critically ill nursing home resident is transferred to the emergency department with severe abdominal pain and hypotension. In the midst of crisis, the physician did not realize that the patient was DNR and successfully resuscitated this elderly patient. This is an important error.

[S]hould that physician be sanctioned for making a decision that flagrantly ignored a patient's preference? I believe that such behavior should receive the same scrutiny as operating on the wrong side of the brain – each is a bodily assault that provides harmful care to which the patient did not consent. Such a case should be reported to the appropriate state authorities, and the resulting sanctions and corrective actions should ensure that informed preferences by future patients are honored.

Clinical Case 14: (p. 163)

A 37 year old woman with primary infertility has had three pregnancies following in-vitro fertilization. The first terminated spontaneously at an early stage; the second was an ectopic pregnancy requiring salpingectomy. The third resulted in a cesarian section for the delivery of twins, performed under general anesthesia. At operation, the single remaining fallopian tube was noted to contain a 3-centimeter mass in its mid-portion. The doctor performing the cesarian was undecided whether to resect the mass leaving the rest of the tube for later attempted reconstruction or to resect the entire tube. After consultation with a senior colleague he elected to resect the tube.

Did he act correctly in resecting the patient's single fallopian tube without her consent?

Clinical Case 15: (p. 164)

A three year old child has pneumonia. When seen by a pediatrician, the child is acutely ill and in respiratory difficulty. The pediatrician urges immediate admission and intravenous antibiotic therapy but the parents refuse, citing their belief that the child is improving and their preference for holistic and alternative medicine. They also express the opinion that antibiotics are harmful and will predispose the child to other illnesses, and their fear that the child may contract additional infections in the hospital. The pediatrician insists on admission and threatens to call for police assistance if the parents refuse; the child is admitted and treated despite the parents' ongoing protestations.

1. Are the pediatrician's actions correct?

2. Should the child be forcibly removed from the parents' care to prevent subsequent similar episodes?

Clinical Case 16: (p. 165)

A 41 year old Down's syndrome patient has diverticulitis. He is treated conservatively and recovers. His surgeons then recommend partial colonic resection for prevention of another acute episode, giving the chance of recurrence as 30%. His parents refuse the procedure.

Should the operation be performed against the parents' wishes?

Clinical Case 17: (p. 168)

A teenage girl agreed to donate bone marrow to a woman suffering from acute leukemia. After the recipient had undergone marrow ablation chemotherapy in preparation for the transplant, the donor refused to continue (she had felt unwell during testing and become afraid). At this stage, the recipient's life depends entirely on receiving the donated marrow, and she proceeded with her own marrow ablation only because she had been assured that the donation would be forthcoming.

Can the donor be forced to go through with the donation?

Clinical Case 18: (p. 169)

A 35 year old single man with early stage uncomplicated localized colonic cancer refuses surgery because he does not want a colostomy as it may interfere with his marriage prospects. His disease has an excellent prognosis with surgery and a disastrous prognosis without it.

Should his refusal be respected?

Clinical Case 19: (p. 185)

An ambulance is despatched to attend to an injured child. En route the ambulance crew receives a call to proceed to the scene of an accident in which five adults have been injured; the extent and severity of their injuries is unknown.

Should the ambulance continue to the child or divert to the injured group?

Clinical Case 20: (p. 185)

A young lady doctor found herself applying lifesaving pressure to a severed artery in the neck of a child at the scene of a terrorist attack. It was clear to her that if she abandoned the child she would almost certainly be able to save others. Should she abandon this single individual in order to save many, or is she forbidden to abandon him since that would directly bring about (or at the very least, allow) his death?

Clinical Case 21: (p. 191)

A young surgeon training in emergency surgery in Johannesburg found himself in the following situation. The hospital's trauma unit had acquired a sophisticated new ventilator for use on severely injured patients; however, the hospital had issued strict instructions allowing its use only for patients thought to be salvageable. Any patient assessed as unlikely to survive was to be treated with older technology; the new machine was to be held in reserve only for those who might be saved in the long term. (The concern was that if a non-salvageable patient were ventilated using the new machine, a patient with a better prognosis arriving subsequently would receive inferior care because the ventilator is committed to the first patient.) In addition, this unit is so busy that the dilemma is inevitable – whenever a non-salvageable patient is given the ventilator, a salvageable patient is sure to be admitted during the time the first patient is using it and therefore be denied its use.

Is the hospital's rule correct? According to halacha, must the surgeon obey it (and consequently be able to save the second, salvageable, patient) or must he defy the rule and use the machine on any non-salvageable patient who happens to be admitted (and quite possibly lose the subsequent salvageable patient because he has already committed the machine to the first)?

Clinical Case 22: (p. 211)

A 37 year old mother of two (a boy and a girl) underwent resection of a breast malignancy and chemotherapy one year ago; it is not clear whether the chemotherapy has affected her fertility. On genetic testing she is found have the BRCA gene; her mother died of ovarian cancer at a young age. Her doctors recommend that she undergo prophylactic bilateral mastectomy and oophorectomy. She is willing to undergo both procedures with immediate breast reconstruction following the mastectomies.

Background facts:

1. Ovarian cancer is usually diagnosed late; in many cases the disease has spread by the time of diagnosis.

2. There is a three-fold risk of breast or ovarian cancer in women who have an affected first-degree relative.

3. The BRCA gene gives a risk of breast cancer of 60-80%. The risk in the general population is approximately 10%. Mastectomy reduces the risk to 5% (but not to 0%).

4. The BRCA gene gives a risk of ovarian cancer of 20-40%. The risk in the general population is approximately 1%. Oophorectomy reduces the risk to 4% (but not to 0%).

5. Current recommendations for women who are BRCA carriers include prophylactic bilateral mastectomy and oophorectomy at age 35-40 or at the age at which the youngest affected family member was diagnosed.

Questions:

This woman has a number of risk factors for developing another malignancy: she has already had breast cancer, her mother was affected at a young age, and she carries the BRCA gene. In this setting, what is the correct halachic approach with regard to the following questions:

A. Surgery:

1. Is mastectomy obligatory in these circumstances?

2. Is oophorectomy permitted? (Female sterilization is generally halachically prohibited.) Is it obligatory?

3. May the patient decline oophorectomy if she wishes to have more children despite the risk? If she wishes to undergo the procedure, does her husband have a right to object on the grounds that he wants more children?

4. May she refuse mastectomy due to intimate marital concerns despite the risk? Is her husband's opinion halachically relevant?

B. Other issues:

1. Is a woman who is BRCA positive obliged to divulge that fact to a prospective spouse before marriage?

2. Is this woman's daughter obliged to undergo genetic testing to ascertain whether she has inherited the BRCA gene? If so, at what age?

3. Are all women obliged to undergo screening for BRCA status? (At present it is not clear that close follow-up of BRCA positive women alters their prognosis.)

BIBLIOGRAPHY
AND SOURCES

Hebrew Bibliography and Responsa

Collections

Hershler M, ed., *Halacha and Medicine* Vol. 1 (Regensburg; Jerusalem, Chicago 5740/1980)

Hershler M, ed., *Halacha and Medicine* Vol. 2 (Regensburg; Jerusalem, Chicago 5741/1981)

Hershler M, ed., *Halacha and Medicine* Vol. 3 (Regensburg; Jerusalem, 5743/1983)

Hershler M, ed., *Halacha and Medicine* Vol. 4 (Regensburg, Jerusalem, 5745/1985)

Commentaries, Codes and Responsa

Alter of Slabodka: R. Nosson Zvi (Nota Hirsh) Finkel, b. Lithuania 1849; d. Israel 1927. Founder of the Slabodka yeshiva and leading figure in the *mussar* movement.

Aruch Hashulchan: Extensive halachic work by R. Yechiel Michel Epstein, b. Bobroisk, Russia, 1829; d. 1908.

Atzei Arazim: Work by R. Noach Chaim Tzvi Berlin, b. Furth 1738; d. 1802. Head of Beth Din of Altona, Hamburg, Wansbeck.

Beis Halevi: R. Yosef Dov Soloveitchik of Brisk; 1820–1892.

Bertinoro: R. Ovadiah Yare b. Bertinoro, northern Italy b. ca. 1440; d. Jerusalem ca. 1530. Primary commentary on the Mishna; printed in virtually all editions.

Bet Meir: R. Meir Posner, b.1725; d. 1807. Koenigsberg and Shotland.

Birchei Yosef: R. Chaim Yosef David Azulai (Chida), b. Jerusalem 1724; d. Leghorn, Italy, 1806.

Brit Yaakov: Responsa on Sh. Aruch by R. Baruch Mordechai ben Yaakov Libshitz, printed Warsaw 1876.

Chafetz Chaim: see Mishna Berura.

Chazon Ish: R. Avraham Yeshaya Karelitz, b. Kosov, Lithuania 1878; d. Bnei Brak 1953.

Darchei Teshuva: Work on Sh. Aruch by R. Tzvi Hirsch Shapira (or Spira) of Munkatch, b. 1850; d. 1913.

Divrei Malkiel: R. Malkiel Zvi ben R. Yonah haLevi Tannenbaum, Poland, b.1847; d.1910.

Eidels: R. Samuel Eliezer Eidels (Maharsha), b. Cracow in 1555; d. 1632. Known primarily for his commentary on the Talmud.

Eiger: R. Akiva Eiger, b. Eisenstadt 1761; d. 1837.

Emden: R. Jacob ben Tzvi Emden (Yaavetz), b. 1697; d. 1776, Germany. Son of the Chacham Zvi. Authored works on Mishnah, Talmud, Kabbalah, the prayer book and responsa, She'elat Yavetz, and Mor u'K'tzia on Orach Chaim.

Feinstein: R. Moshe Feinstein, Rosh Yeshiva and halachic authority, b. Russia, 1895; d. USA, 1986. Responsa collected as Igrot Moshe.

Gaon of Vilna: (gaon: lit. "genius") R. Eliyahu ben Shlomo Zalman of Vilna; 1720–1797.

Grodzenski: R. Abraham Grodzenski, b. 1884 Warsaw; burned to death by Germans 1944. Author of Toras Avraham.

HaChasid: R. Yehuda HaChasid, b. ca.1150 Speyer, Germany; d. Regensburg 1217. Author of Sefer Chasidim.

Igrot Moshe: See Feinstein.

Imrei Esh: R. Meir Eisenstadt, Ungvar, Hungary, 1800's.

Jakobovits: Rabbi Immanuel Jakobovits, b. 1921 Koenigsberg; d. 1999. Chief Rabbi of Britain. Authored work on Jewish bioethics.

Kluger: R. Shlomo Kluger, b.1783 Komarow, Russia; d.1869. Authored over 100 works; most still in manuscript.

Korban HaEda: Commentary on the Jerusalem Talmud by R. David Fraenkel, b. Berlin 1707; d 1762.

Kovetz Shiurim: Work by R. Elchanan Wasserman (see below).

Machzit HaShekel: Work by R. Shmuel Kelin, b. Kelin 1724; d. Boskowitz 1806.

Magen Avraham: Commentary to Shulchan Aruch O. C. by R. Avraham HaLevi Gombiner, b. ca. 1637 Gombin, Poland; d. Kalisch 1683.

Maharal of Prague: R. Yehuda Loewe ben Bezalel, b.ca.1512; d. 1609.

Maharam Bar Baruch: see Maharam MiRotenberg

Maharam MiRotenberg: R. Meir ben Baruch of Rothenburg, b. Worms, Germany ca. 1215; d. in captivity in the Ansheim prison, Germany, 1293.

Maharam Shik: R. Moshe Shik, b. Slovakia 1807; d. Chust, Ukraine 1879. Authored responsa on all four parts of Shulchan Aruch.

Maharit: R. Joseph ben Moshe Trani, son of Mabit, b. Safed 1568; d. Constantinople 1639.

Maharsha: see Eidels.

Maharsham: R. Shalom Mordechai Schwadron, b. 1835; d. 1911 Galicia.

Maimonides: R. Moshe ben Maimon (Rambam), b. Cordova, Spain 1135; d. Egypt 1204. Authored Mishneh Torah (also known as Yad HaChazakah), Guide to the Perplexed, hundreds of responsa and numerous medical works.

Margoliot Hayam: R. Reuven Margolies, b. Lvov 1889; d. Israel 1971.

Mecklenburg: R. Yaacov Tzvi Mecklenburg, b. 1785; d. 1865, Koenigsberg. Author of Ha'K'tav V'HaKabbalah, commentary on Torah.

Meiri: R. Menachem ben Shlomo Meiri, b. 1249 Perpignan; d. 1315. His Talmudic commentary was largely unknown for centuries until being republished in modern times.

Melamed l'Ho'il: R. David Tzvi Hoffman, b. Verbo, Hungary 1843; d. Berlin 1921. His responsa deal with a wide range of modern problems.

Minchat Avraham: Work by R. Abraham Reinhold, Cracow; published 1937.

Minchat Chinuch: Commentary on Sefer HaChinuch (which systematically discusses the 613 commandments) by R. Yosef Babad, b. Pzseworsk, Poland 1800; d. Tarnopol 1874.

Minchat Yitzchak: Work by R. Yitzchak Yaacov Weiss, b. Galicia 1902; d. 1989. After the war he moved to England, later to Israel and became head of a major rabbinical court in Jerusalem.

Mishkanot Yaakov: Work on Shulchan Aruch by R. Yaacov b. R. Aharon Bruchin, b. Minsk 1781; d. Karlin 1845. Leading disciple of R. Chaim Volozhin.

Mishna Berura: Detailed commentary on Shulchan Aruch Orach Chaim by R. Yisrael Meir HaKohen, b. 1839; d. 1933 Radin, Poland. Also known as Chafetz Chaim; authored many influential works on halakhah and ethics including Chafetz Chaim on the laws of speech.

Mishnat Chachamim: Work by R. Yosef Hochgelernter; Zamosc, Poland. First printed Lemberg, 1790.

Mor u'Kzia: See Emden.

Mordechai: R. Mordechai ben Hillel, b. ca. 1240; martyred 1298 with his wife and five children, Nurenberg, Germany.

Nachmanides: R. Moshe ben Nachman (Ramban), b. Gerona, Spain 1194, died Israel 1270. Authored commentaries on the Bible and Talmud, halachic codes, responsa, works on mysticism and philosophy.

Noda B'Yehuda: Work by R. Yechezkel ben Yehuda Landau, b. 1713 Opataw, Poland; d. 1793 Prague. Also authored Dagul Mervavah on Shulchan Aruch and Tziyun l'Nefesh Chayah (Tz'lach).

Ohr Sameach: R. Meir Simcha HaKohen, b. 1843 near Vilna; d. 1926 Dvinsk. Authored commentary on the Rambam and Meshech Chochmah on Chumash.

Palaggi: R. Chaim Palaggi, b.1788, Smyrna, Turkey; d.1869 there.

Pilpula Charifta: Work by R. Yom Tov Lipmann Heller, b. Wallerstein, Bavaria, 1578; d. Cracow, 1654. Prague and Poland. Also authored Tosafot Yom Tov, and Ma'adanei Yom Tov on the Rosh.

Pitchei Teshuva: commentary on Shulchan Aruch by R. Avraham Tzvi Hirsch Eisenstadt, b. 1813; d. 1868 Lithuania.

Pri Megadim: Commentary on Shulchan Aruch by R. Yosef Teomim, b. 1727 Steritz, near Lvov, Poland; d. 1792 Frankfort.

Ra'avad: R. Avraham ben David, b. ca. 1120 Narbonne; d. Posquieres 1198. His commentary on the Rambam's Mishneh Torah printed in almost every edition of this work since 1509.

Radbaz: R. David ben Shlomo ibn Avi Zimra, b. Spain 1479; d. Israel 1573. Chief rabbi of Egypt; authored thousands of responsa.

Ran: R. Nissim ben Reuven of Gerona, b. Catalonia 1320; d. 1380. Authored Talmudic commentaries and essays.

Rashba: R. Shlomo ben Aderet, b. Barcelona 1235; d. there 1310. Authored thousands of responsa; many still in manuscript. Many of his halachic decisions were included in the Shulchan Aruch.

Rashi: R. Shlomo Yitzchaki (R. Shlomo ben Yitzchak), b. Troyes, France 1040; d. there 1105. Pre-eminent commentator on Torah and Talmud.

Recanati: R. Menachem Recanati, b. ca. 1250 Italy; d. ca. 1310.

Rekanti: See Recanati.

Rema: R. Moshe Isserles, b. ca. 1520 Cracow; d. there 1572. His additions to Shulchan Aruch reflect Ashkenazic practice.

Ritva: R. Yom Tov ben Avraham Ashvili, b. ca. 1250 Saragossa, Spain; d. there 1320.

Rivash: R. Yitzchak ben Sheshet Perfet, b. Barcelona 1326; d. Algiers 1408.

Rosh: R. Asher ben Yechiel, b. ca. 1250 Germany; d.1327 Toledo. Authored commentary on the Talmud and more than 1,000 responsa. Father of the Tur.

Sefer Halachot Gedolot: Compendium of halachic decisions composed during the Geonic period in the ninth century by R. Shimon Kayyara; Basra in Babylonia.

Seridei Esh: Work by R. Yechiel Yaacov Weinberg, b. Poland 1885; d. Montreux 1966.

Shach: R. Shabtai ben Meir HaKohen, b. 1621; d. 1662, Lithuania. Authored primary commentary on Shulchan Aruch.

Shem Aryeh: R Aryeh Leibush Bolchover, d. 1851. Zaslaw (district of Walin), Russia.

Shevet Halevi: Work by R. Shmuel HaLevi Wosner, b. Vienna 1914.

Shevut Yaakov: Work by R. Yaacov ben Yosef Reischer, b. ca. 1670; d. 1733. Prague, Ansbach (Bavaria), Worms, and Metz (Germany).

Shik: See Maharam Shik.

Shulchan Aruch: Code of Jewish Law by R. Yoseph ben Ephraim Caro, b. Toledo 1488; d. Safed 1575.

Shulchan Aruch HaRav: Halachic code by R. Shneur Zalman, b. 1745 Liadi; d. 1813. Chassidic leader; author of Tanya.

Soloveitchik: R. Chaim haLevi Soloveitchik, b. 1853 Volozhin; d. 1918 Otwock, near Warsaw. Introduced a particular analytical methodology to Talmudic study.

Steipler: R. Yaacov Yisrael Kanievsky, b. Hornosteipel 1899; d. Bnei Brak 1985. Author of Kehillot Yaakov, also several volumes of letters, Karyana d'Igerta.

Taz: see Turei Zahav.

Tiferet Yisrael: Commentary on the Mishna by R. Yisrael Lipschitz, b. 1782; d. 1860. Dessau and Danzig.

Tosafot: Set of classic commentaries on the Talmud composed during twelfth to fourteenth centuries, printed in all standard editions of the Babylonian Talmud. Included Rashi's grandson R. Yaacov ben Meir Tam (Rabbenu Tam), and Rashi's nephew R. Isaac ben Shmuel (Ri).

Tosefot Rid: Talmudic commentary by R. Yeshaya diTrani, b. Trani, Italy ca. 1180.

Tosefot HaRosh: see Rosh.

Tur: Major halachic compendium by R. Jacob ben Asher, b. Cologne ca. 1269; d. Toledo ca. 1343. Son of the Rosh.

Turei Zahav (Taz): Primary commentary on the Shulchan Aruch by R. David HaLevi, b. Ludmir, Poland 1586; d. 1667.

Tzitz Eliezer: Responsa work of R. Eliezer Yehuda Waldenburg, b. Jerusalem 1917; d. there 2006. Over 20 volumes, deals with many contemporary halachic problems and medical issues in particular.

Volozhin: R. Chaim Volozhin (Volozhiner), b. Volozhin 1749; d. there 1821. Leading disciple of the Vilna Gaon. Founded the Volozhin yeshiva (the "mother of all Lithuanian-style yeshivos") in 1803. Author of Nefesh HaChaim.

Wasserman: R. Elchanan Wasserman, Rosh Yeshiva and Torah leader, Baranowitch, b.1875, martyred 1941 Kovno; leading disciple of the Chafetz Chaim. Authored Talmudic commentary and essays.

Yaavetz (She'elat Yaavetz): See Emden.

Yad Avraham: Commentary on Shulchan Aruch (printed in Vilna Shulchan Aruch) by R. Avraham Maskil L'Eitan, b. Minsk 1778; d. 1848.

Yad Rama: Work by R. Meir ben Todros HaLevi Abulafia, b. ca. 1170; d. Burgos, Spain ca. 1244.

Zer Zahav: Issur veHeter Ha'Aruch by R. Yona Ashkenazi was first printed in Vilna in 1891 with the commentary Zer Zahav by R. Avraham Broin.

Zevin: R. Shlomo Yosef Zevin, b. Kazimirov 1888; d. Israel 1978. Author of numerous books and other halachic publications; co-founder and editor of the Talmudic Encyclopedia.

English Bibliography

Avraham AS, *Nishmat Avraham* (3 Vols; ArtScroll, 2000)

Beauchamp TL and Childress JF, *Principles of Biomedical Ethics,* 5th ed., (Oxford, 2001)

Bleich JD, *Contemporary Halachic Problems* Vol. I (Ktav, 1977)
Bleich JD, *Contemporary Halachic Problems* Vol. II (Ktav, 1983)
Bleich JD, *Contemporary Halachic Problems* Vol. III (Ktav, 1989)
Bleich JD, *Contemporary Halachic Problems* Vol. IV (Ktav, 1995)

Bleich JD, *Bioethical Dilemmas* Vol. I (Ktav, 1998)
Bleich JD, *Bioethical Dilemmas* Vol. II (Targum, 2006)

Bleich JD, *Time of Death in Jewish Law* (Z. Berman, 1991)
(includes English and Hebrew material)

Gillon R, *Philosophical Medical Ethics* (John Wiley, 1986)

Hauser M, *Moral Minds* (Little, Brown 2006)

Hogan, DE, Burstein JL, *Disaster Medicine* (2nd ed; Lippincott, Williams and Wilkins, 2007)

Jacobovitz I, *Jewish Medical Ethics* (Bloch, 1975)

Steinberg A, *Encyclopedia of Jewish Medical Ethics* (3 Vols; Feldheim, 2003)

Glossary

aggada: Torah sources of more metaphysical, less halachic nature

bar-mitzva: age of majority; 13 years for boys; 12 years for girls

beth din: Jewish court of law

brit: covenant; circumcision

chacham (pl. chachamim): wise man

chayei sha'a: situation of terminal illness

chayei olam: long term (normal) life; as opposed to *chayei sha'a*

Chumash: the Five Books of Moses

dayan: rabbinical judge; member of *beth din*

gemara: Talmud; more specifically the analysis and discussion of the Mishna

goses: imminently terminal situation

halacha: Torah law

Hashem: lit. "the Name" of God

kabbala: esoteric Torah wisdom

masechta: tractate (section of Talmud)

Midrash: Torah sources which delve deeper than the plain meaning of the Scriptural text

Mishna: the definitive statements of the Oral Law

mitzva (pl. mitzvot): commandment

mussar: the study and practice of Torah character building

neshama: soul

parsha: Torah portion

pasuk (pl. p'sukim): Scriptural verses

posek: halachic authority who decides cases at law

p'sak: halachic ruling

Rebbe: Rabbi, teacher

Rishonim: 10th – 15th century Torah authorities

Rosh beth din: Head of Jewish court of law

Rosh Yeshiva: dean of a Talmudic academy

shiur (pl. shiurim): lesson; lecture

Shulchan Aruch: Code of Jewish Law

talmid (pl. talmidim): student

Talmud: the Oral Law; comprising Mishna and *gemara.*

Tanach: Scripture

Torah: the Five Books of Moses; or more generally all of Scripture, the Oral Law and commentaries

treifa: person with lethal injury or lesion

yeshiva (pl. yeshivot): Talmudic academy